European Issues in Children's
Identity and Citizenship **2**

Young People's Understanding
of Economic Issues in Europe

*Edited by Merryn Hutchings, Márta Fülöp
and Anne-Marie Van den dries*

Children's
Identity &
Citizenship
in Europe

Trentham Books
Stoke on Trent, UK and Sterling USA

Trentham Books Limited

Westview House	22883 Quicksilver Drive
734 London Road	Sterling
Oakhill	VA 20166-2012
Stoke on Trent	USA
Staffordshire	
England ST4 5NP	

First published 2002

British Library Cataloguing-in-Publication Data
A catalogue record for this book is available from the British Library

1 85856 256 2

Designed and typeset by Trentham Print Design Ltd., Chester and printed in Great Britain by Cromwell Press Ltd., Wiltshire.

Contents

Series Introduction: European Issues in Children's Identity and Citizenship

Young People's Understanding of Economic Issues in Europe is the second volume in the series *European Issues in Children's Identity and Citizenship*. This series arises from the work of the ERASMUS Thematic Network Project called Children's Identity and Citizenship in Europe (CiCe). This network brings together over 90 University Departments, in 29 European states, all of whom share an interest in the education of professionals who will work with children and young people in the area of social, political and economic education. The network links many of those who are educating the future teachers, youth workers, social pedagogues and social psychologists in Europe.

This series as a whole is designed to discuss and debate the issues concerned with the professional and academic education of teachers, early childhood workers, social pedagogues and the like. These professionals, and those who will educate and train them, need to understand the complex issues surrounding the socialisation and social understanding of the young, and to be aware of the similarities and differences in professional practices across Europe. They will need to work with young people learning to be citizens – citizens both of the traditional political entities, and of the developing new polities of Europe.

This particular volume is the second in the series, and focuses on the important area of economic understanding. The European Union began as an economic coalition, and economics have been one of the key driving factors in the growth of the European movement, and one of the major forms in which European unification is being developed. There has also been a series of major economic changes and developments in Europe. Not only have the economies of the larger states of the EU grown and developed in a way that was barely conceivable 50 years ago, but many of the smaller and newer members of the Union have seen recent rapid transformations in their economies. And in East and Central Europe, where a dozen states are in various stages of the accession process, there have been even more radical economic transformations with the ending of Soviet hegemony. Economic understanding is thus developing in social contexts that are themselves changing at a very rapid rate. This volume explores the implications of these changes for the ways in which children and young people come to construct an understanding of their economic context.

The CiCe Network began in 1996, and has been supported by the European Commission since 1998. This series arises from our conviction that changes in contemporary European society are such that we need to examine how the processes of socialisation are adapting to the new contexts. Political, economic and social changes are under way that suggest that we are developing multifaceted and layered identities, which reflect the contingencies of European integration. In particular, children are growing up in this rapidly changing society, and their social behaviour will reflect the dimensions of this new and developing social unit. Identities will probably be rather different: national identities will continue alongside new identifications, with sub-national regions and supra-national unions. Our sense of citizenship will also develop in rather different ways than in the past: multiple and nested loyalties will develop, more complex than the simple affiliations of the past.

Those who will work with children and young people have a particular role to play in this. They will have to help young people develop their own relationships with the new institutions that develop, while at the same time being mindful of the traditional relationships known and understood by parents and grandparents, and their role in inter-generational acculturation.

CiCe welcomes enquiries from potential members of the Network. These should be addressed to the CiCe Central Coordination Unit, at the Institute for Policy Studies in Education, University of North London, 166–220 Holloway Road, London N7 8DB, United Kingdom.

Alistair Ross
Series Editor

On behalf of the editorial committee: Tilman Alert, Márta Fülöp, Yveline Fumat, Akos Gocsal, Søren Hegstrup, Riita Korhonen, Emilio Lastrucci, Elisabet Näsman, Panyota Papoulia-Tzelpi and Ann-Marie Van den dries

Chapter Synopsis

Chapter Two: Economic socialisation: How does one develop an understanding of the economic world?

Economic socialisation is a specific concept referring to the whole process by which a child will develop an understanding of the economic world. It is related to 'naive economics', the economics of non-specialists. Even though children, as well as many adults, are 'naive subjects', they are familiar with parts of the economic world and possess some knowledge and understanding of how it works. Economic socialisation concerns the acquisition of the knowledge, skills, behaviour, opinions, attitudes and representations that are relevant to the economic world. The concept refers to the maturing child who is learning how to apprehend the world of adults. In the past twenty years, there has been an array of research concerning the influence, decision power and buying power of children. In order to understand economic socialisation, different authors use a variety of methods and techniques which will be described in this chapter. In a final part, we will consider the implications for educators, both parents and teachers.

La socialisation économique est un concept spécifique qui renvoi à l'ensemble des processus par lesquels l'enfant développe et appréhende le monde économique. Ce concept est lié à l'idée 'd'économie naïve' ou encore, de l'économie vue par les non-spécialistes. Bien que les enfants, comme beaucoup d'adultes, soient des sujets 'naïfs', ils sont en contact de plus en plus précocement avec des éléments de la consommation et du monde économique, ce qui leur facilite l'acquisition de connaissances spécifiques. La socialisation économique traite aussi de l'acquisition de compétences propres au monde économique, de conduites économiques, d'opinions, de valeurs et d'attitudes, sans oublier les représentations d'objets économique. De nombreux travaux de recherche s'intéressent à l'étude de l'influence, du prise de décisions et du pouvoir d'achat des jeunes et, de façon à décrire la socialisation économique, les différents chercheurs se servent d'une grande variété de méthodes et des techniques multiples basées sur l'utilisation de matériel concret facilement manipulable. En conclusion quelques éléments utiles aux éducateurs, qu'ils soient parents ou enseignants, seront évoqués.

Chapter Three: Young people, socialisation and money

This chapter looks at the international psychological literature stemming from the early 1900s that has examined how young people (children and adolescents) come to understand the economic world. It will concentrate on three areas of research:

• stage-wise theories of the development of economic understanding

• the acquisitions of very specific concepts like profit, ownership, poverty taxation as well as understanding of institutions like banks, trade unions, etc.

• studies of pocket money or allowances that examine how parents try to socialise their children into the meaning of work and money

It will also consider what areas of research have been neglected and some of the problems with the methodologies that have been currently used to study how young people operate in the economic world.

Chapter Four: Economy and knowledge acquisition: Obstacles and facilitation

Many studies have focused on the acquisition of economic knowledge and different aspects of this process: economic competence in problem solving, informal reasoning in economics, mental representation of economics and their roles as obstacles in social reasoning, the development of economic notions in children of different ages, the role of economic curricula in knowledge acquisition. These studies are based on different research frames because the researchers belong to different areas such as economics, pedagogy, social psychology, developmental psychology, educational psychology. The chapter presents a review of these studies and a critical discussion of their characteristics aimed at building a picture of the acquisition of economic knowledge and the factors that obstruct or facilitate this process.

Economia e processi di conoscenza: ostacoli e facilitazioni
L'acquisizione di conoscenze economiche è tema di parecchie ricerche che focalizzano aspetti diversi: il ruolo della conoscenza economica nella soluzione di problemi, le caratteristiche del ragionamento informale di tipo economico, le rappresentazioni economiche di tipo quotidiano e il loro ruolo nell'ostacolare il ragionamento su temi sociali, le caratteristiche dell'acquisizione di nozioni economiche a diversi livelli di età, la funzione di curricoli di economia appositamente messi a punto. Le prospettive teoriche alla base di questi studi sono diverse perché sono condotti da psicologi dello sviluppo, da psicologi dell'educazione, da psicologi cognitivisti 'generalisti', da pedagogisti e da economisti: risulta perciò un panorama molto vario e articolato alla cui composizione contribuiscono studiosi diversi. Il saggio darà conto di questo panorama evidenziando gli elementi che risultano fattori di facilitazione e quelli che al contrario emergono come ostacoli per ricostruire le caratteristiche dell'acquisizione di conoscenze economiche.

Chapter Five: How children construct ideas about work
Children learn about work through participation, observation and interaction in a variety of social settings: home, school, after-school clubs and classes, the community and through the media. From these different resources children construct work in a variety of ways that are complex and contradictory. This chapter draws on interviews with children in London primary schools to explore their constructions of work in different settings, and the resources that they drew on in these constructions. It will consider the ways in which children draw on their experiences of work in familiar contexts (e.g. at school) to construct ideas about work they have less experience of

(e.g. in a factory), and will discuss the processes involved in such 'transfer of learning'. The chapter focuses particularly on the fact that some children appear to have very much more experience than others to draw on, and considers the range of reasons for this. Finally it discusses what schools might do to compensate for these differences in experience.

Chapter Six: The representations of wealth and poverty: Individual and social factors
Anna Silvia Bombi, Università degli Studi di Roma 'La Sapienza'
In this chapter I discuss the individual and social factors that are likely to influence the ideas of children and adolescents about rich and poor people. First, I review the pertinent literature, contrasting the studies about individual developmental factors (e.g. Berti and Bombi, 1988) with those about environmental factors (e.g. Dickinson and Emler, 1996). Although based on different theoretical assumptions, most of these studies rely on the same method, namely, interviews. I then summarise some studies I conducted with a different tool, drawings, including a very recent investigation that combines drawings and interviews with children and adolescents from radically different social backgrounds. The results will help to understand how verbal and non-verbal means of assessment are suited for studying different aspects of the development of economic representations, with special reference to the impact of experience and social values.

La rappresentazione della ricchezza e della poverta: fattori individuali e sociali
In questo capitolo prendero' in esame i fattori individuali e sociali in grado di influire sulle idee dei bambini e degli adolescenti sui ricchi e i poveri. Iniziero' passando in rassegna la letteratura pertinente, confrontando gli studi sui fattori evolutivi individuali (ad es. Berti e Bombi, 1988) e quelli sui fattori ambientali (ad es. Dickinson e Emler, 1996). Benche' basati su premesse teoriche diverse, molti di questi studi si basno sullo stesso metodo, l'intervista. Riassumero'

quindi alcuni studi da me condotti con uno strumento diverso, il disegno, incluso un lavoro recentissimo che combina interviste e disegni di bambini e adolescenti provenienti da ambienti sociali nettamente diversi. I risultati ci aiuteranno a comprendere come metodi di valutazione verbali e non verbali siano adatti a studiare aspetti diverso dello sviluppo di rappresentazioni economiche, con particolare riguardo all'impatto dell'esperienza e dei valori sociali.

Chapter Seven: Economic education and attitudes towards competition, business and enterprise among adolescents in Hungary

The decline of the socialist system during the late 1980s and early 1990s in Eastern and Central Europe resulted in dramatic social, political, and economic changes. Phenomena that had previously been ideologically denied and banned, such as competition and enterprise, became highly valued and praised at all levels of society. All these changes resulted in the need to increase understanding of new economic concepts and to change attitudes towards the free market economy and business, and towards their active agents, the entrepreneurs. This chapter focuses on five main topics:

- views about the economic consequences of the political changes among different age groups

- adolescents' ideas about the role and effects of competition in their rapidly changing society

- attitudes towards entrepreneurs

- economic education in Hungarian secondary schools

- attitudes towards business, enterprise and entrepreneurs among secondary school students participating in a one year long economic and business education programme.

Gazdasági oktatás és a vállalkozások, az üzleti világ és a versengés iránti attitüd magyar serdülők körében
A szocialista rendszer bukása a nyolcvanas évek végén és a kilencvenes évek elején drámai társadalmi, politikai és gazdasági

változásokat hozott Közép-Kelet Európában. Az olyan korábban ideológiailag tagadott és tiltott jelenségek, mint például a versengés vagy a vállalkozás kívánatossá és értékessé váltak a társadalom minden szintjén. Ennek következtében új gazdasági fogalmak megértésére lett szükség, valamint arra, hogy megváltozzanak a piacgazdasággal és az üzleti élettel valamint ezek aktív résztvevőivel, a vállalkozókkal kapcsolatos értékek és attitüdök. A jelen írás öt fő témára koncentrál:

* A politikai változások gazdasági következményeinek percepciója különböző korosztályok körében

* Miként gondolkodnak a serdülök a versengés szerepéröl és következményeiröl a gyorsan változó társadalmukban és gazdaságukban.

* A vállalkozókkal kapcsolatos attitüdök

* Gazdasági oktatás a magyar középiskolákban

* Milyen attitüdökkel rendelkeznek az üzlet, a vállalkozás és a vállalkozók iránt azok a középiskolások, akik gazdasági és üzleti oktatásban részesülnek.

Chapter Eight: Pocket money, spending and sharing: Young children's economic understanding in their everyday lives

Young children are often described as incompetent in economic matters. In their everyday lives, however, they indirectly experience and take part in economic transactions. In the research project Children's Economic Understanding, we interviewed some 70 children aged three to six years at their daycare centre in small groups. The focus is on their everyday life economy in their families and at their daycare centre. The children's descriptions are related to examples of the ways in which staff in daycare centres value children's competence in economic matters, and the ideas of economic socialisation of young children at daycare centres. The following questions are discussed in this chapter:

- Do young children have money of their own?
- What are their views on this and on children's role in making decisions about their own money?
- Can young children work to earn money?
- How do they use their money in terms of saving and consumption?
- What norms do children identify in relation to transactions involving private property?
- How do daycare staff consider young children's economic competence and what economic norms do they refer to?

Fickpengar, utgifter och att dela med sig: Små barns förstående av ekonomi i sitt vardagsliv

Små barn beskrivs ofta som inkompetenta i ekonomiska frågor. Ändå får de indirekt erfarenhet av och deltar även själv i ekonomiska transaktioner i vardagen. I projektet Barn och ekonomi har vi bland annat gruppvis intervjuat ett 70tal barn 3-6 år gamla. Fokus har legat på deras vardagsekonomi i familjen och förskolan. Barnens beskrivningar relateras till exempel på hur personal inom förskolan förhåller sig till små barns ekonomiska kompetens och idéer om ekonomisk socialisation som finns i förskolan. Följande frågor diskuteras i det här bidraget:

- Har de små barnen egna pengar och hur ser de själva på detta och på barns del i beslutsfattandet om sina egna pengar?
- Kan barn tjäna pengar genom eget arbete?
- Hur använder de sina pengar i form av sparande och konsumtion?
- Vilka normer kring privat egendom och att dela med sig uttrycker de?
- Vilka föreställningar om barns kompetens och vilka ekonomiska normer har personal i förskolan?

Chapter Nine: Children's reflections on income and savings

In today's society children are often looked upon as consumers and they have their own money to manage, sometimes from an early age. Even though children's pocket money has been studied, little is known about how children think about and value their own money. This chapter is based on data from a research project, Children's Economic Understanding. Interviews were conducted with ten children, girls and boys, eight to ten years old, all attending the same class at school. Among the topic areas in these interviews were the children's ideas concerning their income and their saving. The following questions are discussed here:

- What sources of income do children have, such as pocket money, pay for work, etc.?

- To what extent and in what ways can children increase their income?

- How do children understand saving and, if they save money, what does it mean to them?

Barns tankar om sina inkomster och sitt sparande: En studie av skolbarn i Sverige
I det moderna samhället ses barn ofta som konsumenter och barn har ibland från tidig ålder egna pengar att hantera. Även om studier gjorts av barns fickpengar är dock föga känt om hur barn tänker om och hanterar sina egna pengar. Det här bidraget bygger på data från ett forskningsprojekt Barn och ekonomi. Intervjuer genomfördes med tio barn, flickor och pojkar, i åldrarna 8-10 år, alla från samma skolklass. Bland de ämnen som togs upp i intervjuerna var barnens tankar om sina inkomster och sitt sparande. Följande frågor diskuteras här:

- Vilka källor till inkomst har barnen såsom fickpengar, betalning för arbete etcetera.

- I vilken utsträckning och på vilket sätt kan barn öka sina inkomster.

- Hur förstås barn sparande och, om de sparar, vad betyder det för dem?

Chapter Ten: Earning money of your own: paid work among teenagers in Sweden

The purpose of this chapter is to give young teenagers a voice and to let them use their own words to explain their understanding of their everyday lives, focusing on work and money. As part of a research project, Children's Economic Understanding, young teenagers who had a regular paid job in parallel to their school work were interviewed. The sample is teenagers who are employed to distribute a local weekly newspaper to its subscribers. The newspaper has been distributed by young people for the last 80 years. The working hours are one-and-a-half hours per week and the pay is about 450 SEK per month. Questions discussed in this chapter are:

- Why do young people work?

- How much money do they dispose of each month?

- How do they spend their money?

- What is the attitude of their parents towards their work?

- Are the moral aspects of paid labour in Sweden expressed by the teenagers?

Tjäna egna pengar: Betakt arbet bland yngre tonåringar i Sverige
Syftet med den här uppsatsen är att låta yngre tonåringar själv komma till tals och med egna ord förmedla sin bild av sin vardag, med fokus på arbete och pengar. Som en del av ett forskningsprojekt Barn och ekonomi, intervjuades yngre tonåringar som hade ett regelbundet betalt arbete parallellt med skolarbetet. Ungdomarna var anställda av en lokal veckotidning för att distribuera tidningen till prenumeranterna. Tidningen har distribuerats av ungdomar under de senaste 80 åren. Arbetstiden är cirka en och en halv timme per vecka och lönen cirka 450 SEK per månad. Frågor som diskuteras i det här bidraget är:

- Varför arbetar ungdomar?

- Hur mycket pengar förfogar de över varje månad?

- Hur använder de sina pengar?

- Vilka attityder har föräldrarna till ungdomarnas arbete?

- Uttrycker ungdomarna de moraliska aspekter som finns kopplade till arbete i Sverige?

1

Introduction: young people's understanding of economic issues in Europe

Merryn Hutchings, Márta Fülöp and
Anne-Marie Van den dries

When writing about the economic understanding of children and young people, it has become almost customary to begin with a justification of the importance of the subject, and many of the contributors to this book have followed that custom. However, this is in itself a sign that we share a belief that there is insufficient recognition of the value of work in this area. Authors of books about understanding of mathematics or of chemistry do not feel the same need to justify the interest of their topic. However, in the case of economic understanding the arguments have not yet been fully accepted, so we begin this book by setting out the reasons why we believe this subject is an important one, and considering why it has been relatively neglected by both researchers and educators. We introduce the themes that are taken up in more depth in later chapters, and explain the structure of this book.

Why should we be interested in young people's economic understanding?

The development of young people's understanding of economic issues is important both at an individual and at a national level. It is vital that individuals are empowered to cope with the everyday economics of earning, consuming, borrowing and saving in a world that is increasingly economically complex. The ordinary citizen in Europe today needs to understand about interest rates, loans, credit and debit cards, share-holding, pension schemes, public and private funding arrangements, and so on. Those who fail to understand are disempowered, and may find themselves financially disadvantaged. Similarly, patterns of work are rapidly changing from the single career to a more flexible and contract-based culture, and the skills needed for the individual to succeed have changed.

Understanding of economic issues is also important at a national level. It is an essential attribute of an informed and questioning citizen and voter. National economies rely on enterprise and wealth creation. In this volume Fülöp and Berkics argue that in the Eastern European countries, whose economies are still recovering from the years of communism and the change to a market economy, there is a need for young people to develop entrepreneurial skills and to enter the business world. Similarly Bamford (2000) argues that as a consequence of Scotland's shortage of entrepreneurs setting up new businesses, there has been a considerable commitment to enterprise education in Scottish schools. In England and Wales *Curriculum Guidance 4: Education for Economic and Industrial Understanding*, one of the cross-curricular themes of the National Curriculum, stated that:

> Pupils need education for economic and industrial understanding to help them to contribute to an industrialised, highly technological society. With increasing economic competitiveness, both in the European Community and world-wide, the nation's prosperity depends more than ever on the knowledge, understanding and skills of young people. To meet this challenge, pupils need to understand enterprise and wealth creation and develop entrepreneurial skills. (National Curriculum Council, 1990, p.1)

Yet despite this potential for the empowerment of the individual and for national development, both economic education in schools, and research into young people's economic understanding, have been very limited. The next two sections consider the reasons for this comparative neglect.

Reasons research is limited

One reason why research in this area is limited is perhaps that it extends into different disciplinary fields. This has the effect that studies come from different perspectives, adopt different methods, and tend to focus on the debates and previous work in their own fields. This has led to some fragmentation, with small pockets of research interest, and other areas that are widely neglected.

Economists could examine how Economic Man, characterised by Maital (1982, p.24) as 'an obstetric marvel' who 'springs to life' from the pages of economics journals, actually comes into being: that is, the development of economic rationality. Alternatively they might focus on how children understand the economic world of adults. Lea, Tarpy and Webley (1987) point out that the economic behaviour of children is interesting, not simply as a prelude to the economic behaviour of adults, but also in its own right; there is a 'playground economy' through which children swap, borrow, lend and sell items. This theme is taken up in two contributions to this volume, Elvstrand, and Näsman and von Gerber, both investigating children's accounts of the wide range of their economic activities. But despite this potential, economists' contribution to research about children and young people has been limited.

Another focus of interest is the part that children and young people actually play in the economy, both through their work (see Justegård in this volume) and their purchasing and 'pester' power. Manufacturers and advertisers recognise that children have considerable influence on what is bought, and so they carry out research that will support their sales efforts. It is notable that regular surveys of children's pocket money or allowances in the United Kingdom (referred to by Furnham in this volume) are carried out by Birds Eye Walls, manufacturers of food and ice cream.

The efforts of researchers in psychology are also fragmented in that, as Ajello points out in this volume, studies of young people's economic understanding can fall within a number of different branches of the discipline. Some psychological studies have started from an interest in whether development of understanding of the social world

3

proceeds through the same stages and in the same rhythms as have been proposed for learning about the physical world. This has led to a number of studies identifying stages of economic thinking. Some have adopted the more recent 'domain-specific' approach, which originated in studies of thinking about science, and applied this to research into children's economic thinking (e.g. Berti and Monaci, 1998). Roland-Lévy and Ajello (both in this volume) examine the range of theoretical orientations and methods used by researchers.

Sociologists tend to come to research in this area with a rather different perspective. Their starting point is the structures in society, and they are concerned with how society reproduces itself and/or changes, and in the socialisation processes through which children become members of society. A recent perspective in the sociology of childhood emphasises investigating children's own social worlds, and research in this volume illustrates the equivalent investigation of children's economic worlds (see chapters by Näsman and von Gerber, Elvstrand, and Justegård).

Sociological and psychological perspectives come together in studies focusing on how children come to understand the structures of society. Some place more emphasis on what children understand, and others on how they come to understand it. In this volume, Bombi's chapter about the representations of wealth and poverty of children of different socio-economic backgrounds illustrates this approach.

Educational researchers come from a different perspective again; their main concern is to provide information that can underpin the efforts of parents and teachers to develop children's understanding in this area, and to evaluate the curricula that are being offered. Furnham (this volume) points out that recently a number of books have been published aimed specifically at parents who want to encourage their children to learn effective money management; it is unclear how far such books of advice are based on research, but their sales demonstrate parental concerns about economic socialisation. Furnham also reports on a variety of studies that show how parents can socialise children through particular practices in relation to giving pocket money or allowance. Pocket money is widely given to children throughout Europe, and forms an important aspect of their economic experience and learning (see Elvstrand, this volume).

In schools, teaching of any aspect of economic skills or understanding is limited, and this offers little encouragement to researchers seeking to underpin the curriculum in this area. Nevertheless, some of the research discussed in this book is linked to school efforts to increase young people's economic understanding. Fülöp and Berkics's chapter is concerned with the evaluation of an economics programme for young people in Hungary, and Ajello reports on the curriculum development activities of Berti and her fellow workers in Italy. Other authors bemoan the lack of activity in schools, and argue that their findings offer schools a potential basis for curriculum input.

The extent of economic education in schools

The extent and form of economic education varies across Europe. In many countries it forms part of the social studies curriculum, particularly for younger children. In Sweden, elements of consumer economics are taught within the home economics curriculum (Klingander, 1998); in some Hungarian secondary schools the American Junior Achievement Program offers courses in economics and business as an optional extra.

The importance accorded to this aspect of the curriculum has also varied through time. In England and Wales, for example, the 1980s saw a greater interest in activities such as school links with industry and mini-enterprise. The efforts of those wanting to promote this area culminated in the inclusion of Economic and Industrial Understanding as a cross-curricular theme in the first National Curriculum for England and Wales, published in 1990.

However, the cross-curricular themes (and particularly Economic and Industrial Understanding) had limited impact on practice because at that time the new curriculum was very much too large, and schools were suffering from massive overload. Inevitably the 'core' subjects (mathematics, English and science) were prioritised, and the themes that were intended to permeate the curriculum were almost ignored. While some of them have been revived under other names (careers, citizenship) the Economic and Industrial Understanding theme has largely disappeared from schools and from public debate.

However, curriculum overload is not the only reason for the limited impact of the activities of those supporting curriculum activities in this area. Another commonly cited factor is that teachers lack enthusiasm, and several reasons have been put forward for this. Klingander (1998) found that teachers in Sweden paid little attention to Consumer Economics, a subject that has always been included in the curriculum in Sweden. They reported limited interest from themselves and from pupils. One teacher is quoted as saying:

> Household economics doesn't move the deeper qualities of a personality. Of course one can teach it in school, but I don't think it is of much importance. Personally I have never been taught this subject, have never planned a budget, I play it by ear. My economics is excellent. (1998, p.58)

As well as expressing lack of interest, this teacher is questioning the validity of household economics as part of the school curriculum because she herself was never taught it and she has managed perfectly well. The tendency of teachers and those involved in curriculum design to take their own education as a model for what should happen in schools today is well known, and militates against change. However, it fails to take into account the dramatic changes that have taken place in the economic world that children today have to cope in.

Another concern has been that teachers themselves lack experience of the business world, and may not feel confident teaching in this area. In England and Wales, a response to this concern was the Teacher Placement programme through which teachers spent short periods of time in industry. There has always been a suspicion that those who choose to work in education see themselves as avoiding the 'nastiness' and competitive attitudes that are found in the business world. This was encapsulated in a speech made in 1976, by the then Prime Minister, James Callaghan, in which he stated:

I have been concerned to find that many of our best trained students who have completed the higher levels of education at university or polytechnic have no desire or intention of joining industry. Their preferences are to stay in academic life (very pleasant, I know) or to find their way into the civil service. (1976, p.72)

Around this time Wiener (1981) published his thesis that the decline of British industry could be attributed to anti-industrial attitudes, which he argued were encouraged through the school curriculum. This analysis was given considerable exposure and appears to have influenced politicians' views (Ahier, 1988; Ross, 1992a, 1995) that education should be made to foster more positive attitudes to industry.

However, the education system has changed dramatically in the last two decades through increasing marketisation, greater control by schools over their own budgets, performance-related pay, testing of pupils and league tables. These changes have now transformed the pleasant backwater that education could be seen as in 1976, and the charges that teachers may be avoiding the values that they associate with the business world no longer ring so true.

Nevertheless, there is still a tendency for teachers to avoid economic issues. In this volume Näsman and von Gerber show how staff in Swedish pre-school centres have avoidance of conflict as their first priority. Since economic activities such as swapping, lending and selling tend to lead to conflict, they are generally not permitted. The suggestion is not that teachers *deliberately* limit economic activities, but that they are completely unaware of the potential that exists for supporting children's economic learning. This echoes, but reverses, an earlier observation by Pollard (1985). He identified ways in which primary school teachers encourage productivity, efficiency, order and discipline, which, he argued, could be said to meet industrial needs for a productive and compliant workforce. However, he pointed out that teachers act in this way as a result of their pragmatic concern to cope with their own working conditions, rather than from a desire to inculcate the dominant values of society and reproduce the capitalist system. This, then is a 'hidden' curriculum: teachers are not consciously promoting (or failing to promote) economic concerns.

Teachers' anxieties about the economic curriculum also stem from their concerns that the government's intention is to indoctrinate children. For example, Costello (1992) quotes Perry (1989) who argued that government advice that children should 'acquire an understanding of the values of a free society and its economic ... foundations' (DES, 1984: Annex, para. 12) is potentially indoctrinatory:

> teachers are asked to explore with their pupils value-laden concepts such as profit; wealth distribution; exploitation; the right to work; the dignity of labour; pollution; state ownership; capitalism – and so on. What is more, the wording of the circular suggests that the value-laden nature of such concepts should in no way be addressed in a neutral fashion but that they should be taught in a way which directs the young towards the predominant values of their own society, and how these relate to its economic structures. (Perry, 1989, quoted by Costello, 1992, p.83)

Ross argued that 'there are clear dangers of schools uncritically reflecting capitalistic structures to children' (1992a, p.59), and proposed that teachers should encourage critical enquiry into social and economic structures and relationships. Similarly, Ford stressed that:

> economic and industrial understanding is not concerned with a blind acceptance of neo-classical free-market economics... it is not about developing positive attitudes to industry ... [It] is concerned ... to develop individual capacity in critical thinking and informed decision making. In this way it can empower pupils. (1992, p.26)

Thus the inclusion of economic understanding in the curriculum has been supported by groups with very different motivations; such input has been seen in terms of empowering children and promoting greater equality of opportunity, but may also be used to teach children more about existing capitalist structures and to make inequalities seem 'natural' and acceptable.

There are, then, a number of reasons for the limited extent of economic education in schools. These include curriculum overload; the dominance of 'core' curriculum subjects; a reluctance and lack

8

of interest on the part of some teachers; a failure to see the potential in this area; suspicions about the motivations of those promoting this area; and concerns about indoctrinatory potential.

The form of economics education

The previous section has shown that economics education is often limited. But even among those who agree that it is vital that we teach children about the economic world, there is considerable disagreement about the way in which we should do so.

In Britain, education in this area has traditionally involved a large experiential element. In much of the curriculum advice offered, schools have been encouraged to adopt an experiential approach, including workplace visits, visits from industrial workers and managers to schools, mini-enterprises and simulations (Ross and Hutchings, 1987). This approach fitted in well with British traditions of primary education: the 1931 Hadow Report insisted that the curriculum 'should be seen in terms of activity and experience, rather than of knowledge to be acquired and facts to be stored' (Consultative Committee of the Board of Education, 1931, p.75). This emphasis on provision of experience has been a continuing theme: the 1990 National Curriculum stated that 'Pupils ... should visit and investigate industries and other places of work ... have opportunities to talk and work with adults from industry and the community ... [and take part] in small-scale business and community enterprise projects...' (NCC, 1990, p.6). The value of this experiential approach is frequently claimed in case studies of classroom practice. Teachers have drawn attention to the value of experience in creating enthusiasm (e.g. Benfield, 1988) and motivating children (e.g. Fitzpatrick, 1988), though Ross (1990a) pointed out that some, worryingly, tend to assume that if the children have enjoyed themselves then learning *must* have taken place, and Atherton, Davis and Parr (1992) question the assumption that economic and industrial understanding necessarily develops by spending time in an industrial context. At a more analytical level, some case studies show how shared experience creates opportunities for discussion and interaction between children, which may lead to increased knowledge and understanding (e.g. Ross, 1983).

9

Ross (1990b, 1992b) has examined the effects of providing specific experiences. He investigated the understandings of hierarchy and of capital of children in classes which had visited different workplaces. He concluded that: 'One of the most important factors affecting children's development in this conceptual area seems clearly to be the kinds of experience they have of industrial and commercial life' (1990b, p.139). A further reason for an experiential approach is that this offers the best potential for developing critical awareness of work arrangements. Ross (1988) argued that listening to the range of views put forward by workers, trades unionists and management would preclude the possibility of indoctrination with any single view.

Arguably, some aspects of economics education can only be delivered through an experiential approach. Bamford (2000) argues that the development of entrepreneurial skills and attitudes is best done through experiential learning with a period of reflection. This is partly because skills such as leadership and cooperation can only be developed by practising them. She also refers to the excitement, creativity and imagination generated in enterprise activities. These are aspects that may stimulate young people to become entrepreneurs.

However, school visits increasingly have to justify their value, in terms of both time, in an increasingly crowded curriculum, and money. An alternative is to draw on children's out-of-school experiences; Fox (1978) pointed out that all children bring to school an 'economic knapsack' of attitudes and unprocessed direct experience of various economic activities including work. Blyth (1984) argued that educators have frequently ignored the duration and range of children's experience outside the school. He claimed that it is important for teachers to know about such experience, and to take it into account in their curriculum planning. It is only in this way that schools can provide experiences that enable children to learn. This is the perspective taken in the chapters written by Näsman and von Gerber, Elvstrand and Justegård. Elvstrand argues that '[the] financial knowledge that children possess could be more extensively utilised in schools and that children's daily experiences related to

10

economic issues should form the basis of improved economic education'. Similarly Hutchings focuses on experience. She investigates the specific experiences that children draw on in their accounts of adult work, arguing that some children have very much more limited experiences than others. In these circumstances, schools should provide experience to compensate for, or redress, societal inequalities.

However, others argue that experience is not essential for learning, and that economic experience may be a source of children's confusions and misunderstandings. Linton (1990) examined the relative importance of cognitive growth and experiential learning in the development of children's understanding of supply and demand, profit, interest and income differentiation. He found that 'Children's experience if anything tended to impede rather than promote economic understanding, with eight year old children regarding the store's till as the terminal part of the process' (p.100).

Thus the older children's greater understanding was not 'a product of their greater experiential involvement' (p.101) but rather resulted from cognitive development. Ajello *et al.* (1987) argued, like Linton, that everyday familiarity does not in itself constitute an advantage, and that the vividness of direct experience in some cases may make it more difficult to understand. They concluded that it is the cognitive complexity of certain concepts, rather than children's lack of experience, which limits understanding. As Ajello points out, direct experience of some economic phenomena can confuse rather than enlighten. The use of cash-dispensing machines does not offer children any insight into the functioning of a bank.

Thus in such areas the approach to instruction may need to be rather different. Italian researchers including Berti and Ajello have designed instructional units for schools in which they teach children about economic institutions such as shops and bank, without providing direct experience, and these interventions in children's learning have been extremely successful (Ajello *et al.*, 1987; Berti and Monaci, 1998). But as Ajello points out, this approach may be so successful precisely because children have not already developed their own theories from previous experience.

11

Similarly economics education programmes in the United States focus on 'instruction' rather than 'experience' (Ahier, 1992). A frequent starting point is a definition of the concept by the teacher which is then elaborated through examples (e.g. Laughlin and Odorzynski, 1992; Reinke, 1992; Schug and Lephardt, 1992).

It is possible that instructional approaches are more appropriate for learning about some aspects of the economic world, and experiential approaches for others. Further research and evaluation is needed if we are to support effective curriculum development across the whole range of economic aspects.

Structure of this book

This series has an explicitly European dimension. In the current volume authors are from Sweden, France, Italy, Hungary and the United Kingdom. The book is organised in three broad sections.

The first three chapters give an overview of research in this field, addressing methodological and theoretical concerns. Christine Roland-Lévy (Chapter Two) reviews different theoretical orientations to economic socialisation, and illustrates the range of theoretical and methodological approaches that have been used in research, describing surveys using interviews and questionnaires, and experimental studies. She discusses the implications of such research for educators. Adrian Furnham (Chapter Three) offers an overview of research into the economic beliefs and behaviours of young people. He summarises a wide range of research into children's understanding of different aspects of money, and focuses particularly on investigations related to pocket money, or allowances. Anna Maria Ajello (Chapter Four) discusses theoretical approaches in psychology to research in this area, and identifies the difficulties that children have in correctly understanding some economic issues.

The next three chapters are in-depth discussions that focus on particular economic issues that concern young people: work, wealth and poverty, and attitudes towards competition, business and enterprise. While these three contributions address very different topics and age groups, a common theme is a concern about inequality. Anna Silvia

Bombi (Chapter Six) finds that children from wealthy backgrounds perceive a very much wider gulf between rich and poor than do children from poorer families, and speculates that this may tend to make each group more satisfied with their own position, and less concerned to challenge inequality. Merryn Hutchings (Chapter Five) is concerned with the vast differences in the experiences available to children, and argues that schools may have to compensate for societal inequalities. Márta Fülöp and Mihály Berkics (Chapter Seven), from a very different perspective, are concerned that economic education is vital in countries like Hungary in order to close the economic gap between Eastern and Western European countries, and create a more united Europe. These three chapters also illustrate very different approaches to research. Hutchings draws on data from semi-structured interviews in which children were encouraged to speculate and use imagination in talking about adult workplaces; Bombi analyses children's drawings of rich and poor people; and Fülöp and Berkics analyse data from a questionnaire. All three chapters also consider the ways in which experiences are used to construct ideas. For Fülöp and Berkics, focusing on the transition from a communist system towards the free market economy, this involves the difficulty of changing the ways of thinking that characterise a society. Bombi and Hutchings both discuss the specific sources that are available to children, including first-hand experience, observation, and indirect sources such as television.

The final three chapters all come from a group of researchers in Linköping University in Sweden. These three chapters take us away from the wide-ranging and more theoretical arguments of earlier parts of the book and paint a vivid picture of the economic activities that children and young people are actually engaged in. The researchers come from a perspective that emphasises the need for adults to understand the social and economic worlds of children. The demand to 'give children a voice' has been an increasingly important trend in child-related research and practice (Lavalette, 1999). As Qvortrup put it, children are not merely 'human becomings' (1994a, p.4); they have views about their own lives and status. So rather than emphasising economic understanding, these researchers focus on

13

the children's interests and concerns. The three chapters focus on different age groups from pre-school to teenagers.

Elisabet Näsman and Christina von Gerber (Chapter Eight), re-searching children aged three to six years, demonstrate the importance these children attach to having money of their own. They identify the variety of economic activities that go on among the children in the pre-school centre, including swapping, lending, and selling second-hand toys. Helene Elvstrand (Chapter Nine) underlines how among older children, pocket money leads to financial responsibility, makes one aware of freedom, and can be seen as a mechanism of economic socialisation and family solidarity. Helén Justegård's study of teenagers who have part-time jobs (Chapter Ten) shows that young people enjoy the independence and rewards offered by work.

These three chapters illustrate the way in which having one's own money gives children and young people a sense of power or control, and offers them opportunities to make their own decisions. Without exception, these young people describe their economic activities in a positive way. Here we should perhaps sound a note of caution. While Justegård is quite clear that there are no concerns in Sweden about exploitation of children who work, or negative effects on school work, these have been raised in some other European countries. In Britain there is evidence that many teenagers are exploited by their employers (Hobbs and McKechnie, 1997), and that employment can have a negative effect on school achievement (Dustmann et al., 1996). Thus while young people themselves feel that they benefit from working, Lavalette (1999) questions how far we can act on research that draws only on children's voices. Similarly one could point to the unhappiness that is sometimes caused when some children are celebrating their own wealth or possessions. However, the main concern in these three chapters is not whether children should work, have pocket money, etc., but rather, how schools are missing the opportunities available to them to use their pupils' experiences as a basis for teaching about economics and ethics.

While the chapters in this volume cover a wide range of issues, this concern that schools are not capitalising on the economic experiences of children and young people is an over-arching theme.

2

Economic socialisation: how does one develop an understanding of the economic world?

Christine Roland-Lévy
Université René Descartes, Paris 5, France

What do children understand about their economic environment? How do they gain control over their economic conditions? Does understanding develop in the same order when the social, economic and political systems are radically different? These are some of the main questions that those interested in children's education might ask. The purpose of this chapter is to provide tools to study these questions in terms of economic socialisation. Economic socialisation is a specific concept referring to the whole process by which a child will develop an understanding of the economic world. It is related to 'naive economics', the economics of non-specialists. Even though children, as well as many adults, are 'naive' subjects, they are familiar with parts of the economic world and possess some knowledge and understanding of how it works. Economic socialisation refers to the maturing child who is learning how to comprehend the world of adults. Furthermore, it refers to the adult's evolving outlook on the economy as his/her role in life changes in line with various economic events such as getting his/her first job, being unemployed or retiring. In the past fifteen years there has been a great deal of research concerning the influence, decision-making power and buying power of children. In this chapter the reasons for studying economic socialisation will be outlined. This will be followed by an overview of the different theoretical orientations used to define economic socialisation. In order to understand economic socialisation, different researchers have used a variety of methods and techniques, which will be described later in this chapter. In conclusion, some useful suggestions for educators, whether parents or teachers, will be given.

1. Why study economic socialisation?

If socialisation is, as Zigler and Child wrote in 1968, 'a broad term for the whole process by which an individual develops, through transactions with other people, specific patterns of socially relevant behaviour and experience' (p.455), then one might easily presume that in order to define economic socialisation more specifically, it is necessary to include particular elements around the idea of exchange. An economic way of defining potential transactions with other people would include specific ideas related to production, trading, or commerce. In this case, economic socialisation covers the process by which individuals develop competence in dealing with the economic world; this competence is gained through their experience of using money to purchase items, and also through the experience of negotiating exchanges of any kind, as well as of persuading others to buy, exchange or sell a product. Such behaviour related to money provides a better understanding of the need to budget, and develops skills of negotiating and bargaining with others. Linked to the economic world of production, this experience provides specific natural training which gradually develops skilful knowledge via an appropriate perception of economics, which in turn, little by little, constructs economic socialisation. Economic socialisation is concerned with the acquisition of the knowledge, skills, behaviour, opinions, attitudes and representations that are relevant to the economic world. An early understanding of the notions implicated in the economic world may, during adult life, help avoid some of the outcomes of unemployment or of credit, such as excessive levels of debt. In that sense, studying and understanding the mechanisms related to the development of economic socialisation can be very useful both for parents and for teachers.

2. Different theoretical orientations

Although the literature proposes various definitions, the main conceptual contents are widely accepted; socialisation refers to the problem of general education in any society, implying a process of interaction between the subjects and their environment. In fact, two main theories dominate the field: the Piagetian developmental-cognitive approach and the environmental learning theory. Piaget proposed a transactional process which links children's cognitive stages to their experience of the world and emphasises the primacy of children's actions in their development and maturation, while learning theory (behaviourism) stresses the effects of the environment on children's behaviour. According to this theory, a functional behaviour will be imitated because it previously appeared to be rewarding. As Youniss (1978) indicates, these two models are not really incompatible. The cognitive model is applied to the development of thinking processes, while learning theory explains behaviour. Piaget's approach deals with the framework, while the behaviourists supply information concerning the content of socialisation. The first model stresses intra-individual differences as the child grows up, while the second describes inter-individual variations among children of the same age. Both theories assume that contacts with social reality are necessary for the construction of a predictable pattern of behaviour.

An example of the use of the Piagetian developmental-cognitive approach in dealing with economic socialisation is the research of Berti and Bombi (1988). By testing children of different ages corresponding to the stages defined by Piaget, the authors investigate the effects of the Piagetian developmental stages on economic socialisation. This type of study speculates that adults have a fully developed knowledge and understanding of the economic world. It is therefore incompatible with theories that suggest that economic socialisation evolves as the individual is modified by different experiences and phases of life: for example, changing school, graduating, getting his/her first job, having a child, buying a house or being laid off, and also retiring, which is a specific phase of re-socialising and a further step towards economic socialisation.

Two fundamental theoretical orientations constitute the basis of research in the field of economic socialisation: the analysis either centres on children's understanding of the economic world of grown-ups, or on how children solve the economic problems of their own world (Roland-Lévy, 1998a). Depending on the orientation chosen by the authors, the methods and techniques used are often different, each bringing complementary data and results. However, Lea and Webley (1991) argue that research in economic socialisation is unsatisfactory when it adopts an adult-centred view of the economic world. These authors believe that researchers should be more concerned with the real economic world of childhood and suggest several lines of investigation focusing on how children solve the economic problems that face them. For example, they provide stimulating ways of dealing with the question via what is described as a 'play-economy', which will be discussed in section 3.2 of this chapter.

3. Methods and techniques

In order to provide ideas for new studies in the field, it is important to note the diversity of research methods that exist and the originality of the various techniques used. We will first give examples of different types of surveys including studies using observations and/or projective tests, and then we will provide descriptions of laboratory studies with experimental tasks.

3.1 Surveys using interviews and questionnaires: unemployment and money as examples

As mentioned earlier in this chapter, economic socialisation is concerned with the acquisition of knowledge, skills and behaviour, as well as the construction of opinions, attitudes and the sharing of social representations of economic notions and ideas. In order to study all these aspects of the socialisation of the child or adolescent, investigations are frequently carried out with different kinds of semi-structured interviews. This technique is very convenient for young children, especially for those under ten or eleven years; it has, for example, been used in an international research project conducted in fourteen different countries dealing with the major domains of the economic world and involving three age groups – seven-, eleven- and fourteen-year-olds (Leiser, Roland-Lévy and Sevòn, 1990). In this study, the interviews were conducted in schools and each child was interviewed individually for about half an hour, allowing enough time for the children to discuss and explain different concepts in their own words. The results allowed us to highlight interesting cultural differences: for example, comparison of French and Algerian children showed that the Algerians have a better understanding of prices; monetary exchanges; the general economic mechanism of production and profit; and of their social and economic systems, particularly of their government's role in the problem of employment versus unemployment. On the other hand, French children more often fail to answer the questions, but when they do answer, they give a wider range of responses; they seem to have a better understanding and ability to reason about the purpose of taxes, seeing them both from the point of view of the individual and from that of society (for more detailed results, see Roland-Lévy, 1990a).

Among the different surveys used to study economic socialisation, unemployment is one of the topics that have often been investigated as an interesting situation related to economic problems. For example, Despierre and Sorel (1979) analysed adolescents' understanding of unemployment. They showed photographs depicting various degrees of unemployment to eleven- to twelve-year-olds and fifteen- to sixteen-year-olds who were asked to describe the images. Their ideas and representations were collected through questionnaires and semi-structured interviews. The older group could distinguish between retirement, vacation, and unemployment, whereas many of the younger ones had confused ideas. The spontaneous theories of unemployment given by adolescents differed with age but not with social class. Important insights into children's understanding of unemployment were also provided by Webley and Wrigley (1983). The authors asked children to define unemployment and to explain how unemployed people differ from others. The results showed that understanding of unemployment became more abstract and more global between the ages of eleven and fifteen. Compared with the younger children, the older ones offered more societal and fatalistic explanations for unemployment; they saw the unemployed as very similar to the employed and regarded the main effects of unemployment as social-psychological rather than economic. This study gave a clear picture of the children's understanding of such a situation, and identified many specific elements in understanding unemployment and how it feels to be unemployed. Furnham (1984) studied 240 school-leavers' perceptions of employment prospects in an interesting survey. He showed that young people for whom unemployment was statistically more probable tended to develop external explanations for unemployment, and girls tended to emphasise external factors more than boys. But the main difference found was between the working class teenagers, who tended to stress external and educational factors, and the middle class group who tended to stress internal and effort factors. An interesting result is that these attributions were reflected in the number and in the type of job-search strategies adopted by young people, along with the barriers and assistance that they considered to operate in job-hunting. In a recent study, Giron (2001) analysed both social representations and knowledge of unemployment and work conditions among a group of French adolescents, using a series of items which had to be classified and characterised. Like other authors, such as Singer and Stacey (1986), she found no gender or age differences in the adolescents' causal attributions concerning unemployment, and like Webley and Wrigley (1983), she found that younger children tend to put greater emphasis on economic consequences whereas older ones regard social consequences as more important.

Other authors, such as Roland-Lévy (1991), have studied specific aspects of financial behaviour including various uses of money, credit and debt. In these studies, children or teenagers often had to classify items, to rank or to group phenomena or to match notions related to the economic world with, for example, classifications of objects which either must be insured, may be insured or cannot be insured. Pictures of situations were also used in this study as a basis for the semi-structured interviews concerning various objects related to the economic world (Lassarre and Roland-Lévy, 1989). This allowed the authors to gather very rich information about how children and teenagers apprehend and organise economic ideas. Burris (1981) investigated the children's understanding of buying and selling with a list of items which were presented to four- to five-, seven- to eight- and ten- to twelve-year-old children. The subjects were asked to classify the items, making one pile of 'those which can be sold or bought' and another of 'all the rest'. In another study the same author explored children's concepts of economic value by presenting them with a pair of objects and asking them to indicate which of the two would cost more and to explain why. Other authors have used scales for measuring opinions and attitudes; Cummings and Taebel (1978), for example, used scales to measure American children's opinions about private property, government, unions, etc. Like other researchers, such as DeFleur and DeFleur (1967), they noted that conformity and consistency of opinions and attitudes increase as children get older.

Researchers mainly study economic cognition, which implies knowledge of situations, concepts or phenomena. To study children's understanding of the economic world, most surveys tend to construct attractive visual material based on pictures, drawings, films or objects, thus giving the child the chance to manipulate materials related to complex concepts. This seems to be especially appropriate when working with young children or for investigating abstract topics such as insurance or employment. In various studies, pictures of situations have therefore been used in order to obtain descriptions of abstract notions. For example, Lassarre and Roland-Lévy (1989), by showing photographs of various objects (e.g. cars, motorcycles, houses, jewellery), led children to express clearly the notion of insurance by distinguishing which objects could be insured and which could not. This would have been impossible for such young children (seven-year-olds) if they had not been able to handle images of concrete situations.

In combination with interviews, observation is also often used either as participant observation, as described in Willis (1977), or as direct observation of a child's behaviour in a particular environment. For example, Watiez (1987) observed children visiting small supermarkets in order to study the behaviour of children in a store. The observations were based on 'behaviour episodes' as a combination of actions and speech; at the end of their shopping excursion the children were interviewed about 'the different things that they found interesting in the supermarket'. It is stimulating to note that, in this particular study, gender differences appeared in terms of economic knowledge. One of the possible explanations for these arose from the observations of behaviour: girls seemed to be more 'at home' in stores than boys, and adopted a behaviour very similar to that of adults when shopping. Another innovative study using observation should be mentioned: this was conducted in a school playground and involved observing children's games of marbles (Webley and Webley, 1990). In this study, the authors showed that children, in a game, reproduce the same economic behaviour as adults. In the playground, children appear to have excellent economic thinking which is well adapted to their economic world, and this can, potentially, be transferred to the real world of economics.

Occasionally, a projective approach is also utilised. For example, as part of a longer interview Lassarre *et al.* (1987) used pictures in a projective test concerning economic situations. Four hundred eleven- to twelve-year-old children were shown four simple drawings: two of potential consumerism (a woman looking at a shop window, and a view of an open-air market) and two that presented different employment situations. For each, the children were asked to tell the story the picture evoked and expand on it. This projective approach allowed the children to talk about themselves and their relations with the economic world, and thus demonstrated their capacity to describe complex situations in a very natural way.

Since 1992 Vergès has focused on the study of social representations of the economic world (e.g. 1992, 1998), and especially of economic concepts such as the market, buying, advertising, profit, production and money; he uses word association tasks to investigate the spontaneous representation of an economic domain such as money. In a recent chapter (2001) Vergès and Bastounis describe new research methods and techniques used to investigate social representations of the economy. As they explain, when studying social representations of the economy, one should understand that the economic object is not isolated from the reality of its social components. Social representations of the economy are involved in the relationship that social subjects, children for example, have with daily reality. This relationship is both real and imaginary; consequently representations are at the same time knowledge and ignorance.

Economic representations are representations in the sense of a cognitive organisation, which in turn is socially defined, as it lies within the social debate. Economic representations are socially determined through three social processes involved in the construction of common sense. The first process pertains to the economic experience of the social agent. As adults, social agents may hold a job; as children, they are already consumers. The daily experience of subjects interacts with their system of representations. The second process determining economic representations is practical ideology appearing in the form of a discourse diffused through conversation and the media. The last process attests the historic depth of social representations: each society carries a collective memory made up of events as well as ideas, values and norms (cf. Vergès and Bastounis, 2001, pp.20-21).

This long-term shared social thought manifests itself in the form of cultural matrices of interpretation which constitute one of the main elements in the construction and transmission of economic socialisation.

3.2 Laboratory studies with experimental tasks

The second major theoretical orientation, behaviourism, leads to the second research method used in the field of economic socialisation. In this section, studies focus on economic behaviour and, in particular, on how children solve the economic problems they are faced

25

with; these studies tend to use experimental tasks. In an attempt to examine the real economic behaviour of childhood, experimenters have organised a variety of creative and ingenious laboratory studies. Authors have constructed artificial economies for children, within which they can work and earn tokens which they can save or spend (Webley, Levine and Lewis, 1991; Sonuga-Barke and Webley, 1993). Experimentation is used to explore both the handling and the understanding of the concepts, and, when employed with young children, appears frequently in the form of a 'play-economy'.

Abramovitch, Freedman and Pliner (1991) organised a laboratory experiment with children aged six, eight and ten; this study dealt with differences in children's behaviour toward money, especially credit versus cash. The children received $4 either in cash or in the form of a credit card to spend in an experimental toy store; what they did not spend in the store could be taken home. The observers noted what they did, how much they spent, how they spent it, what they spent it on, and so on. The results showed that the children who did not normally receive pocket money spent more in credit than those who were given a regular allowance.

Webley, Levine and Lewis (1991) studied children in another 'play-economy'. Subjects received money (tokens) and were put in a setting that consisted of different rooms in which they could either save their money in a bank or spend some – as little or as much as they wanted – on various activities. Some of the activities were free, while others were not. Over a period of time the children had to find ways of spending as little money as possible and of saving some in order to buy a toy that they wanted.

In another experimental study – based on the assumption that in economic experiments about voluntary donations to charitable organisations adults are more altruistic than the narrow definition of self-interest would seem to predict – Harbaugh and Krause (1997, unpublished) carried out an investigation to explore whether, among six- to twelve-year-old children, contributions to charities would have the same significance as for adults. In fact, the authors found that the overall pattern of children's altruistic behaviour is similar to that of adults, but sometimes in repeated experiments it varies.

A last example, in which various experimental tasks were created for a sample of 34 young people, aged fifteen to seventeen, can be briefly described here to show how this method is also used in order to study social representations of economic ideas. The subjects were tested in an experiment composed of three phases. (i) All underwent the same first task, in which their ideology and the social representations of unemployment were studied. (ii) They were then randomly distributed into three groups: in the first experimental group, the subjects were given a document created for the occasion, presented as a page from a newspaper with obviously left-wing political comments on unemployment. In the second group, the conditions were identical except that the document presented was clearly right-wing. A neutral document was presented to the control group. All the pupils had to read the document they had been given, and summarise it. (iii) After a short break, they all completed the third phase in which they had to evaluate various items. Comparison of the social representations, before and after the experimental phase, showed that the core of the representation had changed. In the two experimental groups, after reading and studying the text, many new elements appeared in the peripheral structure. This was especially clear among teenagers who had unemployed relatives. These results imply that the experimental phase had an impact on social representations and that a potential radical change can be obtained with this method (Roland-Lévy, 2000). This example demonstrates that, with various helpful techniques, it is possible to facilitate the understanding of specific objects; it should therefore be profitable for educators to refer to some of these in order to develop economic socialisation for underprivileged children.

All these examples, whether they refer to experiments, interviews or questionnaires, illustrate that in order to study abstract economic notions it is necessary to ask children to solve the kind of economic problems they are faced with in their everyday lives. It seems necessary to put the child in a situation that might be meaningful, and one of the best solutions is the combination of various attractive materials that can be manipulated by the child in order to help him/her develop notions which s/he already possesses. The second-best

27

option is to focus on how children understand and solve the economic problems that they are actually faced with, rather than considering economic socialisation as a steady process of adaptation to the economic behaviour and concepts of adults. This implies being more concerned with the child, and as Webley and Lea observed, 'only a determined effort of observation, empathy and imagination will enable us to enter children's own economic world and assess the relative importance of the events that happen in it' (1993, p.466).

4. Some differentiating factors

Many researchers, when investigating how children observe and perceive economic conditions, tend to present their results in terms of differentiating factors such as age, gender, social class and cultural background, or educational environment.

Most studies based on Piaget's theory remain descriptive and demonstrate that conformity and consistency increase as children get older (DeFleur and DeFleur, 1967). Studies of economic thinking have found no fundamental differences between boys and girls. Gender differences do appear when dealing with economic knowledge; this may be explained, as in Lassarre *et al.* (1987), by the fact that girls still participate more in activities related to consumption, such as shopping.

Social class is one of the most frequently investigated factors in studies of economic knowledge. These studies reveal that middle class children are more familiar with banking vocabulary and professional prestige, while those who come from the working class seem to understand more about industrial relations. For example, it has been found that children whose fathers are workers in large factories have a thorough knowledge and understanding of the world of manufacturing and production (Jahoda, 1981). It should be emphasised that, in many cases, the observed differences cannot be directly related to the economic level of the family, but rather to the type of occupation, or the educational background of the parents, especially the mother. It was also shown by Lautrey (1980) that the consistency between the parents' educative behaviour and the cognitive structures expected in schools is very important. He demonstrated that the parents' educational style directly influences the quantity, type, and diversity of economic information known by the children; this is reinforced by the effect of informal socialisation through discussions about, for example, the family's consumption habits.

The last main differentiating factor seems to be the combination of the children's social and cultural background. It is evident that children from different countries have more or less the same knowledge and understanding of economic phenomena at approximately the same age. Where there are differences, the social, cultural, economic and political situation of the countries should be taken into account. For example, French and Algerian children offer different responses which are clearly related to their cultural backgrounds. French children would 'invest the amount in a bank' in order to increase the amount of money they have, whereas Algerian children, deeply influenced by the words of the Koran forbidding the practice of usury and interest, say that they should 'work more' (Roland-Lévy, 1990a).

Such findings illustrate the importance of collective representation in the construction of knowledge and practices related to the economy. The field of economic socialisation today is taking a new direction with more studies focusing on the influence of parents' lay conceptions of the economy and on the links between social representations of economic phenomena and economic behaviour (Roland-Lévy, 1994, 1998b).

5. Implications for educators

Both parents and teachers can and should try to introduce a more systematic education oriented towards a better understanding of the economic world. A good way of assuring an early economic education is to give pocket money on a regular basis, starting early in childhood. This money-giving should be accompanied by regular discussions about what it stands for; how it is earned; how it can be saved in order to accumulate and later buy something more expensive; how money can be borrowed; and particularly the consequences of borrowing money. Educators could really help the cause of economic socialisation for underprivileged children by

29

introducing a specific budget in the classroom. Some initiatives of this type have been very successful in classes in which a year-long experiment was conducted in order to save money for a specific project (e.g. a trip, a picnic, getting new books) that could not be financed by the school budget. If it is the social and cultural background, rather than age or gender, that determines the economic socialisation of children, then educators can play an active role in this process. In order to enhance the economic socialisation of children, they should find ways to relate to children's everyday lives, their previous experience, and their relations with other people such as peers, teachers and family, and with social institutions.

3

Young people, socialisation and money

Adrian Furnham

University College, London, United Kingdom

Introduction

This chapter examines the economic beliefs and behaviours of young people, concentrating specifically on three things: stage-wise theories about the development of economic ideas; research into the development of specific economic concepts like profit and bank interest; and recent research on pocket money.

Until recently there had been comparatively little research into the economic beliefs and behaviours of young people (Berti and Monaci, 1998; Furnham, 1999a, 1999b; Lunt and Furnham, 1996; Thompson and Siegler, 2000). Even less had been done on *how* knowledge and beliefs are acquired as opposed to the *content* of the knowledge base (Berti and Bombi, 1988). Furthermore it has not been until comparatively recently that researchers have looked at young people's reasoning about economic issues such as consumption, saving, marketing and work-related knowledge. There are a few books on the psychology of money but these tend to say little about children (Ealy and Lesh, 1999; Forman, 1987; Furnham and Argyle, 1998; Matthews, 1991).

What is special about economic understanding is that it forms the basis of the understanding of power in society, and the concepts/ ideology a child develops are therefore of concern to educationalists and politicians (Webley, 1983). The need to relate to the economic structure of any particular society (an idea more radically expressed by Cummings and Taebel, 1978), and the importance of characterising a child's own economic environment, are therefore aspects that might distinguish the development of economic concepts from others. Social values and ideology can influence understanding profoundly. It is, quite simply, impossible to understand the concept of poverty or wealth without understanding the structure of society and the concept of inequality.

Educationalists have been interested in economic understanding in children for a very long time (Bas, 1996, 1998; Goodnow, 1988, 1996; Goodnow and Warton, 1991; Gunter and Furnham, 1998). Indeed there is a stream of papers going back to the turn of the century that concern themselves with children and money (Dismorr, 1902). There has been a vigorous research interest in such things as children's knowledge of money and work experience since then (Mortimer and Shanahan, 1994; Witryol and Wentworth, 1983). Indeed, because of the perceived importance of children's and adolescents' economic understanding, there are now various books aimed at parents and young people that attempt to help them understand and behave responsibly in the economic world (Estes and Barocas, 1994; Gruenberg and Gruenberg, 1993).

For instance in a book subtitled *A smart kid's guide to savvy saving and spending* Wyatt and Hinden (1991) claim to provide a perfect 'hands-on introduction to managing money'. Rendon and Krantz (1992) aimed their book specifically at teenagers. It explains such things as the difference between capitalist and socialist economies; the nature of inflation and recession; how the stock market works; and the government's role in the economy. They believe various factors affect young people's attitudes toward money. These include: whether they have more, less, or the same amount of money as other people in their community; how closely they live to people who have either a lot less or a lot more money than they do, and how much they hear about such people; whether their parents' current money situation is very different from the one they (their parents) grew up with; and how they and their family feel their situation compares with the situations of people they see on television and films or in their textbooks.

There are also a number of interesting books on money specifically for parents. Davis and Taylor (1979) wrote *Kids and Cash* for 'parents who ... want answers about allowances ... want their kids to earn and save money ... believe a job teaches responsibility ... are interested in preparing their children for the realities of the adult world'. They believe all children need to learn money skills such as: *spending money* (understanding concepts like scarcity, price differentials and the necessity of choices); *budgeting* (planning and keeping to money plans); *saving* (the importance and benefits of postponement of gratification); *borrowing* (the concepts and costs of borrowing); and *earning money* (by such things as selling ability, learning to take risks, understanding the competition).

They stress the importance of the allowance/pocket money system in teaching children about the value of money and the basis of responsibility. They argue that parents use five systems that do not work:

1. Money given when needed: irregular, unplanned, capricious.

2. Commission system: effectively a pay-for-work-done system.

3. Allowance tied to responsibility: money conditional upon chores done.

4. Allowance with no strings: paid regularly without responsibilities.

5. Allowance with no strings: but supervised spending.

They also offer advice to parents about how to educate their children through allowances by following quite specific rules.

Godfrey (1994, 1996) aims to help parents teach their children the value and uses of money. The author, a banker who founded a children's bank, suggests that school-aged children should be told that they are 'citizens of the household' and 15 per cent of their allowances goes into tax. They also need to give 10 per cent to charity, and they should be given interest on any savings. Family meetings

33

should discuss economic affairs openly and honestly; a written agenda and a log should be kept. Issues might include product testing the purchases of major items, holiday planning, charity and gift giving. It is also recommended that there is a pool of family money, called the family bank, and the family as a whole should discuss how it is administered and the money spent. Further the family bank should have an explicitly stated credit policy: if a child borrows money they have, say, three weeks to pay it back, with interest. The message to be given is that children, as citizens of the household, should volunteer to do chores and odd jobs, and to take responsibility for these. As children get older and they borrow, lend and trade, they can be taught the importance of verbal contracts, negotiation and the general rules of trading. Family and community values on breakages, shoplifting, etc. need to be discussed, along with consumer affairs. For instance, it is proposed that pre-adolescents are taught the following simple, but important, consumer concepts: get the best buy for the best price; make sure you know the store's policy; don't forget to keep receipts; shop during sales; know your rights. In the teenage years, they need to be taught good practice about credit cards and budgeting, as well as starting a financial portfolio. Clearly the growth of such books is an indication of the importance of this issue to parents who want advice in how best to instil good monetary habits and understanding.

The development of economic ideas and concepts in the children

There is a long and patchy history of research into the development of economic ideas in children and adolescents (Leiser, Sevòn and Lévy, 1990; Roland-Lévy, 1990b). Lunt's (1996) review of research into children's economic socialisation identifies three phases. First, there was a small amount of descriptive work that established that children had a clearly developing understanding of economic life. Second, researchers attempted to map descriptions of children's comprehension of economic matters onto Piaget's theory of the stages of cognitive development producing classic stage-wise theories. Third, an attempt is being made to introduce social factors into the explanation of the development of economic understanding. There has been a burgeoning of research into economic socialisation since the mid 1980s and even more so over the past five years.

Although there have been a variety of studies which have claimed to support the Piagetian view about the development of economic concepts in the child, these studies have found different numbers of stages. There are several possible reasons for this: the age ranges and number of subjects in each study were different, and the precision in the definition of stage boundaries varied.

Table 3.1 shows that there has been disagreement about the number of stages, points of transition and content of understanding at each stage. These stages suggest, though, that the child's understanding of *different* economic concepts always advances *simultaneously* which is clearly not the case. For example, knowledge about wealth lags in development. Stage-wise theories appear to have a number of implicit assumptions: the sequence of development is fixed; there is a specific end state towards which the child or adolescent inevitably progresses; some behaviours are sufficiently different from previous ones to enable us to identify which stage a child or adolescent has reached.

Table 3.1 Dates, samples and stages found in studies of the development of economic understanding

Researcher	Year	Number of subjects	Age range	Number of stages
Strauss	1952	66	4.8-11.6	9
Danziger	1958	41	5-8	4
Sutton	1962	85	grade 1-6	6
Jahoda	1979	120	6-12	3
Burris	1983	86	4/5. 6/7, 10/12	3
Leiser	1983	89	7-17	3

There is increasing criticism of the cognitive stage-wise approach. Dickinson and Emler (1996) believe that economic transactions take place between people in a variety of social roles and there is no clear and simple domain of economic knowledge separate from the broader social world into which the child is socialised. Different social groups possess different economic knowledge; Dickinson and Emler suggest that there are systematic class differences, in that working class children emphasise personal effort as the basis of wage differentials, whereas middle class children recognise the importance of qualifications. They argue that these differences in attribution bring about a self-serving bias that acts to justify inequalities and therefore reinforces the status quo of socially distributed economic resources. In this sense social class determines understanding, which maintains the system.

Leiser and Ganin (1996) report a study of the social determinants of economic ideology that revealed a complex relation between demographic, social and psychological variables. Increased economic involvement was related to support for free enterprise. Middle class adolescents supported a version of liberal capitalism, whereas the working classes were most concerned about inequality. Thus the social conditions influence the system of financial allocation within the household, which then creates consumers with particular orientations towards the economy, which in turn reproduces the existing social organisation of the economy.

There is clearly a movement from a strictly Piagetian, exclusively cognitive view of the growth of economic understanding to one that recognises social factors such as social class which may both promote understanding of the economic world and help maintain it. In this sense, children from different social classes may have slightly different understandings of the economic world. However, social class is difficult both to define and to measure, and research in this area has only begun to scratch the surface.

The development of economic thinking

Although numerous studies of children's understanding of different aspects of the economic world have been carried out, it appears they have concentrated on some topics rather than others (Berti and Bombi, 1988). For example, relatively few studies exist on young people's knowledge of betting, taxes, interest rates, the up and down of the economy (boom, recession, depression, recovery, etc.) or inflation, though the recent work of Thompson and Siegler (2000) may be an exception. Berti and colleagues in Italy have extended the work on understanding economic concepts (Berti and Monaci, 1998) to the judicial system (Berti and Ugolini, 1998) and the nation state (Berti and Benesso, 1998). There is detailed and replicated research on topics like possession and ownership, wealth and poverty, entrepreneurship, prices, wages, money, buying and selling, profit and the bank. However, the common denominator to all economic interactions in the western world is obviously money, and therefore its understanding is a prerequisite for all other concepts.

Money

Children's first contact with money (coins and notes and more recently credit cards) often happens at an early age (watching parents buying or selling things, receiving pocket money, etc.) but this does not necessarily mean that they fully understand its meaning and significance, even though they use money themselves. For very young children, giving money to a salesperson constitutes a mere ritual. They are not aware of the different values of coins and the purpose of change, let alone the origin of money, how it is stored or why people receive it for particular activities.

Pollio and Gray (1973) conducted a study with 100 subjects, from age seven to college students, on 'change-making strategies' and found that it wasn't until the age of thirteen that an entire age group was able to give correct change. When giving change, the younger subjects showed a preference for small value coins (with which they were more familiar) whereas the older ones used all coins available.

Berti and Bombi (1979) interviewed 100 children from three to eight years about where they thought money came from. At *Level 1* children had no idea of its origin: the father takes the money from his pocket. At *Level 2* children saw the origin as independent from work: somebody/a bank gives it to everybody who asks for it. At *Level 3* the subjects named the change given by tradesmen when buying as the origin of money. Only at *Level 4* did children name work as the origin. Most of the four- to five-year-olds' answers were in Level 1, whereas most of the six- to eight-year-olds were in Level 4. The idea of payment for work (Level 4) thus develops out of various spontaneous and erroneous beliefs in Levels 2 and 3, where children have no understanding of the concept of work, which is a prerequisite for understanding the origin of money.

Berti and Bombi (1981a) later identified six stages in the development of children's understanding of the use of money for payment: *Stage 1*: no awareness of payment; *Stage 2*: obligatory payment – no distinction between different kinds of money, and money can buy anything; *Stage 3*: distinction between types of money – not all money is equivalent any more; *Stage 4*: realisation that money can be insufficient; *Stage 5*: strict correspondence between money and objects – correct amount has to be given; *Stage 6*: correct use of change. The first four stages are clearly to be found in the pre-operational period whereas in the last two, arithmetic operations are successfully applied.

More recent studies have looked at such things as children's actual monetary behaviour. For instance, Abramovitch, Freedman and Pliner (1991) found that six- to ten-year-old Canadian children who were given allowances seemed more sophisticated about money than those who were not.

Despite these studies there is a lot we do not know: for instance how socio-economic or educational factors influence the understanding of money; when children understand how cheques or credit cards work, and why there are different currencies. Both attitudes towards and symbolism of money have been studied in adults but not children, and this too awaits empirical enquiry.

Prices and profit

There are a number of prerequisites before children are able to understand buying and selling. A child has to know about the function and origin of money, change, ownership, payment of wages to employees, shop expenses and the shop owner's need for income/ private money. This shows the complexity of the simple act of buying and selling.

Furth (1980) identified four stages in the acquisition of this concept: (1) no understanding of payment; (2) understanding of payment of customer but not of the shopkeeper; (3) understanding and relating of both the customer's and the shopkeeper's payment; (4) understanding of all these things. Jahoda (1979), using a role play where the child had to buy goods from a supplier and sell to a customer, distinguished between three categories: (1) no understanding of profit – the two prices were consistently identical; (2) transitional – mixture of responses; (3) understanding of profit – selling price consistently higher than buying price.

Berti, Bombi and De Beni (1986) pointed out that the concepts about shop and factory profit in eight-year-olds were not incompatible. They showed that by training, children's understanding of profit could be enhanced. Both critical training sessions stimulating the child to puzzle out solutions to contradictions between their own forecasts and the actual outcomes, and ordinary, tutorial training sessions (information given to children) that consisted of similar games of buying and selling, proved to be effective. The authors suggested that although arithmetical abilities are essential, 'making children talk about economic topics they have not yet mastered, far from being an obstacle to learning, may contribute to their progress, constituting in itself a kind of training, as Jahoda (1981) also found in different circumstances' (p.28).

In a study with eleven- to sixteen-year-olds, Furnham and Cleare (1988) also found differences in understanding shop and factory profit. Only 7 per cent of eleven- and twelve-year olds understood profit in shops, yet 69 per cent mentioned profit as a motive for starting a factory today, and 20 per cent mentioned profit as an explanation for why factories had been started. Young children (six to eight years) seemed to have no grasp of any system and to conceive of transactions as simply an observed ritual without further purpose. Older children (eight to ten years) realised that the shop owner previously had to buy (pay for) the goods before he can sell them. Yet they do not always understand that the money for this comes from the customers, and that buying prices have to be lower than selling prices. They thus perceive buying and selling as two unconnected systems. Not until the age of about ten are children able to integrate these two systems and understand the difference between buying and selling prices.

Because of the obvious political implications of the ideas of profit and pricing it would be particularly interesting to see not only when (and how) young people come to understand the concepts but also how they reason with them. It is equally important to investigate when young people understand how competition (or lack of it in monopolies) affects profit, the pressure of shareholders for profits, and the moral concept of profiteering.

Banking

There have been a surprisingly large number of studies on children's understanding of the banking system. Jahoda (1981) interviewed 32 subjects of each of the ages twelve, fourteen and sixteen about bank profits. He asked whether one gets back more, less, or the same as the original sum deposited and whether one has to pay back more, less, or the same as the original sum borrowed. From this basis he drew up six categories:

- no knowledge of interest (get/pay back same amount)
- interest on deposits only (get back more; repay same amount as borrowed)
- interest on loans and deposits, but more on deposits
- interest same on deposits and loans
- interest higher for loans (no evidence for understanding)
- interest more for loan (correctly understood).

Although most of these children had fully understood the concept of shop profit, many did not perceive the bank as a profit-making enterprise (only a quarter of the fourteen- and sixteen-year-olds understood bank profit).

Ng (1983) replicated the same study in Hong Kong and found the same developmental trend. The Chinese children were more precocious, showing a full understanding of the bank's profit at the age of ten. A later study in New Zealand by Ng (1985) proved the New Zealand children to 'lag' behind Hong Kong by about two years. Ng attributed this (at least in part) to socio-economic reality shaping socio-economic understanding. This demonstrated that developmental trends are not necessarily identical in different countries. A crucial factor seems to be the extent to which children are sheltered from, exposed to, or in some cases even take part in economic activity. In Asian and some African countries quite young children are encouraged to help in shops, sometimes being allowed to 'man' them on their own. These commercial experiences inevitably affect their general understanding of the economic world. This is yet another example of social factors, rather than simply cognitive development, affecting economic understanding.

Takahashi and Hatano (1989) examined understanding of the banking system among Japanese young people aged eight to thirteen. Most understood the depository and loan functions but did not grasp the profit-producing mechanism. They suggested several reasons for this: opportunities for children to take part in political and economic activities are very limited; they are not taught about banking in schools; humans do not have any 'pre-programmed cognitive apparatus' to understand human organisations; and banks themselves do not attempt to educate consumers about what they do. However, in most countries, banks are now very eager to educate young people into the world of banking.

More recently, Berti and Monaci (1998) set out to determine whether third grade (seven- to eight-year-old) children could acquire a sophisticated idea about banking after twenty hours teaching over a two-month period. It was a before and after study that involved teaching concepts such as deposits, loans and interests. They concluded:

> While the notion of shopkeepers' profit was successfully taught to third graders who already possessed the pre-requisite arithmetic skills in only one lesson, in the present study it took 20 hours to teach the notion of banking at the same school level. Should this notion be retained in a third grade curriculum nevertheless? Or should that great amount of time be more profitably spent teaching children more fundamental skills, such as writing and arithmetic? Considering the key role of the bank in the economic system, and the pivotal role of the children's widespread misconceptions of banking in supporting their misconceptions of other economic institutions, we think that children's understanding of banking should be promoted as early as possible. Further, it should not be forgotten that some of the hours needed to teach banking were in reality spent on arithmetic exercises, which allowed children to practice operations which in any case they would have had to practice (even if not calculating for exercising arithmetic skills meaningfully). (p.269)

It would be of particular interest to examine the understanding of children in certain Muslim countries where usury is considered to be a sin. It is also interesting to know whether children can differentiate between banks, building societies, merchant banks, offshore banks, etc.

Possession and ownership

The topic of possessions and ownership is clearly related both to politics and economics but has been investigated mainly through the work of psychologists interested in economic understanding. Berti, Bombi and Lis (1982) interviewed 120 children aged four to thirteen years to investigate their knowledge about (a) ownership of means of production, (b) ownership of products (industrial and agricultural) and (c) ownership of product use. Children's ideas about ownership of means of production develop through the same sequences but at different speeds. The notion of a 'boss-owner' seems to occur at eight to nine years for the factory, ten to eleven for the bus, and twelve to thirteen for the countryside, perhaps because 85 per cent of the subjects in the study had had no direct experience of country life. Although very few had had direct experience of their father's working environment, they heard him talk a lot about his work and thus acquired their information, though obviously not all the fathers worked in factories.

Cram and Ng (1989) in New Zealand examined 172 children of three different age groups between five and twelve years about their understanding of private ownership, by noting the attributes the subjects used to endorse ownership. Greater age was associated with an increase in the endorsement of higher-level (i.e. contractual) attributes and in the rejection of lower-level (i.e. physical) attributes, but there was only a tendency in that direction. Nearly 90 per cent of the youngest group rejected 'liking' as a reason for possessing, which increased to 98 per cent in the middle and oldest groups. This indicates that surprisingly most five- and six-year-olds are aware of the distinction between personal desires and ownership.

Concepts relating to means of production seem to develop similarly to those of buying and selling. They also advance through phases of no grasp of any system, to unconnected systems (knowledge that the owner of means of production sells products but no understanding of how he gets the money to pay his workers) and to integrated systems (linking workers' payment and sales proceeds), depending on the respective logico-arithmetical ability of the child. Although these concepts seem to follow the same developmental sequence, it cannot be said whether, to what extent, and how, the same factors (experimental, maturation, educational) contribute to the development of each concept.

Poverty and wealth

In an early study Zinser, Perry and Edgar (1975) tried to determine the importance of the affluence of the recipient to pre-school children's sharing behaviour. Most of the children favoured sharing with poor recipients rather than rich recipients. They were also more generous with low value items than with high value items towards both groups equally, and these findings were consistent among those aged four, five and six.

Winocur and Siegal (1982) later asked 96 adolescents (twelve to thirteen and sixteen to eighteen years old) to allocate rewards between male and female workers in four different cases of family constellations. Concern for need decreased with age: older subjects preferred to distribute rewards on an equal pay for equal work basis whereas younger subjects supported the idea that family needs should be reflected in pay, but there were no sex differences in the perception of economic arrangements. This confirms Sevòn and Weckstrom's (1989) suggestions that younger children judge from a homo-sociologicus and older children from a homo-economicus point of view.

Leahy (1981) asked 720 children and adolescents of four age groups between five and eighteen and four social classes to describe rich and poor people and to point out the differences and similarities between them. The answers were grouped into different types of person descriptions: peripheral (possessions, appearances, behaviour); central (traits and thoughts); and sociocentric (life chances and class consciousness). Adolescents emphasised central and sociocentric categories, perceiving rich and poor as different kinds of people who differ both in observable qualities and in personality traits. Lower class subjects tended to refer more to the thoughts and life chances of the poor, taking on their perspective, while upper-middle class subjects tended to describe the traits of the poor, perceiving them as 'others'. Two theoretical models are discussed to explain these findings: a cognitive developmental model, suggesting that later adolescence is marked by an increased awareness of the nature of complex social systems, and a general functionalist model, suggesting that socialisation results in uniformity within different classes and races as to the nature of the social class system and thus retains stability in social institutions.

Stacey and Singer (1985) had 325 teenagers from a working class background complete a questionnaire, probing their perceptions of the attributes and consequences of poverty and wealth, following Furnham (1982). Regardless of age and sex all respondent groups rated familial circumstances as most important, and luck as least important, in explaining poverty and wealth. With internal and external attributions for poverty and wealth rating moderately important, these findings differ slightly from Leahy's (1981) results, as here adolescents clearly thought sociocentric categories to be more important than the other two.

Wosinski and Pietras (1990), in a study with 87 Polish subjects aged eight, eleven and fourteen, discovered that the youngest had better economic knowledge in some aspects (e.g. the definition of salary, the possibility of getting the same salary for everybody, the possibility of starting a factory) than the other groups. They attributed this to the fact that these children were born and had been living under conditions of an economic crisis in Poland. They had experienced conditions of shortage, increases in prices and inflation, and had heard their families and television programmes discuss these matters.

Again it seems that socio-economic experience shapes the speed of acquisition of economic concepts. This is particularly the case for wealth and poverty, which are often featured in children's story-books.

Saving

Parents are often very eager to encourage saving in their children (see also next section on pocket money). Sonuga-Barke and Webley (1993) argue that children's behaviour and understanding of saving are constructed within the social group and are fulfilled by particular individuals aided by institutional (particularly school) and other social factors and facilities. Researchers need a child-centred view of economic activity, examining children as economic agents in their own right, solving typical economic problems such as resource allocation.

There have been comparatively few studies on children's saving (Ward, Wackman and Wartella, 1977). Webley and colleagues have done pioneering research in this area (Webley, Levine and Lewis, 1991). Sonuga-Barke and Webley (1993) believe that saving is defined in terms of a set of actions (going to the counter and depositing money) made in relation to an institution (bank or building society), but is also a problem-solving exercise; more specifically it is an adaptive response to the income constraint problem. Children have to learn that there are constraints on spending and that money spent cannot be re-spent until more is acquired. Thus all purchases are decisions against other goods, or between spending and not spending.

In a series of methodologically diverse and highly imaginative experimental studies, Sonuga-Barke and Webley found that children recognise that saving is an effective form of money management. They realise that putting money in the bank can perform both defensive and productive functions. However, neither parents nor banks and building societies seem very interested in teaching children about the functional significance of money. Yet young children value saving because it seems to be socially approved and rewarded; it is understood as a legitimate and valuable behaviour, not an economic function. However, as they get older they appear to see the practical advantage in saving.

Some countries like Japan show a particularly high rate of personal saving. The welfare state, the inter-generational transfer of money, and inability to postpone gratification have all been suggested as reasons for poor saving in Britain. There remains a good deal of research to be done to establish when, how and why adult saving habits are established in childhood and adolescence.

More recently, Furnham (1999b) examined the saving and spending habits of young British people between eleven and sixteen years. Nearly 90 per cent of the respondents claimed to have a regular source of income, the vast majority of which (70 per cent) came from pocket money (around £2.50 per week[1]). Over 90 per cent said they received money for Christmas and birthday presents: over five weeks pocket money equivalent on birthdays, and about four weeks pocket money equivalent at Christmas. Most respondents (80 per cent) noted that their parents would not give them more money if they spent it all, confirming their middle class status. Just under three-quarters (72.5 per cent) claimed that they lent money to friends, but 54 per cent claimed that they borrowed money from friends.

Most (92 per cent) reported that they had between £100 and £500 in a building society account. About two-thirds claimed to save regularly, with a quarter saving half of their pocket money, but another quarter of the sample saving almost none. The most commonly cited reason for saving (71.1 per cent) was to buy something special. About two thirds (66.5 per cent) said they had a bank account (though it may well have been in their parent's name), and most of those that did not, simply reported that they had not got around to opening one. A quarter, in fact, reported that they intended to open a new bank account in the forthcoming year, though there is no way of checking whether they did. Of those who already had a bank account, just over a third reported having had it for more than four years.

When asked why they had opened a bank account, the main reasons given were to keep money safe and earn interest; because their parents had opened it for them or advised them to open it; and because there were special offers for young people opening bank accounts. Nearly 80 per cent of the respondents held accounts at one of the 'big four' banks in Great Britain. About a fifth had changed banks for a variety of reasons. Visits to banks were relatively infrequent (once or twice a month). Curiously, the respondents reported withdrawing money more frequently than depositing it, presumably because they deposited comparatively large amounts and withdrew small amounts. Nearly two thirds (63 per cent) claimed to keep a regular check on their bank balance, mainly by requesting a bank statement on a monthly basis.

Economic socialisation: pocket money

One important way in which parents socialise their children in monetary and economic matters is through their *pocket money*, a weekly or monthly *allowance* given either unconditionally or for some household work. The British tend to use the term pocket money; the Americans allowance. Until recently there has been little academic research in this area and most of the information comes from marketing studies. In Britain, for example, a regular survey of pocket money has been carried out by Birds Eye Walls. This reveals that the average pocket money in 2000 was £3.10 per week, that it increases with age, that boys get on average slightly more than girls and that the highest rates of payment are in Scotland, where average payments are almost half as much again as in the south-west of England.

Surveys in France paint a similar picture but also reveal that parents report giving much lower amounts than children report receiving, essentially because parents focus only on pocket money whereas children count all money they receive (Micromegas, 1993). This finding gives an idea of the age at which pocket money may be an important socialising agent, since it constitutes 100 per cent of the income of those aged four to seven years, but only 14.5 per cent of that of thirteen- and fourteen-year-olds (half of French fourteen-year-olds work regularly).

Over fifty years ago, Prevey (1945) studied the practices of a hundred American families in training their adolescents about money. They concluded that boys were provided with more valuable experiences than were girls. Parent practices such as encouraging earning experiences, and discussing family financial problems and expenses with high-school-age children tended to be positively re-lated to later ability to utilise financial resources in early adulthood.

Marshall and Magruder's (1960) study appears to be the first that specifically investigated the relationship between the parents' money education practices and children's knowledge and use of money. They found, as they had hypothesised, that children's know-ledge of money is directly related to the extensiveness of their ex-perience of money: whether they are given money to spend; their opportunities to earn and save money; and their parents' attitudes to, and habits of money spending. Thus it seems that socialisation and education have important consequences for an adolescent's under-standing of economic affairs. In a later study Marshall (1964) found there was no difference in financial knowledge and responsibility between children given an allowance and those not given an allowance. But parents who gave their children allowances differed from those who did not in (a) providing their children with a wider variety of experiences in the use of money, (b) making the purposes of spending money clearer to their children, and (c) permitting or encouraging their children to earn money away from home. The two groups of parents did not differ in other money-education practices and attitudes.

Abramovitch, Freedman and Pliner (1991) have investigated how spending in an experimental store was affected by children's experience of money. After they had finished in the store the children were given a pricing test in which they had to say how much familiar items (e.g. running shoes, television sets) cost; children who received an allowance scored higher on this test, as did the older children. These results suggest that receiving an allowance may facilitate the development of monetary competence.

Though the limited evidence does suggest that allowances are effective, it seems as if parents make only limited use of their potential as a vehicle for economic socialisation. Sonuga-Barke and Webley (1993) focused specifically on whether parents used pocket money to teach children about saving. They found that for most parents, pocket money was seen as money to be spent, not money to be saved. Though there were some half-hearted attempts to foster saving (e.g. by parents offering to match any money saved by the child) this opportunity was rarely taken up. Newson and Newson (1976) in an extensive study of over 700 seven-year-olds, found some differences related to social class in children's unearned income and savings. Middle class children received less pocket money than working class children, but more of them saved some money at the end of the week (90 per cent, in comparison to 48 per cent of the working class children). Furnham and Thomas (1984a) found a similar pattern in their investigation of age, sex and class differences in the distribution and use of pocket money among seven- to twelve-year olds. Working class children received more money, but saved less, than middle class children. Middle class children also reported more than working class children that they had to work around the house for their pocket money and tended to let their parents look after the pocket money that they had saved. The older children received more money and took part in more 'economic activities' such as saving, borrowing and lending.

Furnham and Thomas also investigated adults' perceptions of the economic socialisation of children through pocket money (1984b). Over 200 British adults completed a questionnaire on their beliefs concerning, for instance, how much and how often children should be given pocket money, as well as such things as whether they should be encouraged to work for it, save it, and so on. In comparison with males, females were more in favour of agreeing with children in advance on the kinds of items pocket money should cover; giving older children pocket money monthly; and reviewing a child's pocket money annually. This shows that females are more willing to treat children as responsible individuals. It is possible that this is due to the tendency for women, both at work and in the home, to have greater contact with children and therefore a better understanding of their capabilities.

Over 90 per cent of the middle class adults, but only 70 per cent of working class adults, believed that by the age of eight children should receive pocket money. All middle class adults, but only 84 per cent of those in the working class, believed that by the age of ten the pocket money system should be introduced. Indeed some working class respondents did not believe in the system of pocket money at all. A similar class difference was revealed in the question concerning when children should receive their pocket money. Whereas 91 per cent of the middle class believed children should receive it weekly (and 4 per cent when they need it) only 79 per cent of working class adults believed children should receive their pocket money weekly (and 16 per cent when they need it). Furthermore, significantly more working class adults believed that boys should receive more pocket money than girls.

Miller and Yung (1990) found, contrary to adult conceptions, no evidence that American adolescents understand pocket money to be an educational opportunity promoting self-reliance in financial decision making and money management. Most adolescents see pocket money as either an entitlement for basic support, or earned income. The authors argue that the significance of allowances for adolescents is not the receipt of money per se but how the conditions of receipt are evaluated, the extent of work obligations, and monetary constraints on the amount, use, and withholding of income. In families pocket money allowances are systematically related to all other areas of socialisation.

Feather (1991) examined the relationship between parental reasons and values, and parents' allocation of pocket money to their Australian children. He found the amount of pocket money provided was related quite naturally to the child's age, but also to parents' belief about the need to foster a strong and harmonious family unit. For the older children, parents saw independence training and meeting the child's needs as more important factors and there was some evidence of the difference between mothers and fathers. The parents' work ethic did not affect the amount they gave, yet there was evidence that pocket money is bound up with other parental values and practices.

In Canada, Pliner *et al.* (1996) conducted a number of experiments comparing children who received an allowance with those who did not. Those who received an allowance were found to be better able to make use of credit and to price goods. These skills also increase with age and it appears that the allowance system brings forward the acquisition of consumer skills. Pliner *et al.* suggest that the allowance system works because it engenders a relationship of trust and expectation which requires the child to become financially 'literate' and experienced.

In France, Lassarre (1996) found that the best allocation strategy is the giving of allowances paired with discussions of the family budget. The mechanism that makes the allowance system so effective is the possibility it affords for discussions about financial matters within the family. Lassarre suggests that the reasons why parents give allowances change as the child develops. The allowance is an attempt to control the increasing demands made by the child. Thus a straightforward pocket money system is often the first thing to be introduced, which then gradually evolves into a full allowance system which includes a variety of obligations on both parties.

Three recent British studies examined the issue of pocket money and allowances. Furnham (1999a) asked 400 British adults to complete a questionnaire about their attitudes towards, and behaviour concerning, pocket money in order to investigate the relationship among various beliefs about the use of pocket money, and the extent to which viewpoints are widely shared or vary with parental demography. Most parents (91 per cent) were in favour of starting some weekly-based system by the age of six, with the amount of money increasing linearly over time. The greatest increase was found to occur between seven and ten years, and the least between fifteen and eighteen years. Around three-quarters of the sample believed allowances should be given weekly, and that children should be encouraged to save and take on a part-time job. They strongly endorsed attitudinal items that suggested that parents and children contract the rules under which the children receive money. There were clear age, but relatively few sex and class differences with respect to all the issues examined in the questionnaire. Parents had consistent ideas about rules and responsibilities associated with the allowance system they established, and how it educated their children into the world of money.

Furnham and Kirckaldy (2000) replicated the above study on 238 German adults and compared their results to those of Furnham (1999a). The results were similar overall. In all 91 per cent of British and 99 per cent of Germans believed in the early introduction of pocket money: the British favoured starting at 6.73 years, the Germans at 6.40 years. The recommended amounts given to children at the seven ages specified showed that in both samples there was evidence of a clear linear progression. British parents believed children aged five and six years should get 62p per week while the Germans advocated 72p. For seven and eight year olds the difference was smaller: British £1.98, Germans £2.10. The major difference was for those aged seventeen and eighteen, for whom the British suggested £6.40 and the Germans £9.67.

Furnham and Kirckaldy found 91.3 per cent of Britons and 91.5 per cent of Germans agreed that children should be encouraged to save money; and 38 per cent of Britons and 39 per cent of Germans believed that from age eight, children should be encouraged to donate money to charity. Both groups were strongly against their children borrowing and lending money. However, there were also some interesting differences. More Germans than British (96 per cent v. 86 per cent) believed children should do household chores whereas more British than Germans believed this should be an opportunity to earn more money (66 per cent v. 44 per cent). Over 90 per cent of Germans, but only 72 per cent of Britons believed that parents and children should agree in advance what items pocket money should cover. Interestingly, twice as many Britons (80 per cent) as Germans (40 per cent) believed children should be forbidden to buy particular items. Over three-quarters of the British parents but less than half of the Germans believed children should be given money on special occasions. Further, 88 per cent of the British but only 54 per cent of the Germans believed children should be encouraged to have part-time jobs, but whereas Germans believed children should start at eight years the British suggested ten was more appropriate. Germans agreed much more strongly than the British that pocket money should be paid to those over thirteen years old on a monthly basis, and that pocket money should never be withheld as a punishment.

When the parental samples were asked to report on their own experience as children, the only major difference between the two groups lay in the relationship between allowances and household chores. In all 42 per cent of the British but only 14 per cent of the Germans recorded that they were expected to do household chores to receive their pocket money. Nearly a quarter of the British but less than 10 per cent of the Germans noted that payment of their pocket money was actually dependent on completing tasks.

Furnham (2001) reflected more specifically on individual difference factors associated with parental allowances beliefs. Previous studies have concentrated on demographic and national differences. This study focuses on three types of parental individual difference variables in addition to demographic differences. Many of the attitudinal questions asked in the studies by Furnham (1999a, 1999b) and Furnham and Kirkaldy (2000) served as the dependent variables.

As has been established in previous studies, results indicated that most parents were in favour of pocket money schemes and believed that they should begin at around six years old. They favoured a linear relationship between child's age and amount received, and believed that saving should be encouraged, but that borrowing and lending from other children discouraged. They clearly approved of the establishment of clear rules around pocket money (when it should be received, and what to do when it runs out). Attitude statements were factor analysed to produce clear interpretable factors. These factor scores plus the answers to specific questions served as the dependent variables in a series of regressions which has four sets of independent variables pertaining to individual participants: demographic variables (sex, age, education, income); beliefs (religious and political); 'money pathology' score; and a measure of 'money smarts' (parental allowance style) that assessed related behaviours. Political beliefs, parental 'money pathology' and 'money smarts' were related to attitudes to child socialisation rather than to actual (self-reported) behaviours. Results are discussed in terms of parental socialisation styles.

Overall the various multiple regressions performed showed that the independent variables selected were not particularly powerful predictors of the money attitudes. Three of the six regressions were significant but there is an interesting pattern in that one variable, 'money smarts', was by far the most consistent predictor of attitudes. As in Furnham (1999a), demographic factors accounted for little of the variance, and age and class turned out never to be significant. Religious and political beliefs, which in previous studies have been shown to be relatively powerful predictors of monetary attitudes (Furnham, 1990, 1993, 1996, 1999a, 1999b) were powerful predictors on only one factor, albeit the most important. Money pathology was also a weak predictor of allowance and related attitudes.

However, the 'money smarts' (or money style) test was a logical predictor in each of the significant regressions (Bodnar, 1997). This was a multiple choice 'situational test' that required respondents to indicate how they would behave in a range of money-related situations with their children. The test had clearly been devised as a self-assessment quiz but the results from this study showed both a normal distribution and a satisfactory internal reliability. In essence the test measured how 'sensible' parents were with regard to their children and came at the beginning of a book that attempted to teach children to be better informed about money. The results showed that the higher participants scored on this test, the more they approved of parental involvement in the economic socialisation of their children, and believed in stressing regularity, but the less 'liberal' they were. 'Money-smart' parents clearly believed it is their responsibility to model monetary behaviour and to discuss such things as advertisements, buying decisions and family budgeting with their children. On the other hand they did not endorse ideas that pocket money should not be based on chores or that it should never be withheld. This may be seen as an example of what the book called 'tough love'.

Certainly the growth in books for researchers, practitioners and parents suggests that there is considerable interest in how, why and when young people acquire a working knowledge of the economic world. One obvious other factor that must account for this rise in interest is the increasing spending power of young people.

Conclusion

The importance of how and when children and adolescents begin to understand money and the working of the economy cannot be underestimated. It is important to parents, schools, financial institutions and governments. Parents want to instil sensible habits; schools to find syllabus time and methods to educate; banks to get young customers; and governments to have educated consumers and voters.

Research on what young people (children and adolescents) know about and do with money is clearly important not least because of their increasing purchasing power. Their ideas and understanding are affected by motivation and social experience. Whilst the former is not easy to influence, the latter is. Various groups are interested in increasing the monetary literacy and sensible behaviour of young people.

Studies have shown how economic understanding is acquired gradually and often goes through recognisable stages. However, personal experiences mediated by gender, social class, ethical and national culture often powerfully shape how, and when, young people acquire monetary understanding. Thus whereas in many aspects of cognitive development children from the first (developed, western) world seem to be more advanced than comparably aged children from the third (developing) world, the reverse is often true of economic and monetary understanding. This is primarily due to children from the developing world having to be much more involved in day-to-day economic activity. Five-year-olds may sell fruit while their parents are away, and soon acquire knowledge of change.

Social and economic understanding seems to lag behind understanding of the physical world. Similarly there seems to be less research on the former than on the latter. There are jobs in the public understanding of science: perhaps we need to do as much research on the scientific understanding of the public!

Note

1. The exchange rate at the time of writing is £1 = €1.62.

4

Economy and knowledge acquisition: obstacles and facilitation

Anna Maria Ajello

University of Rome 'La Sapienza', Italy

Introduction

In literature about the acquisition and/or development of social knowledge, it is a commonplace to observe that studies on this subject are not so numerous as those on physico-mathematical subjects. There are several reasons for this: the most frequently mentioned refers to the cultural aspects of social knowledge that reduce the potential for making comparisons, which can be useful in studies concerning the physical world. As we often say, dropping a stone can be seen as a similar experience at every latitude, while making use of public transport and buying a ticket is an operation that is strongly influenced by the cultural, social and economic environment in which it takes place. Moreover, following Piaget's researches, the characteristics of verbal transmission have been identified as a further element of difficulty in the mediation of social knowledge. Direct experience of the social world, which could simplify its comprehension, is an impossibility. After about 50 years of research in this area (since the pioneering studies of Anselm Strauss, 1952), the limitations of the literature are still apparent, not because there have *not* been any studies on the development of social notions, but because they have been following specific directions which this chapter will explore. We will start from the identification of these directions, trying to single out some way to confront the difficulties that are encountered in the course of research in this area.

In outlining economic studies, we immediately notice three things. First, they constitute the majority of all studies dealing with social knowledge. Even though the data are not physical (as in the example of the falling stone), economic ideas are always more accessible than other social notions such as sociological or historical ones. This results from the nature of economic experiences, and our participation in the processes of acquisition and production of goods.

Secondly, the different origins and the variety of paradigms of reference used in this research are apparent; investigations arise in developmental psychology, cognitive psychology, social psychology, economic sociology, educational psychology. This variety is evidence of the wide range of concerns addressed in the findings of such research, ranging from developmental issues to the elaboration of information; and including, for example, the kinds of obstacle that informal reasoning finds in problem-solving; 'expectations' as a cause of different behaviours in financial speculation; the consumer role produced by constant exposure to advertising messages; the function of the socio-economic origin of subjects in their perception of social inequalities; the persistence of moralistic connotations in economic judgement; and so on.

The last aspect to note is that research into economic knowledge often begins from more general problems, such as *conceptual change*. On the one hand, this enables us to see problems through a broad perspective, and on the other hand, it helps us to compare the acquisition of this knowledge with the comprehension of similar notions in the social area, or with totally different notions in the scientific-mathematical area.

The development of economic knowledge

Studies in developmental psychology have made a remarkable contribution to the knowledge of the 'economic world of the child'. In particular, the deep and methodical researches conducted by Anna Emilia Berti and Anna Silvia Bombi (1988) have provided the key to tracing the outline of children's socio-economic notions, by identifying the progression and conceptual articulation which, with the passing of time, characterise the social thinking of younger people.

Some years earlier, the research of Anselm Strauss (1952) and Kurt Danziger (1958) had identified several aspects of children's perceptions of the meaning of money, and of trading and business relations. However, the interest of the results was obscured by the cultural climate, which turned developmental psychology to other models of research.

We will now discuss these models in order to explain the possible causes of children's difficulty of acquisition. According to Strauss, the progression of the capacity to reason allows children to make links among an increasing number of roles. Thus roles that at first are seen as excluding one another – for instance, in children's perception, a mother cannot be a daughter – usually develop into more flexible concepts that are no longer mutually exclusive. In this sense, the ability to reason is considered as an increasing capacity to handle several classes of objects with a progressive expansion of its limits and mutual relations. It is interesting to notice that this way of explaining the difficulties of acquiring a correct understanding involves a return to the formal aspect of reasoning, following Piaget's perspective; in other words, the specificity of economic notions is not examined to identify intrinsic factors which could offer a different explanation for the difficulties of acquisition.

Berti and Bombi's research can be seen as a change of direction. Their investigations start from some specific economic notions – the dealer, the bank, the boss, trading, the factory, jobs and salaries, ownership of the means of production – and trace these back to their origins. The research is focused on children of different ages with their different conceptualisations, and it tries to determine how children progress in dealing with an increasing number of variables and different relations, according to the subjects' ages and to their position in the socio-economic system.

The reference to Piaget's model of cognitive development is used exclusively as a background element. In the absence of more specific and contextual perspectives, it could provide a probable interpretation of children's difficulty of conceptualisation; however, while the two researchers could have relied on a previous study of such notions, they instead proceeded with a close examination of their results in order to continue and develop their research and draw conclusions.

In that way they provided an outline of the economic knowledge of children from the age of four to around fourteen years, beginning from the specificity of each of the economic notions above. Let us consider, for example, the complexity of the term 'boss'. For young children this seems to have a meaning that is similar to, and not distinguishable from, the concept of 'owner', because the ideas of command and possession are closely associated. Cognitive development is then based on the capacity to dissociate and to distinguish the two functions. This can happen when the subject is able to establish hierarchical relations in which at least three elements are included: the owner, the boss, and the subordinates.

A different analysis is used in connection with the notion of the bank, in order to elucidate children's difficulty in understanding the concept of loans and of interest received and paid. Several hypotheses concerning the difficulty of acquisition start with the observation that in order to fully comprehend how a bank works the subject must consider the different functions executed by the bank: safekeeping of money, its issue to customers, and its investment. It is interesting to remind ourselves of Jahoda's (1979) analysis of the difficulty children have in understanding this institution. He argued that they need to distinguish between different types of interpersonal and societal relations if they want to understand the reason why you must repay the bank a higher amount of money than the sum that you borrowed, and why this does not happen in the interaction with a friend who lends us some money; the difference between interest received and interest paid is the financing source for the functioning of the bank itself.

Even for this notion we identify a developmental progression linked to the construction of an increasing number of complex relations in which we can determine the central connections: teenagers of thirteen to fourteen years are able to understand that the two functions of receiving money on deposit and putting it into circulation through loans are mutually linked, but this comprehension is a goal attained slowly and with difficulty. To achieve this understanding, the subjects must overcome all their partial conceptions and abandon their tendency to recognise the various functions in isolation, because this prevents the construction of an articulate and complex system.

During the seventies and eighties, research on economic notions focused its interest on the characteristics of social knowledge in the developing child; in these studies Piaget's model has represented a sort of background and a source of explanations in that it was used, like the theory of equilibration (Furth, 1980), to relate the characteristics of the social ideas to the ages of the subjects. This was done neither to prove the validity of the Piagetian model, nor to extend it to other contexts. In a related, but rather different move, researchers felt the need to examine, as anthropologists do, the world of childhood, from which 'the world of grown-ups' appears as an 'alternative' culture. Research in both these areas confirmed Piaget's message of the originality of childhood conceptions, which has been widely developed in Berti and Bombi's researches (1981b, 1988), but at the same time they implicitly admitted the absence of a general model of reference which could steer the comprehension of children's conceptions in the light of the previous studies.

Furth (1978, 1980) proposed that the development of economic cognition should be seen in terms of a progressive increase of sensitivity to cognitive conflict resulting in the construction of more and more consistent conceptual systems. On this basis he outlined a sequence of five developmental stages:

> *Personal elaborations with the absence of general interpretative systems* (from five to six years). In this phase children acquire new data without connecting them to the previous ones, so they do not perceive the conflict between their ideas and the reality

from which they get the information. For example, they can retain the idea that the shopkeeper gives his money to customers because they need it.

Understanding of basic societal functions (from seven to nine years). In this phase children recognise some functions linked to specific forms of action of which they have direct experience, such as the shopkeeper's action of 'giving change'. But in relation to more general economic aspects, their conceptions are playful and person-centred, and are typified by a harmonious vision with no conflict between their ideas and reality.

Partial conceptual systems in conflict (ten to eleven years). In this phase children perceive some inconsistencies among the systems of ideas they have constructed, since they are able to identify several implicit aspects of economic reality, even if these aspects are not visible to them. Children react to these conflicts by finding some compromise solutions that will enable them to avoid recognition of the conflict.

Systematic but concrete conceptualisations (pre-adolescence). In this phase, which has only been found in a limited number of the subjects, there are some consistent conceptions resulting both from the solution of the conflicts through the articulation of logical thinking, and from the acquired differentiation between personal interactions and societal events.

Systematic and analytic comprehension. This phase, typical of older adolescents and adults, is characterised by the development of a detailed comprehension of political functions and of economic relations, which are recognised through their abstract traits.

The developmental sequence above, and the proposal derived from Furth's research, lead us to interpret the changes of children's societal conceptions as an element linked to a mechanism of equilibration which takes place in the presence of conflicting aspects. This is an interesting attempt to single out and set in order the developmental progression of children's societal conceptualisations and it could be a general instrument to interpret the changes which take place in those conceptions.

The references to the organisation of a system and to the overcoming of conflict may be considered as signs of an attempt to set these changes in a general perspective. However, the mechanism of functioning which has been supposed is too generic and adaptable to other sorts of knowledge, so the problem of the different elaborations of societal knowledge cannot be solved. In other words, the sequence is not helpful in explaining why, in certain situations and with particular knowledge, the subject perceives the presence of a conflict, but only in some cases does s/he feel the need to overcome it.

Jahoda and Furth tried to consider social cognition as distinct from logico-mathematical cognition, but assume that it operates under a similar system. They deemed that the different development of the two systems was caused by the greater difficulty in acquiring social knowledge. Their attempts, like all the previous ones, represent this problem in terms that are too generic to produce any interesting results. In this view, we could consider the knowledge of different societal realities (such as economic, juridical and sociological) as a single body. These notions appear similar if we judge them superficially. For example, economic knowledge, like other forms of social knowledge, involves some elements of calculation, of expectation, of organisation, of system and of individualistic perspectives, which definitely contribute to shape that kind of knowledge. Thus the way in which development and acquisition of knowledge of different social realities proceeds could seem comparable. But when we consider things in a more analytic way, as Berti and Bombi did, we discover that even within the same field, say of economic knowledge, we find several lags (*décalages*) in the age of acquisition of particular notions. Presumably this also takes place within other areas of social knowledge, even if they are broadly similar, and it is therefore inappropriate to consider social knowledge as a homogeneous body.

The cognitive development of the subject and the available information

A new perspective on the changes in children's economic conceptions is given by research into the relation between the subject and his external environment; the latter includes the society he lives in, the social class to which he belongs (with its conceptual standards) and finally, the specific opportunities and experiences, which, even within the same age group, social class and district of residence, can produce more developed or more primitive economic conceptions.

While these studies have different specific aims, they share a common concern with the external elements which surround the subjects. Research includes cross-cultural investigations of the universality of stages of development; studies of the determining influence of social class on the economic conceptions acquired; and evaluations of the function of education and/or learning in the acquisition of the correct conceptions. These contributions draw on a great variety of theoretical paradigms through cross-cultural studies, experimental studies, developmental studies and studies of learning psychology. This research has focused its attention, directly or indirectly, on the *content* of the acquisition and this represents a first confirmation of the specificity of these notions.

In Emler and Dickinson's investigation (1985) and in Emler's analysis (1986) a strong critical stance is taken towards the structuralist conception of cognitive development, on the grounds that it does not consider the environment in which this development takes place and the information that is consequently available to the subject. According to these studies, development should be considered a process of *acculturation*, in which the main role is constituted by the social representations of our cultural environment, although children's capacity of elaboration is still seen as a complementary element.

The references to the process of acculturation and to the role of social representations can be seen as an interesting way of outlining the relation between the subject's elaboration and the kind of contents he interacts with. This offers the possibility of identifying some mechanisms that are intermediate between face-to-face interaction and the macro-social dimension of culture in the anthropological sense.

Social representations, considered as structured ideas and images typical of a social group (Moscovici, 1984), constitute the source that gives birth to the elements of conceptual elaboration; without any reference to them, those conceptualisations could only be seen as the primitive forms of economic conceptions. However, viewing social representations as the source of children's elaborations, which can vary according to the different social groups they belong to, allows us to estimate in a more precise way the influence of the external environment on the kind of conceptualisation, and leads us to consider more directly the role of the content of knowledge in the elaboration itself.

Certainly, in this view the range of variation in children's concepts will increase, while the likelihood of finding universal processes in developmental progressions will be reduced. However, in order to be able to support the planning of an effective educational intervention, it would be useful to outline some consistent and reliable developmental tables based on well-founded points of reference. To do this, it is necessary to draw on research which allows us to interpret children's specific conceptualisations, rather than refer to general tables that are too universal to produce further information.

In Leiser, Sevòn and Lévy's studies (1990) we can find an interesting way to consider children's knowledge in relation to their different life contexts; this analysis brings together and compares data from more than 1000 subjects aged eight, eleven and fourteen (about 330 from each age group), gathered in ten different countries (Algeria, Austria, Denmark, Finland, France, Israel, Norway, Poland, Yugoslavia, West Germany). Questions were asked individually and were based on three areas: *comprehension* of economic events (concerning decisions about prices, wages, investments, etc.); *reasoning* about economic matters in connection with economic events and their consequences on a national scale; and the *attitudes* which subjects bring to their consideration of the causes and consequences of poverty, wealth and unemployment. The authors have analysed children's responses using a multidimensional scale in order to obtain a general outline of the similarities and differences between the various groups in the sample, but, as they themselves warn, in this way the fine distinctions that were present in the great variety of responses are no longer apparent.

The general results show a clear developmental trend in responses concerning the comprehension of economic phenomena, which becomes deeper and wider with increasing age; as the authors say, the conceptualisation of economic events changes from the perspective of 'social man' to that of 'economic man'. In connection with reasoning and attitudes, we do not find a developmental trend. Indeed, the children's attitudes suggest a certain stability over time; the main differences found relate to nations of origin. Among these we can identify two general considerations. The first of these concerns the different *institutional conditions* found in different countries; where the state acts as a moving force in economic events, it is frequently mentioned in the subjects' answers. The second concerns *cultural variations*, not only among countries, but also within each country. Thus we can say that the economic condition of an individual is connected to his individual characteristics and to the characteristics of the cultural group of which he is a member.

Apart from these aspects, it is difficult to examine the results of the cross-cultural comparison in greater depth. This is because we must take into account the varied conditions of the interview conducted by different interviewers in every single country. We also need to consider the varied connotations of, for example, 'middle class', which can refer to completely different situations in countries such as Algeria, Yugoslavia and Denmark. A further limitation is the size of the sample: 30 subjects in each age group in each country. This sample is large enough to identify developmental trends within an evolutionary perspective, but if we choose to examine the influence of information given by the environment on children's conceptualisation, then the analysis will be much more complex, and it would be necessary to carry out a larger and more thorough investigation of all the noteworthy issues in each country. The authors conclude: 'In this way we can hope to deepen our comprehension of how the objective factors in the environment of the child can influence his comprehension of economic and social mechanisms' (1990, p.613).

An important aspect of this study is the reflective perspective of the authors. Firstly they attempt to confront the complexity of economic knowledge and to investigate it by distinguishing aspects concerning comprehension, reasoning and attitudes. Secondly, they consider the external environment as a source for the elements of elaboration, distinguishing between the macro-cultural aspects, relevant to national differences, and the micro-cultural groups the subjects belong to. Thirdly, they reflect on the conditions of the interviews, an element that has often been underestimated, but one that is produced by the characteristics of the interviewer and the interviewee, which inevitably affects the responses given.

In short, this study is valuable simply for its effort to consider the different aspects of research into the development of economic knowledge, and for avoiding the trap of experimental reductionism.

Research into informal economic reasoning

A different contribution is made by those studies which, moving away from the human information-processing approach and the neo-Piagetian model, have used a problem-solving methodology to examine the informal reasoning through which adults solve problems about the everyday economic world. James Voss has carried out research examining problems concerning the car market, the federal government deficit, and the cost of money. These were set in the United States, but have aspects common to other western advanced industrial societies. Voss studied problem solving among subjects with different levels of education and competence, from 'naives' through novices to experts (Voss, 1988; Voss *et al.*, 1986). The interesting aspect of this research is that Voss considers the subject matter, or content of the elaboration, and examines its characteristics in terms of the consequences that this could have on the cognitive elaboration itself.

In order to understand this research, it is important to examine the model of reference he used to analyse the subjects' behaviour when they elaborated the solutions of economic problems. The fundamental presupposition of Voss's analysis affirms that, in the solution of problems with social subject matter, the 'solution' is actually a new 'representation' of the problem, so that the whole process, from the initial presentation of the question to its new representation, can be considered as a process of *argument*, created to support this new representation. In Voss's view, this happens because in the social sciences there is no single solution shared by researchers; we can find a number of solutions, and when we choose one of them we have to justify our action. Thus we are dealing, not with an algorithmic process, but with a heuristic one; in the former the reasoning sequences are well known and circumscribed, while in the latter they are linked to the kind of representation that is aimed for, and there is no common method that can lead to that solution.

According to Voss and his co-workers, both specialised reasoning and informal reasoning are used in an argument process; the difference between these two kinds of reasoning lies in the characteristics of the explanations used to support the argument. The explanations used in specialised reasoning are logically connected to their original premises; in contrast, those used in informal reasoning are shown to be reasonable on the basis of a principle of validity shared by all the subjects (soundness); in other words, this means that these reasons are identified with reference to the social group to which the subjects belong.

Moreover, Voss introduces another distinction between specialist and informal reasoning. The expert solver 'turns' the problem into another one; he identifies its historical causes and gives a more precise representation of the problem itself by distinguishing the main aspects from the secondary ones. Therefore in considering the solution, we outline the elements that refer to the central question and from this question we try to derive some subordinate aspects. Those subjects that do not have a specialised competence (novices and naives), limit themselves to 'decomposing' the problem into more limited partial aspects by identifying several separate and circumscribed solutions which cannot be linked in a general perspective.

In relation to the subject matter of the problems (the car market, the federal government deficit and the cost of money), Voss and his associates found that there were some differences between the solutions given by the novice and naive subjects. The researchers considered their attendance at educational courses with economics classes, as well as their professional experience, as possible sources of economic experience. The results show that reasoning about informal economic problems can be divided into two different types. In the first, the subject returns the problem to a disciplinary scheme and expresses the 'algorithm' of the solution; in the second, the subject lacks a familiar solution and/or a theoretical-conceptual scheme to make reference to, and so uses his reasoning to produce answers. Within this second type we can find the most interesting differences between subjects in relation to their educational backgrounds (which ranged up to those who had achieved a first college or university degree). While all the subjects defined the problems in the right way, those with a university education arranged the different concepts correctly; produced higher quality reasons; furnished a larger number of alternative topics; critically checked their declarations; and corrected themselves when their assertions were incoherent. However, there was no distinction between those subjects who had attended economics classes and those who had not. It is interesting to notice that acquired economics knowledge had no influence on the various solutions offered; it was not useful in solving the problems posed. We must therefore consider the difference between 'everyday' economics and that which is taught in school; the results of Voss's research suggests that the latter may not be put into practice in real life.

These conclusions give rise to two other considerations. The first concerns the economics discipline, and in particular the selection of contents and the methods used in class. Currently these elements are not aimed at helping the subject to use his knowledge in everyday life, but rather, they promote the further acquisition of systematic economic knowledge. The second consideration concerns the ability to reason 'in general', which is the main characteristic of subjects who have attended college. In comparison to those who have not reached this degree of education, they were able to furnish more articulate and advanced elaborations and higher quality performances. Moreover, they demonstrated their ability to face new challenges; to link the new concepts proposed by the problem to those they already knew; and to set the information in a hierarchical order, pointing out further conceptual relations. This means that the subject's knowledge, even concerning economics, must be considered on the basis of its organisation and its accessibility, because these are the main conditions for achieving a successful review of useful information to solve new problems, as the study on elaboration suggests.

This discussion of James Voss's theories allows us to begin to consider the different aspects of acquisition of economic knowledge, in that it is closely linked to the results of studies of this kind. The next section will examine this matter more directly.

The acquisition of economic knowledge: a comparison of perspectives

In studies of children's economic knowledge several different explanations have been given of the difficulties and varied rhythms of acquisition; these will be discussed in this section because they represent a way of considering the kinds of obstacle that have to be faced in order to understand economic phenomena.

An interesting branch of research, with some relevance for understanding the learning of economic notions, is that regarding *conceptual change*, in that it offers the opportunity to focus on these aspects more effectively. Vosniadou and Brewer (1992) and Vosniadou (1994) distinguished between *frame* theories and *specific* theories in relation to the acquisition of scientific, physical and astronomical notions (the first areas where these ideas were examined). Frame theories are based on ontological and epistemological presuppositions, and analyse the subject's conception of the world in a general way, while specific theories produce mental models that are more closely targeted.

According to the results of these studies, the intersection between the acquired correct information (e.g. the earth is spherical) and several contradictory notions (e.g. the earth is flat), gives rise to *misconceptions* which are synthesised models that can be derived from attempts to combine two conflicting notions.

Bringing about change in frame theories is complex, difficult, slow and takes place over a long period of time; this is because it implies a change of beliefs that are strongly rooted in the subject's repeated experience. Another way of looking at this is to draw on Carey's (1985, 1991) categorisation of learning in the different fields of knowledge; she distinguishes: *accretion*, defined as accumulation and expansion of knowledge; *weak restructuring*, a sequence of small changes in our system of knowledge; and *radical restructuring*, a substantial change of the perspectives in that field of knowledge. We can say, then, that change in the frame theories takes place only through a radical restructuring.

Why are the results of these studies so relevant to the acquisition of economic notions? They are drawn on in research by Berti and her co-workers; they conducted several studies of conceptual change in connection to the functioning of the bank, in order to analyse the kind of restructuring that can be produced in subjects by a specific didactic intervention. These studies aimed to demonstrate that, under certain educational conditions, it is possible to produce radical and lasting changes which, without intervention, would be reached at a more advanced age. Berti and her co-workers (Berti, 1999; Berti and Ciccarelli, 1996; Berti and Monaci, 1998), through experimental and quasi-experimental studies, provided children aged eight, nine and ten years with several instructional units concerning the functioning of a shop or a bank and the destination of their profits. The result of these interventions was sometimes a weak, but more often a radical restructuring of the children's knowledge of the functioning of the bank. Thus even when the subjects did not conceptualise the bank as an economic business, or did not quantify the interest

71

received or paid, they nevertheless understood that the money deposited did not end up in some 'safe' containers waiting to be withdrawn by its owners, but was put into circulation as loans. This research demonstrates that, through the provision of correct information and the precise identification of the various notions that must be acquired, it is possible to bring about very precocious learning.

These studies are particularly interesting because they involved teaching children about an aspect of economic life of which they had very limited direct experience. Direct experience is the characteristic which is most frequently cited as a factor that facilitates the general acquisition of physical and scientific knowledge; however, it also produces the deeply rooted frame theories that have been found to be a hindrance to a correct and deep comprehension of scientific phenomena. However, in relation to the acquisition of economic notions such as the functions of a bank, the absence of these theories (as a consequence of limited direct experience) becomes an advantage and a resource, in that the correct comprehension of these institutions is no longer in conflict with wrong presuppositions and conceptions that are rooted in the daily experience of the subjects.

An interesting consideration here is that the research of Berti and her co-workers reintroduced the theme of bringing about cognitive development. Piaget ironically criticised such concerns about the possibility of acceleration of progress through the stages; he referred to this as 'the American question', an allusion to the pragmatic attitude that dominated the concerns of US researchers in relation to his model of cognitive development.

In fact, even if the conduct of these experiments of teaching about the bank proves to be correct, and the results are significant, this research raises some questions, in that development, in this case, is linked to a kind of learning that is seen as individual, and involves memorisation of facts. This contrasts with our knowledge that in learning social (and other) ideas, the ability to *argue* has a fundamental role because it involves furnishing the reasons for what we think and, at the same time, working out our knowledge in a wider way. Moreover, considering correct acquisition in the light of the

'American' perspective means assuming a reductionist perspective; socio-economic knowledge acquisition is a very complex pheno-menon and requires careful attention to the variables involved.

Despite these considerations, the research of Berti and her col-leagues still has considerable interest because it makes us reflect upon the other characteristics of macro-social and economic know-ledge in a particular way; it allows us to examine the elements that can hinder (or foster) progression in the acquisition of economic knowledge. In Jahoda and Furth's early studies, two main difficulties were considered: the way in which children fail to distinguish bet-ween societal (macro-social) and interpersonal (micro-social) rela-tions, and the verbal mediation of social knowledge. A further obstacle to achieving correct economic understanding arises from young children's lack of distinction between moral (and moralistic) aspects and purely economic aspects. Their economic evaluations are often interwoven with their moral ones; for example, they cannot identify the activity of an agent as a particular form of work which should be remunerated, because it is considered 'non-productive' and somewhat fraudulent, and thus payment is inappropriate (Ajello *et al.*, 1988).

Earlier research has similarly demonstrated that, in relation to social knowledge, subjects express their evaluations even when they lack information. For example, four-year-olds in the United States were able to distinguish the American flag, and expressed positive feel-ings towards it; they also recognised the Soviet flag, towards which they expressed feelings of hostility. These children did not possess, or express a need to have, any other specific information about the Soviet Union. The researchers underlined the fact that these subjects were strongly influenced by their environment; those were the years of heavy tension between the United States the Soviet Union (Lawson, 1963, Jackson, 1972). The interweaving of moral and economic aspects that dominates children's conceptions is difficult to overcome (and indeed persists in adult thinking), and it must therefore be recognised as one of the main obstacles to acquisition of correct information in the economic field. Efforts to teach children must take this into account. In this sense, the absence of frame theories, which in Berti's studies comes out to be a determining factor for achieving correct understanding, could be considered in the light of moralistic and/or ethical conceptions which can sometimes hinder the correct comprehension of economic phenomena, because the different disciplinary arguments (economic and ethical) are not distinguished. This aspect is a characteristic peculiar to social knowledge, and recognising it means deepening the specificity of these disciplinary fields.

Another consideration for the educator concerns the possibility of children taking part in and observing economic situations of everyday life; this has been seen as an important factor for an easier acquisition. However, the results of even the deepest and most focused interviews, like those of Berti and Bombi's researchers, suggest that even for older subjects it is not sufficient to take part in economic operations or to observe them in order to understand the whole mechanism; to understand those operations completely it is necessary to have some specific interpretative principles. This characteristic is linked to the characteristic of the social sciences which provides the abstract interpretation of daily phenomena: without this element, which acts as a sort of spectacles, everyday reality can be exposed to banal and/or wrong perspectives, like any other kind of experience.

So, in the same way, even the *observation* of external contexts, which is often used in teaching as a technique to facilitate learning, must be related to general abstract principles that are accessible to learners, and do not over-simplify. These principles act as ordering elements that classify the realities observed; in other words they distinguish those aspects worthy of note from the secondary ones. They are useful in reconstructing the general sense of what we are observing and in the attribution of non-explicit meanings. Therefore furnishing those principles in advance is a fundamental step to achieving correct acquisition of social knowledge, even of those notions that seem more straightforward because they belong to ordinary life.

These ideas concerning the selection of ordering principles of experience are linked to the selection of the criteria that must guide the choice of experiences and of disciplinary content to be offered to learners. To determine these, we need to consider the obstacles which must be overcome for a correct acquisition of those notions, and to refer to the results of previous research. From this perspective, we can mention also the ideas of several researchers who, beginning from different interests, have made some valuable contributions towards defining this question in a better way. For example, let us consider Sydney Strauss's proposal (1986) regarding the characteristics of the content to teach in school. He identifies 'intermediary structures' as a useful aid to selection of the content to be transmitted in school. By intermediary structures he means some concepts and explanations which are born from the association between the deep structures of our brain (able to recognise the regularities in the environment) and the intuitions coming from daily experience. For instance, the different temperatures of objects or the different heat they emit, give rise to general intuitive models of thermal concepts, which can be changed through educational interventions. In other words, Strauss's proposal suggests the identification of some principles for the ordering of experience which, through an appropriate educational environment, can favour the acquisition of particular concepts, rules and laws that assume an intermediate position between the general thinking of individuals and some limited specific acquisitions.

In a similar way, for economic knowledge we could single out some constructs that are at this intermediary level; that is what happened, for example, in experiments about the teaching of economic notions in primary schools (Ajello *et al.*, 1986a). The construct of 'productive system' was divided into several 'production chains' and on the basis of this operation the researchers prepared three curricula for pupils from eight to ten years of age. The disciplinary implications and the political or the ideological value of these operations have been discussed in detail elsewhere (Ajello, 1991). The aim here is simply to underline the fundamental educational value represented by the choice of ordering principles for the experiences proposed in the classroom, an element which has not been sufficiently studied by psychologists.

Finally we will consider two contributions: the first is that of Stefano Zamagni (1992). He reflects as an economist on the criteria for selection of theoretical perspectives that simplify acquisition. He believes that the historic-genetic dimension – a useful element to examine the ways in which different historical societies gave rise to different productive systems – is the most appropriate one for this function. In other words, by applying the historical perspective to economic phenomena we would focus on the origin of the different productive systems, and, according to the economist, this is a dimension that simplifies this acquisition. From the disciplinary point of view this means that, in comparison to all the other disciplinary theoretical perspectives, the perspective proposed by classical economics, based on productive systems with the division of labour and exchange, is suggested as the most suitable one to simplify the acquisition of economic knowledge. This suggestion is not currently taken on in the practical teaching of the economics discipline, which is more often based on neo-classical definitions and which considers economic phenomena from the perspective of the individual, dealing with ways of satisfying his needs through the choice of limited and variable resources.

An indirect support for this position comes from Yrio Engestrom's (1991) discussion of the reasons for 'encapsulation'. He uses this word to mean that the correct acquisitions, deprived of connections with other notions in the subject's mind, appear so isolated and closed that they cannot be used in the more general thinking of the individual. Engestrom's explanation suggests that the acquisition of notions that are not connected with the historic-cultural environment they come from somehow makes them sterile and deprives them of those links that could favour their further use. According to Engestrom, if for example we compared textbooks coming from different periods, we would consider knowledge as a product of specific perspectives linked to the interests of societies from different historical phases; in this way its connections with the other dimensions of a certain period would appear more evident. For economic knowledge, that means pointing out the links with the other aspects of the societies it refers to, rather than the presentation of ahistorical and abstract concepts.

In conclusion we can note that in order to facilitate the acquisition of socio-economic knowledge, we have some suggestions from developmental psychologists, from socio-cultural psychologists and from economists. These different disciplinary fields shed light on ways in which we can proceed. Moreover the link between societal characteristics and economic notions is one of the most important issues we can consider in order to facilitate the socio-economic acquisition of children of different ages.

5

How children construct ideas about work

Merryn Hutchings
University of North London, United Kingdom

Introduction

Work, whether paid, unpaid or voluntary, is a central aspect of society. There are ongoing debates about the distribution of both work and rewards for work across society, the changing nature of work, conditions of work, and in the United Kingdom, long hours worked. Young people's perceptions and expectations of work must be a matter of interest in relation to the reproduction of society, how it changes, and in particular, how social and economic inequalities are reproduced and certain groups remain disadvantaged. Yet our understanding is still relatively limited about how children, who are to a large extent cut off from the adult world because they attend school, construct ideas about adult work. This is partly because of the fragmented way in which work has been given attention in academic studies.

The concept of work is a very complex one. We talk about 'going to work' (a place where one works, usually involving employment or self-employment); 'working hard' (making a sustained physical or mental effort which may be for employment, but may also involve studying or pursuing a hobby); 'household work' (usually unpaid, but necessary); 'working out' (to get fit). Work can be regarded as a serious and important activity, not to be interrupted; as an unpleasant

79

and tedious necessity; or as the central fulfilment of life. This complexity has not always been fully reflected in academic writing. Sociological studies of work have traditionally focused entirely on activity that is economically rewarded (e.g. Argyle, 1972; Anthony, 1977). A broader perspective includes a wide variety of productive and reproductive activities such as wage labour, self-employment, household work, childcare and voluntary work. Pahl argued:

> Work can be understood only in relation to the specific social relations in which it is embedded. Specific people in specific sets of social relations and social relationships can be described precisely in terms of whether they are engaged in work or play. The word 'work' cannot be defined out of context. (1984, p.128)

Most sociologists have not considered any children's activities to be work, though Pahl's argument potentially includes school work as a form of social reproduction; Qvortrup (1995) saw it as part of the social division of labour; children work to produce themselves as a form of social investment. White points out that:

> As soon as they begin compulsory schooling, pupils are as much involved in work as lorry drivers or mothers looking after children. They are constrained to engage in activities directed to some end-product or other, whether they want this or not. (1997, p.17).

How do children take on this complexity? This is something we know relatively little about, because most research focusing on children and work has focused on a single context. Those concerned with economic understanding have investigated children's constructions of paid employment (e.g. Burris, 1976; Shields and Duveen, 1983). The developmental framework commonly adopted by such studies has resulted in a tendency to collect data relating to a single aspect of employment, e.g. the boss (Berti and Bombi, 1988), in order to discover the developmental sequence of ideas in that particular aspect.

Children's occupational aspirations have been studied quite separately, though again a major concern has been to document the developmental changes in aspirations (e.g. Ginzberg, 1972; Gottfredson, 1981). Others emphasise the situational factors that determine career entry (e.g. Roberts, 1975). A more recent concern has been the gendered nature of aspirations (e.g. Kelly, 1989; Francis, forthcoming).

Other researchers have focused on children's experiences of employment. Many investigations are concerned with numbers employed, their class and gender, the jobs they do, their earnings, the proportion working illegally (e.g. Hobbs and McKechnie, 1997, 1998; Middleton, Shropshire and Croden, 1998). Other concerns include health and safety (O'Donnell and White, 1998), and the effects of employment on educational achievement (Dustmann *et al.*, 1996). Children's views have been investigated in the west (e.g. Morrow, 1994; McKechnie *et al.*, 1996; Justegård, in this volume) and in other parts of the world (Blanchet, 1996; Woodhead, 1999).

A fourth distinct area of research is concerned with children's contributions to household work. Topics include family relationships (e.g. Goodnow and Delaney, 1989); changing concepts of children (e.g. Zelizer, 1985); development of a sense of responsibility (e.g. Elder, 1974; Solberg, 1990); altruism (Rheingold, 1982; Grusec, Goodnow and Cohen, 1996); work in relation to gender issues (White and Brinkerhoff, 1981; Berk, 1985). Much of this research has been primarily concerned with the views of parents; investigations of children's ideas include Goodnow and Burns (1985) and Warton and Goodnow (1991).

Children's work at school has attracted rather fewer studies; researchers tend to focus on children's learning, or on teachers' organisation of tasks, but only a few have considered what children are learning about work. Examples include Apple and King (1990), who focused on the way in which children in the kindergarten are taught to distinguish between work and play; Pollard (1985), who identified ways in which teachers encourage productivity, efficiency, order and discipline (thus meeting industrial needs for a productive and compliant workforce); and Cullingford (1991), who investigated children's views of their experience at school, and included their comments on work.

These, then are the main fields in which research has been conducted. Bowes and Goodnow, reviewing research in this area, comment that 'the available accounts ... are far from adequate, in large part because the relevant studies are scattered. Each work setting, each aspect of understanding, tends to be considered one at a time' (1996, p.300). They argue:

> Social contexts are in reality interconnected. The analysis of social understanding and of competence should then reflect this reality rather than deal with single contexts in isolation. In addition, the expectations that are carried over from one setting to another may be a critical part of the ways in which people approach and respond to work situations. (p.312)

Bowes and Goodnow found very few studies addressing these interconnections. Some considered the perceived relevance of school to future employment (e.g. Goodnow and Burns, 1985; Roberts and Dolan, 1989). Butorac (1988) examined the extent to which children perceive work rules as being the same in school and in the workplace, and Goodnow and Warton (1992) investigated whether children thought delegation procedures are likely to be the same at home and in employment.

This chapter reports on a different approach to interconnections; it examines how children draw on a range of experiential resources in their constructions of adult work. Children experience work in a variety of contexts: home, community, school, and media. While the school curriculum offers some work-related information, the vast majority of children's experiences of work fall outside the taught curriculum.

- They work themselves at school and at home. Work at home may include household chores, contribution to family economic work, school homework and hobbies.

- Work features in children's play and other imaginative constructions. They imagine themselves in different work roles, and expect to work when they are grown up.

- They observe, and may interact with, people working in a variety of contexts: at home, in the community, in the school, on television, and, for some children, in parental workplaces.

- They hear about the work, or lack of work, of other members of their families.

- They read about people working, both in factual accounts, and in fiction.

It would be interesting to know what children learn about work in each of these contexts. However, it is impossible to investigate directly what someone has learned because we do not have access to the contents of the mind and so we cannot tell what another person perceives or remembers. What we can investigate is the 'output' of the mind: what a person does or says in a specific context. This will inevitably reflect the person's construction of the audience and of the specific situation in which they are talking or acting. Moreover, all talk is co-constructed with conversational partners, even if they say nothing and contribute only through body language suggesting attention or indifference (Wetherell and Potter, 1992; Shotter, 1993). Thus what children say can never be taken to represent what they know, but rather, what they construct in a specific situation.

The metaphor of construction is a useful one in the questions it allows us to ask. It draws attention to the fact that descriptions and accounts are constructed, and also that they construct reality. Thus Potter argues, 'If we treat descriptions as constructed and constructive, we can ask how they are put together, what materials are used, what sort of things or events are produced by them, and so on' (1996, p.98).

The notion that accounts and descriptions are constructed is central to the research that I describe in this chapter. I sought to find out how children constructed work in unfamiliar settings: that is, what resources they used and how they put these together. During the interviews I sometimes asked children directly where they had got their ideas from. These extracts are taken from interviews with two eleven-year-olds:

So how do you know all this about factories?
Well, I don't really, I'm sort of guessing, basically.
Good guessing though.
Well, I've watched TV programmes ... and books, and maybe the newspaper ... we've done sort of projects like machinery ... I visited a cotton factory ...
So, a bit from school, a bit from books, a bit from television?
Yes, bits from everything I think, and the rest was sort of thinking what you would do. (Eleanor: female)

So how do you know all this about factories?
I don't, that's what I said. I don't. I just, like with the shares bit I was thinking about it and I was taking it, because I know my grandma, she's got shares in a petrol station or whatever, and I know what happens there, so I just take a bit from each thing that I know and put it all together. (Chris: male)

Both extracts illustrate vividly how children draw on a range of experiences in constructing an imaginary account of an unfamiliar situation. The focus of this chapter is how children '*take a bit from each thing ... and put it all together*'; that is, the way experiential resources are drawn on and used in new constructions.

The data used here are taken from semi-structured interviews investigating children's constructions of work in a variety of settings:

- work done by the child, at school and at home

- work done by family members

- work done by adults in the school

- work the child might do when s/he grew up: two or more possibilities were discussed

- work in factories: each child was asked to imagine setting up and running a factory making an item of their choice. (This topic was introduced by asking about the origins of goods in shops; if they did not mention making goods, this section was omitted.)

Children were also asked about the sources of their ideas.

The 43 children interviewed were aged four to eleven years, and attended two London primary schools: School A, in a deprived inner city council estate, and School B, in an area of Victorian owner-occupied housing. Their parents engaged in a wide range of work: employment in large and small organisations; self-employment; and voluntary work. Several were unemployed. My intention was to include children with a wide variety of experiences of work, rather than to achieve a representative sample. Children are referred to by pseudonyms; after each name I indicate gender, age in years and months, and school attended. Research findings are fully reported in Hutchings (1997).

In this chapter I will address a number of overlapping questions:

* What experiential resources did the children refer to, and why is it that some children drew on a much wider range of resources than others?

* How are previous experiences drawn on in new constructions?

* What does this tell us about the processes of construction?

* What are the implications for education?

What experiential resources did the children refer to?

The range of experiential resources referred to varied enormously between children. Table 5.1 (pages 88-89) presents the resources drawn on by three children. They cannot be regarded as typical, or as representative of the whole group, but have been chosen to give some indication of the variations between children. Jimmy (m/5.10) and Nicky (m/11.00) came from working class families and attended School A (inner city council estate). Jimmy's father was a manual worker; both Nicky's parents had been unemployed for many years. Heidi (f/8.05) attended School B. Her father was a self-employed business consultant and worked from home. Her mother was employed by a national charity. Her older brothers worked in a local shop during their university vacations. Both her parents also did voluntary work.

It is possible to identify a number of factors that contributed to the differences between children in the number and variety of resources referred to:

Age of child: older children might be expected to have a wider range of experiential resources to draw on, and this was generally so. However, the range and variety of resources drawn on did not necessarily relate to age, as can be seen by comparing Jimmy and Nicky. The youngest children tended to draw more extensively on resources relating to their own activities (rather than observation of or talk with others) and often made very ingenious use of these experiences: for example, Jimmy said that he would use *'loads of packets of Superglue'* to stick bricks together to build an engine shed.

'Work-rich' or 'work-starved' household (Pahl, 1988, p.603): Heidi's household was work-rich, having multiple sources of income, able to engage in self-provisioning (such as decorating, gardening etc.) and to employ others to do some household tasks. Nicky's household was work-starved, having no income other than social security payments, and being unable to afford either to employ others, or to engage in much self-provisioning. Thus, in comparison with Nicky, Heidi was able to draw on a wider range of models of adult work.

Family income: those families with higher incomes are more likely to be able to afford to visit a variety of shops; to go on outings and holidays; and to pursue hobbies and out-of-school classes. Such activities offer children opportunities to observe work in the local community and beyond. Differences in income obviously occur between work-rich and work-starved households, but also relate to socio-economic class.

Social class: Walkerdine and Lucey (1989), commenting on transcripts of children and mothers talking at home, showed how the middle class mothers felt that they had to exploit educational opportunities wherever possible, turning household activities such as shopping and laundry into educational play. In contrast, the working class mothers drew clear guidelines between their work, which took priority, and the time they could then spend playing with their children. Walkerdine and Lucey commented that these differences relate to the social and economic circumstances of the women, but also to 'the way in which these things are cross-cut by their under-standing and familiarity with modern accounts of child develop-ment' (1989, p.83). While I did not observe children and parents to-gether, it seemed that the middle class children's families did provide educational activities for their children:

> *When I'm on half term my mum always wants to take me to museums. So I might go to a few museums or galleries or whatever, and come back and say, for a couple of days and play basketball* [with friends in local playground], *go to a gallery another couple of days.* (Chris: m/11.06/B)

Walkerdine and Lucey also point out that working class mothers may explain some aspects of work more directly to their children. They found that working class children were more aware of the relationship between money and work than middle class children were. However, among the children I interviewed this was less evident, perhaps because a number of the working class parents were unemployed.

Nature of parental employment: some forms of work are easier for children to understand than others. The daughter of a stockbroker knew only the title of her father's job, whereas a boy whose father worked in a radio station had visited his father's workplace regularly and could explain what the job involved. These differences did not relate directly to social class, though many of the working class jobs were easier for children to understand because they were practical.

Having siblings entering employment: those children whose siblings were working or seeking work had a wider range of resources to draw on. In these families work became something to talk about rather than something taken for granted, and assumed greater impor-tance for the younger generation.

Safety concerns: many parents do not feel confident that it is safe to allow their children to play in the street or park. It appeared that

Table 5.1: The resources children drew on in their constructions of their own future work and work in a factory

	Jimmy (m/5.10/School A)	Heidi (f8.05/School B)	Nicky (m/11.00/School A)
own activities hobbies, work, etc.	• going to Kentucky Fried Chicken • buying sweets in a sweetshop • having a bank account • use of Superglue • shopping • playing ar being a pop star with his microphone and guitar • cooking toast • visit to nanny in Newcastle • boat trip to London Bridge	• savings in bank and PO • painting, drawing, art classes • raising money at jumble sales • cooking: icing cakes, mashing potatoes • making pottery at classes • going to the shops, paying, getting change • visits to Macdonalds – observed workers' uniforms • being a monitor at school • buying things from stall in the streets	• drawing • work at school in room with desks, other people and paperwork
family work visit	• observing father's work as a daddy, parents' housework • visiting father's workplace (train workshop)	• visits to brother's workplace (health food shop) • seeing father work at home on his computer	
talk	• talk with father about his work fixing brakes on trains • father's working hours	• talk about brother's work in health food shop • talk about brothers' careers after university • talk with father about his work as a self-employed business consultant • talk with mother about her work for a charity • parents' voluntary work as school governors • father going to do voluntary work at local Community Centre	

Table 5.1: The resources children drew on in their constructions of their own future work and work in a factory (continued)

	Jimmy (m/5.10/School A)	Heidi (f8.05/School B)	Nicky (m/11.00/School A)
community	• observing builders	• shops where paintings are sold • uniform worn by Macdonalds' workers	• talk with other children in the class who had visited a magazine distribution warehouse
school curriculum		• project on pollution	
teacher's work		• teacher's discipline style ('I'll give you three chances'; being fair to avoid fights) • teacher checking work to see if it is correct	
media	• pop stars – Michael Jackson	• Yellow Pages • advertisement in magazines • books, fact and fiction, about factories and pollution • television news items about pollution	• newspaper containing job advertisements
other		• friends of parents who make a living as artists • talk about Council • family talk about homelessness and problems of getting a job if you are homeless • talk about sexism and racism • talk about water charges • giving to charity	• possible talk with someone about being a bank manager • notion of bank as a store for money (source unclear)

more of the boys were allowed to go to the local shops or park on their own, and thus had more opportunities to observe work in the community. However, many of the children in both schools spent much of their leisure time in their households. But for School A children these were small crowded flats, which were often what Medrich *et al.* called 'total-television households' (1982, p.238); that is, the set was turned on whenever people were at home. In contrast, most School B children lived in houses with gardens, and had more space to follow their own interests.

These factors combined to offer Heidi a very much wider range of experiential resources on which to draw than were available to Nicky. However, it was also noticeable that even where children had very similar experiences (e.g. watching particular television programmes; attending school), some children, such as Heidi, drew on these in their constructions of work, while others, like Nicky, did not. More of the children in School B, like Heidi, referred to television, the school curriculum, and the teachers' work at school. Children of long-term unemployed families, like Nicky, were the least likely to draw on these resources. There are a number of possible explanations for this:

- Nicky may have been less comfortable and forthcoming in the interview situation in the way that Labov (1969) identified.

- Heidi may have perceived, or taken in and remembered, more of what went on around her.

- She may have seen the relevance of a wider range of experiences to the questions asked in interview, transferring learning more effectively by making analogies and applying generalisations.

These are not necessarily alternatives; all these explanations could apply. I will consider the first two possibilities briefly before focusing on the third in the next section.

The children's construction of the interview as a conversational context is analysed thoroughly in Hutchings (1997). All the children were volunteers, and most tried to prolong the interview to avoid classroom activities. While some answered more briefly than others there was no evidence to suggest that they were as intimidated as the boy Labov described. Nicky was a willing and enthusiastic participant.

I have already pointed out the difficulty in attempting to examine what goes on in the mind, including activities such as perception and memory. Perception has been theorised by many philosophers and psychologists. Most theorists have assumed that previous experience determines what we actually perceive in any situation, and that perception involves not simply sensing, but also making sense of what is perceived by fitting it into categories or concepts, or into a narrative (see, for example, Sarbin, 1986; Wells, 1986; and Crites, 1986). Willig sums up this view of perception: 'It is the memory store that dictates the stimuli we attend to and those we ignore. It governs what we perceive and determines our interpretation of the objects and events observed' (1990, p.20).

The implication of assuming that perception involves drawing on the memory store is that a person with considerable previous experience concerning a particular aspect of the world tends to perceive more in relation to that aspect. This is apparent for example, when I go for a walk with a geologist or a bird watcher who points out a vast array of things that I have failed to notice. And as they consistently perceive more than I do in relation to that specific aspect of the world, they build up even more knowledge. The same argument can be applied to children's experiences of work; those children who have already had a wide range of experiences may notice more phenomena relating to work – on television, in the community, at school and in conversation. Those who have very little previous experience may be less likely to perceive what is available. However, we can only speculate about what is perceived; we cannot directly investigate it.

How are previous experiences drawn on in new constructions?

Of more direct concern here is the issue of how previous experience is used, not in perception, but in joint constructions in conversation. This process of bringing previous experience to bear has been referred to as transfer of learning.

I distinguish here between two mechanisms for learning transfer: I will refer to these as analogy and generalisation. Both terms have been used in a variety of senses. I use *analogy* to refer to the recognition that certain features of a specific, previously experienced situation are similar to a new situation, and the use of this in structuring thinking about the new situation. By *generalisation* I refer to the formation of a general rule which is abstracted from any immediate context and is applied in specific circumstances. Blyth (1990a, 1990b) refers to these processes as cognate transfer and general transfer. I will consider each in turn.

Generalisation

Ideas about transfer of learning in the form of generalisation are particularly important in the context of school learning: this has been assumed as 'the central mechanism for bringing school-taught knowledge to bear in life after school' (Lave, 1988, p.23). Schools teach skills and understandings that are disembedded from situational contexts (Donaldson, 1978), and children are expected to apply them to out-of-school situations. A number of theorists have cast doubt on whether learning transfer involving generalisation does in fact take place in real-life contexts (and specifically, whether the abstract rules/ideas encountered in school are applied in real-life settings). For example, Lave and Wenger argued that knowledge 'can be gained only in specific circumstances. And it too must be brought to play in specific circumstances' (1991, p.34). Research in this area has largely been concerned with use of mathematical skills. The mathematics taught in school can be seen as a context-free abstraction, and a number of studies have found that the methods taught in school have not been used in everyday settings, by, for example, street children in Brazil (Carraher, Carraher and Schliemann, 1985); adults shopping in supermarkets (Lave, 1988); or employees in a dairy (Scribner, 1984). However, this does not necessarily imply that general rules are not used in other aspects of life.

Generalisation has been implicitly assumed in many investigations of children's economic understanding in the context-free and rather abstract questions that have often been used; for example:

What is work? (Goldstein and Oldham, 1979, p.40)

How do people get jobs? (Goldstein and Oldham, 1979, p.49)

Are some jobs better than others? (Burris, 1976, p.183)

Why are there rich people and poor people? (Berti and Bombi, 1988, p.73)

How do people get rich? (Burris, 1976, p.199)

However, questions asked in a generalised form (e.g. Why do people work?) are likely to receive generalised answers (e.g. to earn money). (As I sit at my computer on a Bank Holiday I am aware that work motivations are complex and multiple, and that money is certainly not the only incentive!)

While the research I am describing was designed to investigate children's constructions of work in specific contexts and to avoid the elicitation of generalisations, it was possible that the children would, nevertheless, apply general rules. I examined responses about payment for work to find out whether they were generalising in this context.

I found that over half the children interviewed linked work and pay in some contexts discussed, but not in all. Thus, for example, shopkeepers were paid, but teachers and ballerinas were not. While there appeared to be no overall generalisation, the children did appear to be using some rules or guidelines such as 'people are paid for their work only when a visible payment takes place'; or 'payment for work only takes place when the source of the payment can be identified'; or 'activities that can be pursued as hobbies cannot be paid work'. I have reported this analysis more fully elsewhere (Hutchings, 1995, 1997).

Analogy

Analogy seemed to be the most common way in which children used their previous experiences during the interviews about work. According to Meadows (1993), making an analogy involves finding an appropriate source in the memory store and mapping this on to the current situation, thus producing a new representation of the situation (and possibly, in the process, reconstructing the source or previous experience). Making an analogy may be a step towards forming a general rule.

While Piagetian theory suggests that children cannot use analogy until they reach the formal operations stage and can reason about higher order relations, more recent research has shown that children as young as three years can solve analogical problems so long as they have adequate knowledge of the causal principles (Goswami, 1991). Research into analogical thinking has generally involved test items of the form: a is to b as c is to ? (see Goswami, 1991; Meadows, 1993). To answer such puzzles correctly involves only a part of the everyday process of analogy: the child has to recognise the similarities in the given situations but is not required to identify previous experience which could be analogous. There has been rather less research into children's spontaneous use of analogy. Hatano and Inagaki (1992) examined the ways in which children who had raised goldfish were able to apply their conceptual learning to other animals; however, the source was assumed to be experience with goldfish. I have not located any research that examines the sources children draw on in creating analogies. Yet, according to Meadows, the effectiveness of children's use of past experience in considering new situations depends on 'whether that prior experience is thought of, and seen as relevant, at the right moment' (1993, p.84).

The children interviewed created a variety of analogies in their constructions of work. Some drew on situations that could be seen as almost identical to the one being discussed: for example, Elsa (f/5.01/A) based her imaginary factory almost entirely on a factory she had visited. However, this process was not simply one of recalling and describing, because in the interview she was positioned as factory manager rather than as an observer, and thus her experience had to be transformed. Very few children used a single experience of a factory in this way; more often they made analogies using experiences that were similar in a particular dimension: e.g. using experience of seeing a car factory on television in describing a basketball factory; drawing on experience of cooking at home when talking about a food factory. Some analogies brought together experiences from domains that seemed less closely related: for example, the processes involved in making pottery and chocolates. Here Heidi (f/8.05/B) describes how she will manufacture chocolates:

> *You'd make a little kind of round base and with sides on it, make two of them ... put the stuff inside and then put the other one on top of it ... cos I've been to pottery so I know how to make pots and stuff ... and I'd, you know, when you put the chocolate down over the gaps with your fingers.*

Another type of analogy involved drawing on another text, or intertextuality. Fox's (1993) account of children's story telling shows how children often draw on other stories that they have heard. Sitara (f/8.00/A) did this several times in her account of a knitwear factory. Here she is explaining what happens to the money from selling the jumpers, and draws on the action of a book used to teach reading: *The Three Pirates* (Griffin Readers: McCullagh, 1959):

> Would you pay them [the workers] to make the jumpers?
> *Well. First we weren't paying them, and say that we have to give the selling and then you can have how much money you like, like after we have sold them and we get lots of money right, and then put them in sacks and ran and ran and then maybe some and each of them gets the same size, even me, I get the same size. Each of them gets a sack right, three pirates getting the sack, black three pirates.*

While many analogies were explicit, it also appeared that children were making implicit analogies when their constructions of work in two different contexts were very similar. For example, it appeared that many of the children were making an analogy between the authority structures and nature of work in school and in their

95

imaginary factories. School is the only large organisation that most children know, so it is hardly surprising that they drew on this in their constructions of another large organisation. The younger children seemed to be drawing almost entirely on their experience of teachers in their accounts of running a factory:

> *You would be at the front ... you would sit in a big chair and you wouldn't help.* (Tarquin: m/5.07/B)

> *I'll say, start to work.* (Chloe: f/4.11/B)

> *Tell them when they gotta have their lunch break.* (Enrico: m/7.08/A)

> *I'd have to look at all the people that are making it ... see if they do it wrong or right.* (Elsa: f/5.01/A)

> *My job is to sort things out, like if they had sort of fights and things like that* (Natalie: f/8.00/B)

Authority in the factory and in the school was described in similar terms, as hierarchical structures involving obedience. Emler (1992) showed that children's representations of formal authority were linked to the particular form of school organisation that they had experienced. Children in traditional schools described a rigid hierarchy in which social relations are based on obedience to those higher up in the hierarchy. But children in experimental schools claimed that influence could also be exerted by those at the bottom of the hierarchy, and that the functioning of the organisation involved consensus achieved through negotiation. Both schools used in my research were traditional, so Emler's finding suggests that children would describe rigid hierarchical structures, and indeed, they did:

> [the headteacher] *usually ... makes rules about the school and maybe tells the teachers and the teachers tell the children ... she's the one who expels children or suspends them.* (Andrew: m/11.08/B)

Similarly in the factory the workers were to be offered very little autonomy. They would do what they were told, or be disciplined:

> *If they kept making mistakes ... I'd probably tell them off and might give them the sack.* (Andrew m/11.08/B)

The children's construction of work in factories had marked similarities to their constructions of school work, which had been discussed earlier in the interview. The vast majority of the older children had said that school work was sometimes boring, and was not enjoyable (see Hutchings, 1997):

> *If you have to do it then it's not a pleasure because you've got no choice.* (Chris: m/11.07/B)

> *Work is kind of hard working, it's not about fun, not about fun.* (Shuel: m/11.00/A)

These comments concur with Cullingford's finding that eleven- and twelve-year-olds tended to 'separate pleasure and work as if work were always some kind of drudgery' (1991, p.120). Similarly in their factories children described work that was boring, tiring, defined and checked by the managers, and not what the worker would prefer to do:

> *It's not very fun just putting things in machines.* (Jade: f/11.02/B)

> *Although the people who just move one things to another, it doesn't seem like very hard work, but really it must be very boring just moving one thing to another so it would be quite hard work really.* (Chris: m/11.06/B)

However, these constructions of hierarchy, discipline and authority were not generalisations applied in children's constructions of other work contexts discussed in the interview; they were restricted to school work and factory work. (See Hutchings, 1999 for a more detailed account of this aspect of the investigation.)

The work that the children talked about doing when they were grown up was described in very different terms; the vast majority of children said it would be enjoyable:

> Gardening: *I like it and it's fun.* (Tom: m/8.08/B)

> Arabic teacher: *I like it. I like teaching children.* (Shuel: m/11.00/A)

> Nurse: *...because I like fixing people's arms and things like that.* (Samantha: f/7.10/A)

Artist: *I like it, it's fun drawing.* (Heidi: f/8.05/B)

Here children most commonly appeared to be drawing on their out-of-school activities. Work would be enjoyable, just as the present activity was enjoyable. Hobbies, sports and play were obviously seen as fun; more surprisingly, many children also described household work in these terms. For example, Joel (m/7.11/B) said he liked hoovering because he enjoyed the noise the hoover makes when it *'crunches up things'*, and Heidi (f/8.05/B) explained:

> *Well, it's kind of work, but not school work. It's funner, and you don't have to do it, but I like helping at home.*

This may be related to the limited demands made by these children's parents; Butorac (1989), carrying out similar research in Australia, found that household work was not seen as fun because, like school work, it was compulsory. This was not the case for the majority of the children I interviewed. Even those older children who had regular responsibilities spoke with some satisfaction of their contribution to the household, though admitted that they did not always want to do what they were asked. (I realise that they may have been constructing themselves in a positive way for my benefit). Some children expressed frustration that they were not allowed to do all the tasks they wanted to:

> *My mum doesn't let me do the washing up when I want to, because she thinks I'll break things. I won't. I've done it before and I didn't break a glass.* (Natalie: f/8.00/B)

It seemed, then, that there was a sense in which carrying out household tasks signalled growing up and ability to take responsibility, and this is perhaps why future jobs were described in similar terms. From a child's perspective, adulthood offers an attractive freedom from constraints and opportunity to be in control of your life.

The vast majority of children also described their future work as offering a high level of autonomy. This partly resulted from selection of jobs in the arts (writer, artist). However, the degree of autonomy that children expected did not always coincide with my own constructions of the conditions of various occupations, or with expectations created by the job title. For example, Darren (m/5.07/A) described a policeman as having complete autonomy; nobody would tell him what to do, and he could become a policeman simply by putting on the appropriate clothing. Here he seemed to be drawing on his current play activities with a police outfit. The analogy between play and future work seems to be based on a sense of freedom from constraint, which comes in play, and is expected in adulthood.

More than half talked about a job possibility that was a direct continuation of a current activity, and thus made analogies between their current activities (say, at ballet classes) and the activities they would be doing in their future job (being a ballerina). Jobs in the arts and sports featured strongly in this category. A five-year-old who attended pottery classes and would become a 'potterer'; an eight-year-old who liked drawing aimed to become an artist; an eleven-year-old basketball enthusiast knew exactly what he would have to do to become a basketball player in the USA. The middle class children had a wide range of hobbies and after-school clubs, and as a result had many ideas for hobby-based careers, but the working class children also talked about pursuing jobs based on current activities: a seven-year-old who played at being a nurse, and had a nurse's outfit, planned to become a nurse – but in comparison with the middle class children her nursing activities had provided her with very little information. However, the main attraction was that she liked doing it (see Hutchings, 1996, 1997).

What does this tell us about the processes of construction?

I have considered the various ways in which the processes of bringing experience to bear in a new construction have been described by theorists, and I have considered how children appeared to be using these processes in their accounts: making analogies, and sometimes creating and applying rules. In this section I want to consider briefly the nature of the thinking involved in doing this.

This may seem somewhat perverse in the light of social constructionist arguments that emphasise the need to focus on interaction and behaviour, and bracket off processes in the mind (e.g. by Potter and Wetherell, 1987; Shotter, 1993; Potter, 1996). However, Parker (1992) argued that a consequence of the refusal to speculate about what goes on inside the mind is that discourse analysts could be accused of behaviourism (as in Neisser's claim that Potter and his colleagues are 'classic behaviourists': 1992, p.451); or alternatively that the undefined space of the mind could be colonised by cognitive conceptions of the individual emphasising rationality.

I want to suggest that the ways in which children drew on their previous experiences to construct work in unfamiliar settings involved imaginative or creative thinking, rather than logic or rationality. I draw here on Warnock's (1976) argument that 'Forming mental pictures, creating or understanding works of art, understanding the real world in which we live, are all of them to some extent dependent on the *same* mode of thought' (1976, p.183). In Warnock's view it is imagination, rather than a rational search of the memory store, which enables us to make sense of information from the senses, by fitting it into categories, and by drawing on past experience to create analogies or rules. It is the process by which ideas or images 'leap' into the mind, and, Warnock argued, necessarily involves feelings.

I believe that children's knowledge and understanding of work can be developed by encouraging imaginative and speculative thinking. In the interviews, children were asked to imagine and speculate. Those who did so constructed more complex pictures of work. For White (1990), an imaginative person is one who sees 'lots of possibilities ... with some richness of detail'. These detailed constructions of work offered the children insights into the adult world, and could then become a resource to enable them to move on to more complex constructions. They also provided some of the children with visions of the potentiality of the future that formed a part of their identity and influenced their current behaviour. In addition, the narratives constructed by these children provided them with a great deal of satisfaction, particularly when they created a plausible solution to a problem. The children's speculations and solutions would not all be considered to be 'accurate' representations of the world, but in a social constructionist view, the way we understand the world is inevitably a construction rather than a representation. Thus questions of accuracy and 'truth' become irrelevant.

While many children did use imagination and speculation to create complex constructions of work, others did not take the risks involved in speculation, and confined themselves to what they thought they knew, or did not know. Their responses ('I don't know') may have been accurate, but did not lead the children anywhere.

Why, then, did some children use imaginative thought more than others? First, children are used to a discourse in school in which they are required to produce right answers; some children may not have recognised that they were being invited to switch into a speculative mode. Secondly, some children may have been more accustomed than others to being involved in talk that involves speculation and imagination. This could be related to Wells' (1986) discussion of the role of stories in encouraging thinking that goes beyond the immediate context. And finally, some children, as I have shown, had very much more experience than others on which to draw. As Hanson (1988) has argued, imaginative thinking is grounded in experience.

What are the implications for education?
Children, like adults, are able to construct work in a wide variety of ways. They recognise very different activities as work, and they are aware of the varied conditions within paid work, ranging from a lowly position in a hierarchical and authoritarian organisation to an autonomous and fulfilling activity. In these constructions they draw on a wide range of resources, including television and books, work activities in the family and neighbourhood, and perhaps most importantly, their own activities (whether these are categorised as work or as play). I have shown that some children have a far wider range of resources available to draw on than others, and I have argued that as a result the children who start with fewer close resources available (those in work-poor households) may be less able to perceive the information from other sources (e.g. television). What, then, is the role of the education system?

It would be possible for schools to offer children very much wider views of work by arranging more visits to workplaces, inviting more workers into school, setting up mentoring schemes, and so on. Such experiences could include opportunities for children to encounter a wide range of perspectives, and should avoid the tendency to focus on 'cosy' views (typical of the infant school project on 'people that help us'). Experiences should be provided from the early years of schooling; I have argued that it is the lack of an early experiential base which has resulted in some children apparently failing to use the resources that are available to them.

It is not enough simply to provide experiences; children also need opportunities to talk about their experiences. If, as social construc-tionists suggest, meanings are constructed between people in con-versation, then the role of talk in education becomes central. In parti-cular, I have suggested that children should be given opportunities to talk in a more speculative way, and that there should be less em-phasis on right answers, and more on imagination and emotions.

To offer substantial experience of work would require the adoption of a rather different set of curriculum priorities; it is clear in England that as optional extras, careers education and education for econo-mic and industrial understanding have had little impact. Work would need to be a much more central element in the curriculum. Rather than having schools in which children are separated from society, we should perhaps try to develop a much closer relationship between children's education and everyday life.

The provision of greater experience might be a first step; however, it seems likely that children from middle class work-rich households, who already have greater experience in this area, would gain dis-proportionately from this experience because they would be able to relate it to a much wider range of other experiences. Thus the same groups would be likely to remain relatively disadvantaged. While children's home lives are so different, offering the same experience to every child in school cannot provide greater equality of outcome (in this case, equal opportunities to enter occupations across the whole spectrum of work available). Thus I suggest that we need to reconsider the range of arguments put forward in the 1960s and 1970s in relation to different notions of equality (equal provision or equal outcome) (e.g. Coleman, 1968). We need to review the extent to which schools can or should compensate for the differences which result from economic and social disadvantage (CACE, 1967; Bernstein, 1970; Halsey, 1972); and in particular to consider how these arguments relate to the children of long-term unemployed parents.

So far I have focused on the curriculum; a second issue relates to the structure and organisation of schooling. I have suggested that the hierarchical structure of schools and the relationships of power within them appeared to be models for children's constructions of factories, and were used to construct a picture of alienated work, controlled from above (cf. Bowles and Gintis, 1976; Jeffs, 1988). We need to consider whether this is a desirable model to offer children.

While it might be possible (though difficult) for teachers to implement some of the suggestions I have made in this section, such actions may raise children's hopes and aspirations, but cannot change the work opportunities available, or the stratified nature of society. These inequalities cannot be laid at the door of any one group, but can be seen as consequences of the capitalist economic structure of society, in which some people have very limited opportunities: 'Poverty is at the root of powerlessness. Poor people ... lack the means and opportunity – which so many of us take for granted – of making choices in their lives' (Archbishop of Canterbury's Commission on Urban Priority Areas, 1985, p.xv).

While equal opportunities policies seek to ensure that those at the bottom have an equal opportunity to compete with those at the top, the economic and social advantages of the more affluent ensure that they remain ahead. This relationship was made much more explicit in the nineteenth century. For example, in 1811, an address to the committee for the Royal Lancasterian Institution for the Education of the Poor claimed that 'reading, writing and accounting render the lower orders more useful ... to us on those occasions in which we stand in need of their services' (Goldstrom, 1972, p.46). Nowadays politicians and industrialists are rather less outspoken in their support for a strongly stratified society, but nevertheless support measures that have increased rather than decreased the gap between the advantaged and the disadvantaged.

While many teachers are motivated by liberal ideals, the notion that education can change society has been shown to be oversimplistic in that it tends to reflect uncritically the structures of capitalist society, to the despair of some teachers (Cole, 1988). Ross proposed that the only course is '... to encourage children to analyse the social and economic relationships, to ask why the current structures prevail, and to question orthodoxy ... and to become critically aware of the multifaceted and complex forms of contemporary economic life' (1992a, p.59-60). In order to produce changes on a scale that would result in greater equality of opportunity, I believe it would also be essential to increase the elements of political education in schools. Many people believe that politics has no relevance for their lives. Changing the organisation of schools towards a more democratic and less authoritarian structure could contribute to the development of political understanding (Cohen, 1981; Strike, 1982; Jeffs, 1988).

Clearly the sort of social critique and political education that I am suggesting would not be to the advantage of the affluent and powerful; greater equality of opportunity for all across the spectrum of jobs available would mean that their relative advantage would decrease. But if teachers are serious in their commitment to equality of opportunities then this is perhaps the only route.

6

The representations of wealth and poverty: Individual and social factors

Anna Silvia Bombi

University of Rome 'La Sapienza', Italy

In this chapter I will try to show the complexity of the process by which children come to know the interconnected concepts of wealth and poverty, which are undoubtedly important for children's economic awareness and are deeply linked to their evaluation of the social world. I will first try to highlight the conceptual network which children have to build in order to give an economic meaning to 'wealth' and 'poverty'. Then I will briefly discuss the sources of economic knowledge available to children. Finally I will present some recent empirical data of my own, which sheds light on a specific, and comparatively under-researched component of the development of notions about economic inequalities: images of rich and poor people.

Words under scrutiny

Wealth and poverty are compelling concepts in our understanding of social reality, and at the same time highly complex and sometimes even contradictory. Taking a quick look at *Roget's Thesaurus of English Words and Phrases* (Oxford, 1984) we find that *wealth* is not only associated with the idea of *material prosperity* determined by concrete possessions, but also linked to terms expressing *individual or social volition* such as *sufficiency, competence, satisfaction, success* and *prestige*. On the other hand, *poverty* has associated with its principal meaning (*scarcity of material resources*) ideas of *deficiency, distress and squalor*. Just as in English, the Italian term for wealth – *'ricchezza'* – can be used to denote some perceptual characteristics of *fullness* (chromatic fullness, or the fullness of a flavour); however, it also includes an idea of spiritual value, which I did not find in English. The Italian term for poverty – *'povertà'* – refers less to the moral domain than *'ricchezza'*, but it can be used to mean *pettiness* and *miserliness of soul*. The long dominance of Catholicism in Italian culture has not in any way undermined the positive connotation of *'ricchezza'* even beyond its strictly moral sense. With the notable exception of some monastic movements, such as the Franciscan order, the Catholic church has always represented itself with elaborately and luxuriously dressed priests, exercising their functions amidst the material abundance and aesthetic splendour of its cathedrals.

Even from these few examples we can see how the categories of wealth and poverty go far in organising much of our surrounding reality, especially the social world, along an evaluative dimension. The contrast between the opposite poles represented by wealth and poverty is not only economic, but also includes a wide range of social evaluations. Certainly, a more in-depth lexical analysis could also show dissonant images, suggested by expressions such as 'disgustingly rich', or by terms connected with a voluntary and admirable poverty such as 'asceticism'. But in general words such as rich and wealthy relate to a positive category, while the adjective poor refers to a much less desirable category.

If wealth and poverty are such expressive and multifaceted concepts, it is reasonable to expect that the developmental path through which they are acquired cannot be linear; on the contrary it should be conceived as the composition of several notions from different experiential sources. Moreover, being inextricably connected with evaluations of opposite signs (which, to make things even more intricate, are sometimes reversed) wealth and poverty are not purely 'technical' concepts like those of physics or chemistry (Dickinson and Emler, 1996). Ideas about economic inequalities are strictly linked to people's attitudes and values. Their development, then, is subjected not only to the cognitive constraints characteristic of different ages, but also to the ideological influences of specific social contexts. Finally, judgements about economic differences are also subjected to the interference of individuals' motivational processes and defence mechanisms, since wealth and poverty represent personal states of very different desirability, in which everybody is directly and inevitably involved.

Developmental paths

Interpersonal differences linked to the unequal distribution of material resources are one of the aspects of economic reality most precociously understood by children. Nevertheless (or, maybe, just because of this), it is very difficult to trace back the intervening processes in the genesis of these ideas, and even more difficult to suggest educational strategies. In fact, to understand economic inequalities is not the result of a unitary cognitive act, as memorising a simple rule would be. Economic notions in general cannot easily be reduced to a combination of a series of components in a clear architecture, such as that proposed to explain the development of physical notions (see the very well-known studies about the understanding of weight and how scales function; Siegler, 1978). On the contrary, children's ideas about this important aspect of social life are the result of a series of interconnected conceptual acquisitions, which are summarised in Figure 6.1.

In the model proposed in Figure 6.1, ideas about wealth and poverty derive from a combination of notions in (at least) three related domains: economic, moral and social. None of these domains constitutes a prerequisite for the others; nor do they progress at the same pace. Moreover, some experiences available to children simultaneously pertain to more than one domain, in that they can be read from different perspectives. For these reasons, a graphic model cannot accurately catch the intertwining of concepts that children actually develop, and should be used simply as an indicative list of components.

Figure 6.1: A model of the developmental components of the ideas of wealth and poverty

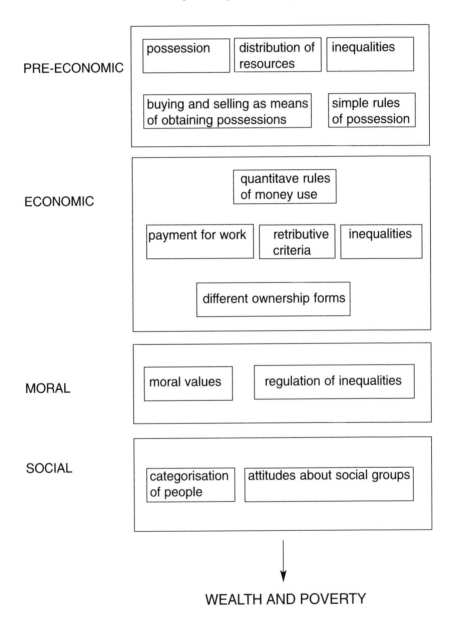

Pre-economic and economic notions

Possession is the first and most 'archaic' milestone in the construction of economic notions that are relevant for understanding wealth and poverty (Snare, 1972). Already around two or three years of age children begin to understand something about possession, as is shown by their use of possessive adjectives and pronouns ('It's my basket', 'This isn't yours'), of verbs indicating desire and ownership ('I want that toy!', 'You've already got one'), very often endowed with compelling references to quantity ('Give me more', 'Don't take them all'). Expressions concerning ownership are used everywhere, even in collectivist cultures, though here they may have a lesser social relevance (Furby, 1978; Rudmin, 1994). Possession is also a matter for explicit teaching, both at home and in the kindergarten (Eisenberg-Berg, Haake and Bartlett, 1981). In these contexts children begin to learn that possession does not follow one's own desires, because it is constrained by rules. This initially happens in simple situations that are directly experienced, such as when children are asked to share something with siblings or classmates, or when they are restrained from touching objects belonging to adults. By the age of five, children not only know that to take somebody else's property is forbidden (Burris, 1983), but they also realise that almost everything around us has an owner, and that the access to ownership is not always easy (Bombi, 1996a). Later, more complex notions will be grasped, such as the difference between 'loan' and 'gift', or the concept of public and private ownership.

The practice of rules about possession becomes in turn one of the earliest ways of knowing about the fairness or unfairness of distribution of resources, about the inequalities between people arising from ownership, and about the meaning of theft (Furnham and Jones, 1987). Children also seem to consider the possession of desired toys or clothes as an important aspect of individuals; this often acts as a motivation for the selection of friends (Selman, 1980). Thus possession appears to be linked both to the moral domain and to the psychological domain: not only is it a matter of prescriptions and prohibitions, but it also informs about the qualities, and consequent value of individuals.

The second step towards understanding of economic inequalities can be found in experiences with the use of money, mainly linked with the shopping script. Children discover very early that one can come to possess many things in those places, sometimes attractive and sometimes boring, that are shops. However, buying and selling is initially conceived as a sort of ritual in which different things (banknotes or coins and merchandise) pass from one hand to another. Nevertheless, given its ubiquity, shopping represents for children one of the main opportunities for learning about economic exchanges, a very instructive daily situation in which they sometimes participate as central actors. Buying an ice cream or a comic book, children come to learn, firstly, that sometimes your money is not enough to obtain the desired object, and then that you must pay with the exact amount of money, corresponding to the marked price. Subsequently, at the beginning of the elementary school, thanks to their increased arithmetic knowledge, children will understand the function of change as a compensation for the discrepancy of value between price and money given for payment (Berti and Bombi, 1981a). In this way, children connect property first with money, then with precise amounts of money.

While they progress in the construction of the 'profit system' (Jahoda, 1979), elementary school children also begin to develop the 'work system', i.e. a series of notions about jobs and their remuneration (Goldstein and Oldham, 1979; Lewko, 1987; Mannetti and Tanucci, 1988); this can be considered another, very important step. Around five years of age children already know, even though confusedly, that 'dad's money comes from work'. But it is important to bear in mind that young children are not consistent in their ideas, and can easily shift back to other, more primitive ideas, when they are faced with difficult questions. For instance, a five-year-old, who already knows that her parents go to work and come home with money, can still suggest 'going to the bank' in case of need, believing that in a bank money is freely available to everyone who asks. Around six or seven years of age, children still believe that money can be produced in a factory like any other object, and they don't suspect its special nature (Delval and Denegri, 1999).

While pre-schoolers know about only their parents' jobs, older children come to understand that all adults work to gain money (and not simply to enable smooth functioning of a world in which trains have to run, schools have to be open, and so forth). Children first recognise that customers pay self-employed workers for their services; subsequently they become aware of the roles of 'bosses', who pay their employees; and connected to this is the discovery that the ownership of means of work, both private and public, rarely coincides with the use of them (Berti, Bombi and Lis, 1982; Cram and Ng, 1994). Understanding that workers are paid by the employer does not mean that children have a precise idea of where the money comes from: children around eight years of age know that 'bosses' have money but they do not know how they come to have it (Berti and Bombi, 1988). The existence of different salary levels is also discovered during the elementary school years, even though the estimate of these differences is far from accurate (Emler and Dickinson, 1985).

Moral concepts

By the age at which children begin to recognise work as a paid activity and to know that different jobs are paid differently, moral understanding has already become quite sophisticated. Children are often taught about fairness, but above all they learn from interactions with their peers that unfair behaviour leads to conflict (Piaget, 1932) and that respect for established rules, including a certain degree of reciprocity, is necessary to preserve relationships (Hartup, 1998; von Salish, 1996). The simplest way to put this into practice is to share with friends on an egalitarian basis, but as they grow older, children also become able to consider remunerative criteria (for instance, more merit, more reward) or the relevance of different needs (for instance, more food for the person who is most hungry). Equity principles are then constructed in an attempt to solve the contradictions arising from strict egalitarianism. Principles of this kind can be considered more advanced, since they require more sophisticated mental operations to be grasped (but see Emler, 1998, for a discussion of the limits of a stage approach to moral development).

Even if we accept the progression from equality to equity as a rough approximation to moral development during middle childhood, we cannot conclude that children who use equity principles in their everyday lives will apply the same kinds of principle when evaluating large-scale social situations. For instance, Bombi, Cacciamani and Pieramico (1990) compared the ideas of elementary school children about situations potentially involving retributive and distributive justice (how to allocate resources to two children, and how much to pay a dentist and a cobbler) and found that there was little or no relationship between the 'lines of thought' adopted by children when reasoning about their peers and about the adult world. Children who were very concerned about justice with friends were ready to take the organisation of the adult world for granted, without in any way questioning its fairness. This result is consistent with the literature about moral development, from which we know that children are not consistent in the principles they use across situations (Enright *et al.,* 1984; Sigelman and Waitzman, 1991).

In fact, it is debatable how we should approach, in moral terms, a problem such as that of wealth and poverty: should economic inequalities, large and small alike, always be considered wrong? Should they be judged in absolute terms, or in the context of historical and political circumstances? In what measure should an individual be considered morally responsible for such a wide and apparently unchangeable phenomenon? Here there is considerable scope for different moral attitudes, and it is not surprising to find that adults themselves do not find it easy to relate their principles of distributive justice to their beliefs about inequality (Shepelak and Alwin, 1986).

Social cognition

Another independent source of knowledge, which is relevant for the understanding of wealth and poverty, is the development of social cognition. Pre-schoolers are already able to classify people according to their personal characteristics: boys and girls, adults and children, black and white. This grouping activity is initially based on external features (body size, facial characteristics, clothes, etc.) and then also on internal psychological cues (attitudes, intentions, needs, etc.). This shift from concrete and 'peripheral' aspects to abstract and 'central' properties of people depends not only on cognitive-developmental factors, as was stressed by the first classical studies on 'person perception' (Livesley and Bromley, 1973) but also on motivational factors (Feldman and Ruble, 1981) and previous experience (Benenson and Dweck, 1986).

Several studies have shown that during middle childhood children become more and more able to categorise people according to economic cues, such as the type of their possessions (clothes, car, house) (Mookherjee and Hogan, 1981). In this way children can also locate themselves in a specific social class, relying on visual information as well as on what their parents tell them. It is important to note that adults are not always reliable informants in this respect. For opposite reasons, poor and wealthy parents can convey inaccurate judgements about the family position in the social scale. In a study on children's ideas about payment for work (Berti and Bombi, 1988), we asked working class children whether their families were rich or poor; we found that the children considered themselves to be 'rich', or at least 'average' on the basis that they had school materials and snacks. Possibly parents draw children's attention to these little possessions to encourage them to feel positive about their own condition, and avoid mentioning the much larger number of things available to really wealthy children. On the other hand, when a family is wealthy, comparison with less favourable positions may be avoided in order to teach children discretion and moderation.

The concepts of wealth and poverty

All of the above mentioned ideas are, in a way or another, relevant for the concepts of wealth and poverty. But what do children say when we question them explicitly about economic inequalities? Berti and I approached this problem (Berti and Bombi, 1988) by asking children from four to eleven years to explain what it means to be rich and what it means to be poor; how people become rich or poor; and whether it is possible to change one's social condition. Our results were in agreement with those obtained by other researchers (e.g. Danziger, 1958; Connell, 1977; Burris, 1983; Leahy, 1983) in different countries. Most of the pre-schoolers thought that a person is rich when he has lots of money or expensive goods, and poor when he is without money and goods; but since there is an unconditional availability of money (because money is believed to be freely available from banks) almost everybody can be, at least momentarily, rich. From six to seven years on, children begin to connect work and money; now they believe that a person is rich when, working and being paid, she has money in her hands. This idea is gradually replaced by a more complex vision, in which wealth and poverty still depend almost exclusively on work, but are now conceived as long-lasting conditions. The rich are now those who 'work more' (eight to nine years of age) or those who get 'good jobs' and are really well paid, regardless of the amount of effort or time put in (ten to eleven years of age). In these latter ideas we see the beginning of a societal perspective, which is evident in studies of older children and adolescents (Leahy, 1983). Adolescents' explanations and evaluations of economic inequalities are not uniform. Some take an individualistic perspective (merit or lack of skills being seen as responsible respectively for wealth and poverty), while others appear more fatalistic; only a small minority assume that society as a whole is responsible for the existence of income and status differences (Furnham, 1982).

Developmental factors

In general, young children receive little or no formal instruction about economic facts. For instance, in Italy some concepts relating to the economic world (work, production, commercial exchanges) are taught in elementary schools as part of 'social studies'; other concepts, such as the processes involved in industrial revolution, are introduced as a part of history teaching in junior high school. But overall we can say that the economy is barely touched on in school curricula for children and pre-adolescents. From what sources, then, do children come to know about economic reality? We can distinguish three sources of information available to children: (a) direct participation in economic exchanges (such as buying something or being paid for a little work); (b) direct observation (such as noticing that shopkeepers receive their merchandise from distributors); and (c) indirect information (such as overhearing your parents discussing father's low salary, or viewing television reports about inflation or the stock market).

Among scholars there is a recurring tendency to suggest that children's actions are central to their acquisition of economic knowledge. For instance, in the seventies Kourilsky (1974) developed a curriculum for economic education based on the reproduction of a mini-economy in the classroom. In the same vein, Webley and his colleagues (Webley, Levine and Lewis, 1991) have argued for the efficacy of a play economy for enhancing children's economic behaviour, and in particular saving. Schug and Armento (1985), in their programme for elementary schools, accord an even larger role to everyday experiences and natural classroom events, as well as simulation of the real world. Recently Thompson and Siegler (2000) have proposed that the situations in which children sell something (used comic books, drinks, etc.) should be regarded as experiences through which the concept of profit can be built.

In pre-capitalistic societies, where there was little separation between domestic activity and the economy at large (Habermas, 1989), the economic socialisation of children took place via first-hand experiences. It is important to note, though, that there is a great difference between a realistic situation of gradual involvement in the family work, as still happened until recently in rural communities in Italy, and a playful reproduction of specific economic exchanges. In my opinion, the complexity of economic processes cannot be approached by these kinds of experience. A playful situation of selling lemonade bottles that were freely provided by the child's mother (Thompson and Siegler, 2000), does not approximate the core features of shop enterprise; even buying lemonade in this context bears little resemblance to the real situations of daily life (for instance, a girl could buy just to be polite to her neighbour, a motivation that is barely relevant in the analysis of economic 'demand').

I don't want to suggest that first-hand economic experiences are totally irrelevant. For instance, the practice of shopping gives children the opportunity to think in terms of trading rules (Webley, 1996). Receiving an allowance on a regular basis, as proposed by Abramovitch, Freedman and Pliner (1991), can help children and adolescents to become judicious consumers. However, we must bear in mind that the money managed by children is not the result of real economic dynamics, but is granted on the unilateral decision of parents. Moreover, children are generally involved only in inessential expenditure: nobody provides a twelve-year-old with all the money s/he would need for food, clothes, medicine, school, etc. In short, the amount of money for which children are responsible is so inessential in their lives that its administration has only a faint resemblance to the economic problems of real life. Hence it is improbable that a realistic view of the economic system could be constructed in this way.

Direct observation seems more promising, at least for young children. For instance, through going to shops, seeing how commercial exchanges function, and reasoning about money, children begin to attach a concrete meaning to certain claims of adults about the limitations of their resources ('we can't buy you the play station, it's too expensive!'). But if young children find these claims quite incredible, it is precisely because of another direct observation: that of seeing adults obtaining banknotes almost magically, simply by putting a plastic card in a slot and pressing some buttons in front of it, or by giving a strip of paper with a few words written on it to the bank cashier. The conclusion is that direct observation is sometimes useful, but it can also be misleading.

The short-lived impact of direct, and necessarily contextualised, experiences (direct participation and direct observation) is shown by the fact that naive concepts sometimes reappear in older children when they try to explain new economic phenomena on a larger scale. For instance, the idea that banks distribute money freely is suggested (even though with some caution) by eight- and nine-year-olds to explain how shopkeepers could make a profit even if they were to sell their goods at the same price they had bought them for. This is an idea which satisfies children's moral principles as well as their criteria for establishing prices: size, utility, materials, all characteristics which obviously remain unchanged from wholesale purchase to retail selling (Ajello *et al.*, 1987). A notion already acquired in a specific context, then, is not used by children as a firm principle, to be verified and generalised. On the contrary, when new problems appear it is all too easy to go back to familiar, catch-all explanations, often with contradictory elements (such as, in the above example, the contradiction between moral rules and children's 'economic' beliefs about pricing criteria). Or, even worse, children can accept the idea that they cannot explain the 'difficult thing' before them because they are accustomed to living with the complexity and the contradictions of the social world, and to receiving little explanation from adults.

Indirect sources are much more realistic then direct participation, but they are almost as incomplete as direct observation. Television is one of the main vehicles of indirect information and it has a large impact on socialisation (Crook, 1998). Unfortunately, television does not provide very clear cues about economics, at least for children: news, quick views of places, even interviews with experts which are often cryptic for adults themselves. Television, then, is much more likely to promote imitation of models and attitude formation than a clear understanding of complex matters, such as economic processes.

In my opinion, the limited educational significance of mass media does not depend on the indirect, verbal nature of the information provided. On the contrary, the possibility of combining words and images could offer enormous potential for economic socialisation. Many studies have shown that a systematic and gradual approach to the provision of verbal information is highly effective with children of elementary school age (Berti, 1993; Berti and Monaci, 1998), especially when supported by visual stimuli (Ajello et al., 1986b). Discussion is another powerful means of promoting conceptual change (Ng, 1983), but it is not always better than a straightforward tutorial procedure (Berti, Bombi and De Beni, 1986).

Wealth and poverty are clear instances of economic notions that cannot be acquired on the basis of direct experience alone. When we reason about economic inequalities, we are confronted with one of the most fundamental aspects of society, which arises from economic, political and historical factors. We are still in the early stages of understanding the developmental path I have traced in this section, a path that will proceed well beyond childhood and adolescence. Nevertheless, what we know about the processes involved in the various steps of the path is enough to allow parents and teachers to provide, for each age group, those pieces of information that will help each individual gradually to construct a larger, more complete picture. For instance, we know that children have limited information about the real amount of salaries, and that they find it difficult to translate into societal terms those moral principles that they practise in their daily life. Educational intervention, then, can be planned around these limits, giving information, and providing opportunities for reasoning and correctly extending those principles that children already possess. It seems to me that the most incomplete data, in this respect, are those about children's early attitudes. Attitudes have been extensively studied among adolescents (Dittmar, 1996) but much less with younger children. Indeed, in middle childhood, many classical instruments of social psychology for the measurement of attitudes cannot be used. Yet it is vital that we learn more about this developmental phase in which long-lasting prejudices may be built. The study that follows represents an attempt to use pictorial and verbal data to explore children's views of wealth and poverty.

Two ways of assessing the impact of social environment on children's ideas about wealth and poverty

I will now present some results from a study about children's representations of wealth and poverty, which was conducted with two aims. First, we wanted to examine the differences between the images of wealth and poverty conveyed in children's verbal responses and in their drawings, two methods which were employed separately in previous research (Bombi and Cannoni, 1995). Second, we wanted to verify which of these methods would be better suited for investigating views of wealth and poverty in children from different social backgrounds. Here I will present only the section of the study aimed at comparing the images of rich and poor individuals.

Hypotheses

Using a procedure that encouraged children to focus on visible cues of wealth and poverty, we expected more differences between social classes than those that emerged when children were questioned about the existence of and explanation for wealth and poverty as general phenomena. From early childhood to adolescence, boys and girls from different classes are equally exposed to 'free floating' information (Connell, 1977) which allows them to construct a first level of knowledge about the existence of economic inequalities, and the most common explanations of these: there is no reason to expect that children from lower (or higher) social class groups understand these facts better. Instead some status symbols, such as expensive or cheap clothes and objects, elegant or shabby houses and streets, and manner of speech and behaviour convey information that is linked to the child's social environment. It is then reasonable to expect that different images of wealth and poverty will be built, according to the degree of familiarity with different social conditions.

The sample in this study was made up of 147 children from two areas of Rome that had contrasting environments and social composition: Tor Bella Monaca (low socio-economic status) and Parioli (high socio-economic status). Tor Bella Monaca is a poor district on the outskirts of the city, inhabited mainly by working class families; Parioli is a wealthy residential district not far from the historical centre and its beautiful monumental zone. The 85 children from Tor Bella Monaca came from low-income families. Only 2 per cent of their parents had a high-school degree and none went to college; accordingly, parents were in employment that offered little responsibility, such as factory work or domestic cleaning. In contrast, in 81 per cent of the Parioli families (N=62) both parents were college graduates and the remainder were high-school graduates; they were professionals, managers, high-school or university teachers. It is important to bear in mind that, in this sample, membership of an economically disadvantaged group does not imply a left-wing political orientation. Even though we were not allowed to gather direct information about the political affiliations of children's parents, we must assume a considerable overlap between the two sub-groups in terms of preference for right-wing parties, and especially for those directly connected with fascist ideology, still widespread in Rome both in working and middle class areas.

In each district children were recruited in an elementary school (aged seven to nine) and a junior high school (aged eleven to thirteen) with permission of the school authorities and parents; for each age level there were approximately equal numbers of boys and girls.[1] All the participants performed three tasks. First, they completed the Draw-a-Man Test (Harris, 1963), following the procedure of the Italian standardisation (Polacek and Carli, 1977); next, they drew, on a single page, a rich person and a poor person; and finally they were individually interviewed about indices of wealth and poverty and about feelings associated with these conditions. The two pictorial tasks were presented as research about representation of the human figure, with or without specific connotations. In the first task (Draw-a-Man test) children were encouraged simply to draw the figure of a man (and subsequently of a woman) as best as they could. In the second task they were asked to draw two people, a rich person and a poor person (or vice versa), to illustrate what it means to be rich and to be poor. Children worked at their drawings in small groups, with their tables spatially arranged in such a way as to make it impossible to copy from each other. The order of the two pictorial tasks was kept constant to avoid any bias over the results of the Draw-a-Man Test, which was administered to control the general pictorial abilities in the two samples. The subsequent individual interviews were proposed as a way of completing the information given in the drawing of rich and poor, and began by asking the child to comment on the drawing, so that his/her attention was focused on visible signs of wealth and poverty. Then the child was asked to name other things that one could look at in order to decide whether a person is rich or poor.

What makes wealth and poverty visible?

The Draw-a-Man Test showed that children from both samples were equally able to draw human figures: the small, non-significant difference in the scores was in favour of the children with lower socio-economic status. Two independent judges examined the drawings and separately evaluated each figure to establish if it was recognisable or not recognisable as 'rich' or as 'poor'. The drawings were then assigned to one of four mutually exclusive categories (figures that were not recognisable as rich or poor, only the rich figure recognisable, only the poor figure recognisable, both rich and poor recognisable). Boys and girls, both in the elementary and junior high school, appeared able to characterise the figures in terms of wealth and poverty, and, most important here, there was no difference between the two samples in terms of ability to do the task (see Table 6.1).

Table 6.1: Frequency of characterisation of figures by socio-economic status

Characterisation of figures	Low socio-economic status %	High socio-economic status %	Total %
neither rich nor poor recognisable	5	2	3
only rich recognisable	11	6	9
only poor recignisable	1	11	6
both rich and poor recognisible	83	81	82
N	85	62	147

Only a few children failed the task completely, presenting two figures lacking any clear indication of their economic status; the vast majority were successful in their efforts to show the wealth or poverty of the drawn characters. Most frequently, children marked wealth or poverty by details such as quality of clothing, and objects either held by the figures (often coins or banknotes) or shown next to them (such as vehicles, houses or other belongings). We found an interesting difference between the groups of children: among those who characterised only one figure effectively, those with low socio-economic status drew a recognisable wealthy person, while in the drawings of the high socio-economic status group it was the poor person that appeared more recognisable (Chi square (3) = 8.48; p = .037). This result gives us a first indication that children from contrasting backgrounds do not differ in the ability to conceive wealth and poverty as separate conditions, but they do differ in the perspective they adopt when thinking about these conditions. It seems in fact easier for each group to focus on the 'other': the rich when you are poor, and the poor when you are rich.

Two figures that are recognisable by some details as rich and poor can still be similar. For instance, put a thick block of banknotes in the hand of one figure, and a little coin in the hand of the other, and you have made clear the contrast between wealth and poverty, while keeping the two figures nondescript and similar in their other features. Again, you might make distinctions in the clothing of the two figures, but not show the difference in any other way. To check the degree of resemblance between rich and poor, we applied to the drawings the Similarity Scale developed by Bombi and Pinto (1993, see also Pinto, Bombi and Cordioli, 1997, and Bombi, 1996b for examples of the use of this scale[2]). The scale involves separate scores from 0 (very different) to 2 (almost identical) for each of four aspects of the figures: Dimensions, Position, Body, and Personal qualifiers; the scores are then summed up to give an overall Similarity score, from 0 to 8.

The mean score in the entire sample was 3.85[3]. Children not only endowed the figures with different qualifiers (as we have mentioned above), but to these material indices of wealth and poverty they quite often added bodily differences, as if being rich or poor were something that involves the person in the most radical, intimate way. For instance, the poor were portrayed as smaller, older, with shabby hair, and even lacking some physical detail. The analysis of variance performed on the similarity scores by age, sex and sample (experimental design 2 x 2 x 2) yielded two principal effects: of age (F [139,1] = 6.64; p=.011) and of the sample (F [139,1] = 6.88; p=.010), without interactions between the two variables. Among the seven- to nine-year-olds the mean score was 4.16, while the mean for

the eleven- to thirteen-year-olds was 3.54; for the low socio-economic status group the mean score was 4.13 and for the high socio-
economic status group 3.53. The similarity between the results for
the low socio-economic status group and the younger children
should not be interpreted as a slower progression of pictorial ability
in this socially and culturally disadvantaged sample. In fact, we have
seen above that children from the low socio-economic status group
were as good artists as those from high socio-economic status
families, if not better. We have also seen that they were equally able
to make a rich and a poor person recognisable in their drawings.
What varies, instead, is the amount of difference introduced: children from wealthy families stressed the different conditions of rich
and poor by adding a lot of pictorial cues, while children from a disadvantaged environment adopted a much more moderate attitude, so
that the difference is not dramatic.

Verbal descriptions of rich and poor people

The comments and elaborations made by children about their own
drawings during the interviews help us better to understand developmental and social differences in their ideas. The interviews were
scored for the number of references made to six indices of wealth, or
to the corresponding indices of poverty: (1) the quantity of money
and goods; (2) the quality of two salient status symbols (house and
car); (3) access or lack of access to work and other life opportunities;
(4) the individual look, opulent or shabby; (5) the availability or lack

Table 6.2: Composition of the three factors about the indexes of wealth and poverty

	Factor 1 Evident characteristics	Factor 2 Material possessions	Factor 3 Inner diversity
eigenvalues	1.47	1.17	1.13
explained variance	24.4	19.5	18.8
Items and saturations	(2) Symbols 0.86 (5) Basic resources 0.73	(3) Opportunites 0.67 (1) Goods 0.66 (4) Look -0.57	(6) Inner spirit 0.89

of the most basic resources (home, food, minimal money); (6) the 'inner spirit' (dispositions and emotions). The score range was from 0 (no reference) to 3 (three or more references). A factor analysis on these six scores using the method of the principal components and Varimax orthogonal rotation yielded three factors, which overall explain 62.8 per cent of the total variance (see Table 6.2).

The first factor corresponds to a dramatic opposition between wealth and poverty, as indicated by the most common symbols of social status, and the most basic resources.

> Giovanni (7 years; high socio-economic status) *Rich people live in castles, they eat a lot of delicacies; poor people eat what they find in the garbage cans, they live in the street with smoke and pollution.*

> Maria (9 years; high socio-economic status) *A rich person has a big, huge house, with big rooms and tables, nice pictures, waiters and cooks. Poor people have damaged homes, dirty clothes, they don't have the same things as the rich, they ask for charity but often they receive very little.*

The second factor also focuses on material differences, but along a dimension that goes from lifestyle to personal appearance: on the positive pole we find the opportunities available (or not available) to rich and poor and on the negative pole the ways in which they look, thanks to their clothes, objects and personal presence.

> Serena (7 years; low socio-economic status) *A rich man can buy all the things that his family needs, clothes, good food; he has money, and a poor man hasn't.*

> Luigi (13 years; low socio-economic status) *A rich man wears designer clothes, has golden objects, is well groomed with hair combed. The poor man has only imitations of the rich clothes, has scars on the face, or bad teeth.*

The third factor is based on a single item, and refers to the psychological and moral differences between rich and poor.

> Mario (11 years; high socio-economic status) *A rich person speaks with good manners, without mistakes, without swearing; he's educated while a poor person doesn't know how to speak properly.*

Three separate analyses of variance (one for each factor) were then performed on the factorial scores, with age, sex and sample as independent variables (experimental design 2 x 2 x 2). Age appeared as an influential variable in all of these analyses. In the first and second factor, scores decreased with age (in both cases, from 0.21 to -0.24; F [139;1] = 5.30; p=.02; F [139;1]= 11.12 ; p=.001). In the third factor, age and socio-economic status interacted significantly, as shown in Table 6.3 (F [139;1] = 4.82; p=.03).

Other significant effects of social background appeared in the first and second factor. For the first factor, children from the high socio-economic status group obtained higher scores (mean = 0.25) than those from the low socio-economic status group (mean = -0.18) (F [139;1] = 4.80; p=.03). In the second factor, in contrast, it is the low socio-economic status group that had higher scores (mean = 0.13) as compared to the high socio-economic status group (mean = -0.18) (F [139;1]=6.46; p=.012). For this factor, there was also a significant interaction with age (see Table 6.4).

Taken together, these results show a different developmental progression for the two social groups. Children from the high socio-economic status group, who were in absolute terms more inclined to

Table 6.3: Mean scores for Factor 3 by age

	Socio-economic status	
	low	high
younger	0.04	-0.04
older	-0.21	0.45

Table 6.4: Mean scores for Factor 2 by age

	Socio-economic status	
	low	high
younger	0.59	-0.16
older	-0.25	-0.22

make sharp contrasts between the economic conditions of rich and poor, moved with age towards a vision of economic inequalities based on interior, psychological differences. Children from the low socio-economic status group, who in general conceived the differences in less radical terms, stressed only material diversity in terms of lifestyle and opportunities at the younger age, and in terms of personal appearance at the older age.

Conclusions

The results presented in the previous sections shed some light on a component of children's ideas about wealth and poverty which has previously received limited attention: children's images of rich and poor. These images reveal a lot about children's attitudes toward economic inequalities. The two research instruments employed, drawing and interview, both proved useful in this respect. Children from seven years of age were able to depict clearly and effectively the figures of rich and poor, as well as to describe them verbally. Young children's descriptions were organised in terms of large-scale contrasts, while older children mainly focused on personal aspects, a finding that concurs with previous research (Leahy, 1983; Dittmar, 1996), and is coherent with adolescents' growing interest in personal characteristics, including thoughts and feelings as well as body image. The 'dramatic contrast' proposed by our younger interviewees is also a result convergent with the literature (Connell, 1977; Berti and Bombi, 1988); however, its disappearance from the interviews of pre-adolescents should not be interpreted as an indication of a less severe divergence between social classes among older subjects. In fact, the eleven- to thirteen-year-olds introduced very little similarity between rich and poor when they represented them pictorially.

Probably the more interesting result is the interaction of this developmental line with social factors. Children from disadvantaged backgrounds, while perfectly able to draw distinct figures, did not stress their diversity, which was, however, emphasised by their more privileged peers. This gives rise to self-protective presentations of the two social conditions in each of the socio-economic groups. On the one hand, wealthy children had every reason for enjoying their affinity with a figure they described as much superior; on the other hand, children from a poorer background, minimising the gap between their own condition and that of wealthy people, avoided humiliation and envy. The contrasting attitudes of the two groups of children became more radical with increasing age, as is shown by the interviews: middle class subjects presented rich and poor as psychologically different, while lower class children only admitted those personal differences which are evident in clothes, manners and faces.

These different images should not be considered superficial aspects of children's economic conceptions, because they mediate the psychological meaning of wealth and poverty: what is it really like to be a rich person or a poor person? And from this, different degrees of moral tolerance can result. The finding that the two groups have rather different perceptions of the gap between rich and poor is likely to make each group more reasonably satisfied with their own position, and thus reproduce existing inequalities. After all, if those who with low incomes believe that to be poor is not so very different from being rich, why should they strive to improve their position?

Notes

1. Claudia Apperti and Roberta Olivanti collected data. The smaller number of children in the high socio-economic status group arises from the difficulty of obtaining permission from their families to interview them about economic differences.

2. The scoring manual in English can be obtained from the author. A version in Spanish can be found in Bombi and Pinto (1998).

3. In a validation study by Cannoni (1993) children from seven to eleven years of age who were asked to draw two identical figures reached a score of 7.6, while the score in the opposite task (figures as different as possible) did not go below 3.8. A score below 4.0 should thus be considered expressive of a dramatic pictorial difference.

7

Economic education and attitudes towards competition, business and enterprise among adolescents in Hungary

Márta Fülöp
*Hungarian Academy of Sciences, Budapest, and
University of Szeged, Hungary*

Mihály Berkics
Hungarian Academy of Sciences, Budapest, Hungary

Introduction

The decline of the socialist system during the late 1980s and early 1990s in Eastern and Central Europe resulted in dramatic social, political, and economic changes. Phenomena that had previously been ideologically denied and banned, such as competition and enterprise, became highly valued and praised at all levels of society. In those countries that are undergoing a transformation from the communist system to the capitalist system there are macro-system changes at both political and economic levels: the process of democratisation and the introduction of a free market economy. After the political changes in Hungary in 1989, democracy lacked an involved civil society and people had limited experience with a market economy. At that time Hungary's economic problems were severe, with Europe's highest per capita debt and a 20 per cent inflation rate leading to rapidly falling standards of living (Echikson, 1992). Parallel to this, Hungarians were just inventing what democracy and a market economy would mean in their society. The new government was committed to a capitalist economy including privatisation and a shift from full employment to a high rate of unemployment. All this meant severe economic and social pressure. Old certainties had been superseded by new and continuing uncertainties. Flexibility became a desirable capacity, and those who were able to adapt fast became the winners in the new society. All these changes resulted in the need to increase understanding of new economic concepts and to change attitudes towards the free market economy and business, and towards their active agents, the entrepreneurs.

This chapter focuses on five main topics:

- views about the economic consequences of the political changes among different age groups

- adolescents' ideas about the role and effects of competition in their rapidly changing society

- attitudes towards entrepreneurs

- economic education in Hungarian secondary schools

- attitudes towards business, enterprise and entrepreneurs among secondary school students participating in a one-year economic and business education programme.

Views about the economic consequences of the political changes among different age groups

Age groups with different status, experiences and knowledge also have differing views about the societal changes in connection with democracy and a capitalist market economy. Status and degree of social and financial success affect the views of the population even in a traditional capitalist society. Furnham (1997) found that those who are successful feel optimistic about potential economic changes while those with less success are pessimistic. Slomczynski et al. (1999) demonstrated something very similar in Poland, namely that the generalised aversion to systemic change depends on social status, and economically deprived segments of the population show a high level of aversion to the systemic change to capitalism.

Andorka, Healey and Krause's (1994) study revealed that the transition period from the socialist economy to the capitalist market economy resulted in a general dissatisfaction among Hungarian adults with their financial situation, the economic situation of the country and the functioning of the democratic institutional system. In comparison with, for example, the former East Germans (who were also found to be dissatisfied with the changes), the Hungarians showed a greater degree of anomie and alienation, and psychological problems and anxiety were more common. Hungarian adults, when comparing the present economic and political system with the former socialist one, evaluated the present system more negatively and showed little trust in the future. However, when asked in general terms about the value of a market economy and democratic institutional system most of the respondents agreed that they are important and necessary. This points to a kind of gap between seeing the capitalist system as attractive in principle or at the ideological level, and alienation from its present-day reality in the post-socialist countries.

In another study Vári-Szilágyi and Solymosi (1999) investigated the views of Hungarian university students and young professionals (economists, agricultural engineers and architects) about the process of moving to a capitalist society. Interestingly enough these views were rather contradictory. While the most important features of a well-functioning society were considered to be free economic competition, market-led economic processes, and significant income differentials, at the same time respondents expressed their wish for full employment and for the state to care for the weak. This picture seems to combine some capitalist and some socialist principles, pointing to the fact that young adults would like to have all the advantages of the capitalist system without losing the social security that was provided by socialist society. There were some gender differences in the responses, in that, in comparison with males; females were much more concerned about full employment and the gap between the rich and the poor.

Van Hoorn *et al.* (2000) called those young people currently growing up in societies under structural change the 'omega–alpha generation' because they are the last children of the old system and the first adults of the new. They conducted a study among young Hungarians and Poles aged between sixteen and eighteen years who were not participating in any special educational programme concerning politics or economics. The aim was to investigate their identity development in connection with the societal changes, and to discover how they understood and responded to the socio-political concepts related to the transitions, such as the free market economy. They carried out the research in three stages with three different groups of students between 1991 and 1995. During these four years the students' knowledge of and attitude towards the economic changes in their respective countries changed. In 1991 most of them had difficulty in responding to questions about the free market economy, because their knowledge and understanding was very limited. They found it difficult to distinguish between democracy and the free market. Approximately 25 per cent were unable to mention any features of the free market economy. Those who had some idea mentioned free commercial competition, free prices and being able to start a business. By 1995 it appeared that young people of the same ages had a more in-depth understanding of the political and economic concept of the free market economy and its underlying processes: for example, that free price is determined by supply and demand. In the later stages of the study they could apply the new concepts to their own lives better, indicating that constructing new meanings takes time and active experience; in other words it is a gradual learning process.

While understanding of the new political and economic concepts had become deeper and more detailed, emotional evaluations of the economic changes had become more negative. In 1991 the general belief among adolescents was that the transition towards democracy and the market economy would positively influence people's lives. By 1995 the majority of the students thought that their life circumstances had deteriorated, and their descriptions of the effects of the changes on Hungary or Poland tended to focus more on the negative economic and political effects, and the worsening economic conditions for ordinary people. Almost three-quarters of them spoke about the financial difficulties that their own families were experiencing. During the years of the political changes Hungarian adolescents in particular expressed a growing sense of pessimism about the new economic system and situation. However, they were still more positive about the changes than their parents' generation were (Van Hoorn *et al.*, 2000).

If they mentioned positive effects of the free market economy, students pointed to increased job opportunities, emergence of new businesses, privatisation of factories, new shops and greatly expanded availability of consumer goods such as cars. Among the negative changes they identified the high inflation rate, a fall in the standard of living for the majority of people, increased unemployment, huge income differentials, a growing gap between the rich and the poor, increasing numbers of homeless people, financial difficulties for the middle classes, and lack of financial security. According to the students, the changes favoured only certain groups in society: young people, new business-people, and those currently in power.

One major criticism made by young people both in Hungary and in Poland was that some people became very greedy and lost their self-control, in some cases using illegal means to become as rich as they could in the minimum time. Money has become the key force in most areas of life and one of the main areas of competition.

There are different views about what drove the political and economic changes in Eastern Europe. One of the opinions shared by many experts is that the weakness and failure of the economic system was largely responsible. So according to this theory we can say that the social desire was to have a society that is economically more successful and can provide a better living for its citizens. However 'standard of living' is a relative category and when people hope for a better life, they have in mind an ideal, something that they would be satisfied to achieve. For those in the Eastern European states this was clearly the western consumer society. In the early stages of the economic (and political) changes the majority of the eastern societies had taken two things for granted: that the western consumer society is ideal, and that a short and dynamic process, called 'political and economic change' would transform the Eastern European societies to match this ideal. Now these two premises were both proved to be false: the first was a naive point of view, formed by people who had not been familiar with the hardships of western democratic market economies. But much more importantly the second statement turned out to be a dream rather than reality. People who were aspiring to a high standard of living had to face the reality: that sometimes they could not even buy the basics, which before the changes, they could easily afford. The times of shortage of goods were over, but people did not have enough money to buy the goods that had now become available. So in the eyes of the average person, the only thing that made their dreams of being western-style consumers impossible was the lack of money, the lack of purchasing power. Therefore money became the centre of hopes, discussions, worries, competition and even crime in Eastern Europe. Those with less than perfect moral standards were led towards corruption and the 'shadow economy'.

The parents of the 'omega–alpha generation' tried to close the gap between west and east, and led their society through a silent revolution to do so, but despite their best intentions and historic deeds they opened up two more gaps: the gap between hopes and reality, and the gap between rich and poor. It is now clear that the fate of these gaps is up to their children, the omega–alpha generation.

Adolescents' ideas about the role and effects of competition in their rapidly changing society

The notion of competition is central to a market-oriented economy. Ever since Adam Smith wrote *The Wealth of Nations*, competition has formed the basis for explanations of the functioning of market economies. In fact, competition is so central to the notion of the market that western economists rarely use the term in discussing markets (Dalgard, 1993). This is not the case in those societies where the introduction of the market economy on a large scale is a recent phenomenon. Discussions of competition and its consequences are part of the everyday discourse used in the media in countries of the former socialist block. Despite this, it seems that young people form their understanding of this important phenomenon mainly from non-economic sources.

Politicians and economic experts emphasise that competition has to be present in the economy, and that this will also involve the development of competitiveness as an important personal quality. Lynn (1991) was interested in the psychological correlates of economic development. In his study he compared a total of 41 developed and developing countries (categorised according to gross domestic product (GDP)) and found competitiveness to be the only significant determinant of economic growth in both groups.

Van Hoorn *et al.'s* (2000) study showed that most of the adolescents participating in their investigation perceived free competition as a central feature of the economic changes. However, they seemed to be overwhelmed by the intensity of competition, and increasing numbers thought that the government should set some limits on competition in society. They used the Darwinian metaphor saying that at present economic competition is governed by 'jungle law' and the market is largely unregulated. This view is not dissimilar to economists' views of these new market economies, namely that they are immature and are not ruled solely by the rules of the market, but by a kind of aggressive coordination (Hámori, 1998).

Furnham, Kirkcaldy and Lynn's (1994) study gives a kind of insight into why competition is so intensive in the former socialist countries. They found that while competitiveness and attitudes to money are negatively related to GDP they are fairly strongly and positively related to economic growth, meaning that when economic wealth has been secured, competitiveness relatively decreases. We could say that the more scarce the resources, the more competitive people be-come in order to secure survival.

In a study comparing Hungarian, American and Japanese sixteen- to eighteen-year-olds' perceptions of the role of competition in their society today, Fülöp (1999) found that while all three groups mentioned the role competition plays in the economy (keeping prices low, better quality products, economic prosperity, etc.), it was the Hungarians that mentioned this area of competition the most frequently, talking about competition for money, jobs and sheer survival. The existence of competition in these areas is a direct consequence of the political and economic changes in Hungary; thus it is a relatively new phenomenon. In general it is much more salient for Hungarians than it is for Japanese or American adolescents, who more frequently mention competition in non-economic and non-political areas such as education or (among the Americans) sport. In this study the Hungarians evaluated the role of competition in the economy either as positive or neutral, but competition for money and for survival were evaluated negatively because they were thought to be connected with immorality and aggression in society. Competition for jobs, a considerable burden for the middle-aged in Hungary who were brought up in a society with full employment, did not evoke positive or negative emotions among the sixteen- to eighteen-year-olds; they were neutral about it and took it for granted.

Attitudes towards entrepreneurs

Entrepreneurs and enterprising behaviour are key factors in allowing organisations to compete successfully in a complex and changing environment. In order to become more competitive and increase national wealth, all countries need people with an interest in entrepreneurship. Western research on entrepreneurs has revealed several characteristics that are important features of those choosing this career path. The earliest and probably the most influential paradigm emphasises that entrepreneurs have a higher than average achievement motivation and activity level (McClelland and Winter, 1969). Another paradigm connects entrepreneurship with creativity and innovation while a third considers risk taking as a crucial characteristic of entrepreneurs (Atkinson, 1957).

More recent studies consider a combination of these characteristics to be important determinants of being an entrepreneur. They normally include risk taking; vigorously striving for and achieving profit and business growth; seeking innovative solutions to problems; seeking out new opportunities; and the propensity to create business organisations (Cromie, 2000). Each author adds some new and important aspect. For example, Kirzner (1979) has developed a theory of entrepreneurial alertness, which asserts that entrepreneurs are more alert to new opportunities and use information differently from others. Gibb (1987) adds such attributes as initiative, flexibility, and imagination. Chell, Haworth and Brearley (1991) ascribe the following additional trait descriptors to enterprising people: pioneering, adventurous, venturesome, daring, go-ahead and proactive. Koh (1996) argues that entrepreneurs have not only a high need for achievement, but an internal locus of control, a high tolerance for ambiguity, and a good deal of self-confidence. Lumpkin and Dess (1996) added autonomy and competitive aggressiveness to the list of entrepreneurial characteristics.

A successful market economy is considered to increase the income and wealth differentials and inequalities among members of society, creating rich and poor people. After the political changes in Central and Eastern Europe, newly established entrepreneurs have become the driving force behind economic change, and have played a very important role in creating a new and, in comparison to the past, much more business-oriented society. Successful entrepreneurs have become the wealthiest people in society, and the financial gap has grown between different groups of the population that have emerged as either winners or losers as a result of the introduction of a competitive market economy. Such material and financial differences are more easily acceptable when they reflect real effort and achievement and more effective work, or in other words, when they are related to quality and/or quantity of work. A healthy society can accept as natural those inequalities that are the result of applying clear and transparent competitive tactics that are available to everyone. However, in those countries that are just trying to recover from the socialist economic system, the dramatically growing financial inequalities are seen to be the result, not of a fair and open competitive market process that functions according to mutually agreed rules, but rather, of political ties, abuse of power and influence, and corruption and crime.

Rule-breaking, which has a special history among Hungarian entrepreneurs, is seen as a mild form of corruption. In the seventies and eighties the 'troublesome people' played a significant role in the emergence of the 'second economy', the semi-legal sphere of small entrepreneurship in Hungary (Vári-Szilágyi, 1992). These people had high achievement orientation; they were creative, intelligent, and highly competent in their fields. They took risks in order to be able to exercise their professional competence. They could be regarded as innovators who made tremendous efforts to promote a more rational economy within the existing socialist bureaucratic system. They frequently came into conflict with dysfunctional institutions and arrangements, and they took the risk of breaking the rules, both because they were persuaded of the social value of their undertakings, and because they gained substantial individual profit by operating independently of the state. In the particular circumstances of that time, rule-breaking was seen as a necessary step to secure both their own interests and those of other people, and this, in a sense, 'legalised' rule-breaking. The silent acceptance of widespread rule-breaking was to a certain degree useful and constructive in the eighties before the collapse of state socialism, but it became highly destructive after the political changes because it turned into cynicism and a more general neglect of all legal rules. Inequalities that derive from such non-economic processes are hard to accept. In other words, when there are basically no rules in competition and almost any means are used in order to win, the losers will tend to perceive wealth with suspicion and even hatred.

Unfortunately, 'availability bias' (Kahneman and Tversky, 1974) can contribute to this general perception. This states that we tend to overestimate events of momentary significance in our decision-making processes, and to consider them more prevalent and more frequent than they are in reality. For instance, the detailed discussion of corruption cases in the media can make people believe that there are no honest people in business life. The result of this is a much more emotionally-regulated economic life than in countries with a long tradition of the market economy. In the post-socialist countries aggression and envy play a significant role in the economy of transition, but traditional market economies are characterised by more rational and neutral processes (Hámori, 1998).

The GLOBE study (Global Leadership and Organisational Behaviour Effectiveness) compared middle-level managers in 61 culturally diverse countries (Bakacsi, 1998; Bakacsi and Takács, 1998) mainly using Hofstede's (1995) categories. It showed that, compared with those in other countries, Hungarian business-people take a very short-term perspective, and they are extreme individualists, considering only their own interests and ignoring those of the group or the community. Interpersonal relationships among them are perceived to be bad, and they have a low achievement orientation in terms of hard work.

Taking all this into consideration, it is particularly interesting to find out how entrepreneurs are perceived by adults and young professionals or adolescents in the countries undergoing social change. Are they seen as positive or negative role models? To what extent is the description of the entrepreneur in western literature applicable to the way the new entrepreneurs of the post-socialist countries are perceived? Vári-Szilágyi and Solymosi (1999) compared the perception of a personally known entrepreneur with the more general 'Hungarian' successful entrepreneur. They found that in the specific case, university students and middle-aged professionals emphasised internal qualities such as hard work, high achievement, self-confidence, intelligence, persistence and high morality, but in the case of the prototype of the 'Hungarian' entrepreneur, they pointed to external factors such as luck, information and connections as the main determinants of success. The inclusion of the moral dimension (being honest, obeying the law, etc.) as a characteristic of the successful entrepreneur seems to be rather specific to Hungarians. Moral qualities are not explicit parts of the picture of the successful entrepreneur in the western countries, but they are important features in Hungary where economic life is generally perceived to lack morality.

Economic education in secondary schools: the Junior Achievement Program

In high-growth, global, competitive economies, entrepreneurship and related issues such as innovation and enterprise are regarded as crucial determinants of economic growth and prosperity, and are closely linked with efforts to create wealth. Economic education is, then, very important in every society, but it is especially crucial in countries where the economic structure is under profound change and the market economy and large-scale entrepreneurial activity are relatively new phenomena. There are completely new concepts and institutions such as share-holding and the stock exchange, the credit card, and the whole world of investments, which were not present in the former political and economic system. This means that not only young people, but also their teachers, have to learn and understand new economic concepts. The role of well-educated economics teachers is very important, because most of the students do not have the opportunity to talk about business with their parents at home, since many parents have not learned about business either.

To prepare students to be able to participate competently in the new economic environment is not only an important task, but also a rather complicated one requiring constant adaptation, because the economic environment is unstable and everything is in flux. In general, changes in the curriculum lag behind social transformations. In the early years of the transition to a free market economy, teachers were not prepared to teach students about the changing economic system, or to help them to gain and understand the importance of market-driven economies; the role of business in a global economy; the commitment of business to environmental and social issues and to operating in an ethical manner; the relevance of education in the workplace; and the impact of economics on their future (Jávorszky, 1999). This is a major concern because it is not enough simply to change the social structure; there has to be a kind of 'mentality' that maintains and develops it. In other words the way of thinking that characterises a socialist planned economy has to change to a market economy way of thinking (Gumpel, 1993). This requires the development of new competencies.

While there always have been some secondary vocational schools that specialise in teaching economics and commerce, the general educational system has not reacted rapidly to this new demand, and no new school subject concerned with economic studies has been introduced into the core curriculum. At the moment economics and business studies are not taught as compulsory subjects in secondary schools in Hungary. This is despite the tremendous growth of interest in business and business-related studies in the last decade among secondary school students. At present the most popular higher education institution is the University of Economics in Budapest; its applicants are among the most successful secondary school students in the country, but they have very limited knowledge in relation to the economy.

This gap was, however recognised by the North American Junior Achievement Movement which offers special programmes to schools; students participate on a voluntary basis. Junior Achievement Inc. was founded in the United States in 1919 with the original goal of giving young people the skills they needed to succeed in a business environment once they entered the workforce. It is currently providing services to 3.6 million school-aged children within the United States. The first international programme began in Canada in 1955 and spread to fifteen countries by 1989. With the rapid changes and high demand for a better understanding of market economics in the new democracies of Central and Eastern Europe, Junior Achievement Hungary was established to educate young Hungarians about the value of free enterprise, to enhance their understanding of business and economics, to develop ethical leadership practices, and to prepare them to join the work force. Since it was founded in 1993 it has provided intensive teacher training for at least 200 teachers, and more than 20,000 elementary and high schools students have participated. Increasing numbers of elementary schools, high schools, colleges and universities recognise the importance of economic education and the significance of the practically oriented teaching (Jávorszky, 1999).

The aims of Junior Achievement Hungary are to develop and implement economic education programmes for young people through a partnership and cooperation between business and education. This provides first-hand information about operating an enterprise and helps students to understand why it is important to maintain ethical business practices, not only as leader and producer, but also as a consumer.

The educational programme consists of several different parts: for example, an Applied Economics Program, a Project Business Program and a Student Company Program. The secondary school Applied Economics Program helps students to gain an enhanced understanding of the challenges and responsibilities of business. They become familiar with how the economy works and how economic incentives influence consumers, business owners and managers, savers and government employees. Their personal skills are developed, they explore career options and discover the value of education. They study topics such as supply and demand; the business of free enterprise; how to finance a business; economic stability; and production and productivity. These studies help graduates to become acquainted with current economic principles, and provide them with opportunities to use them.

Within the Project Business Program representatives of successful companies and enterprises visit schools regularly on a voluntary basis and hold lectures for Junior Achievement students. They talk about their business experiences and provide practical information about the Hungarian market economy.

In the Student Company Program students set up their own firm, elect a president and four vice-presidents and, as a group, make the company's plan into a reality. Students issue shares in order to finance their operations, choose the product, conduct market research, set the price, produce and market the product. Eventually, the company members close the company's books, prepare an annual report, and liquidate the business. In this process students learn economics through experience. They learn the art of communication, teamwork, and leadership skills (Jávorszky, 1999).

Junior Achievement Hungary also publish a textbook of economic studies to be used by teachers who have agreed to teach the programme, and a whole series of further books is planned to address different aspects of the business world, such as ethical business. A separate book will be published outlining 'good corporate citizenship'. This book will probably be unique in the Hungarian market; case studies will present companies that take care of their community and show responsibility for their environment. These companies look after the people who live in their surroundings, and play an important role in establishing a safe environment for people both within and outside the company.

Attitudes towards business, enterprise and entrepreneurs among secondary school students participating in the Junior Achievement Program

We showed earlier in this chapter that studies of the views of adolescents and young adults in the former socialist countries about economic changes and enterprise have found that there is generally a rather negative attitude. We will now report the findings of an investigation into the attitudes of those young people who have, as an extra subject, taken part in a one-year systematic business education course within the Junior Achievement Program (see notes).

A survey was conducted with 403 secondary school students who participated in the programme (55 per cent girls and 45 per cent boys). They all attended secondary schools with good reputations in different cities in Hungary.

The survey consisted of closed and open-ended questions designed to reveal students' attitudes towards business as a career, business-people in Hungary, and different aspects of the business world. There were five sections:

A. Students' attitudes towards choosing a career in business (closed question)

B. The types of business-people and topics that interest students (closed questions)

C. Students' attitudes towards the market economy, entrepreneur-
    ship and business-people (attitude scale consisting of 30 state-
    ments)

D. Students' images of the typical Hungarian business-person (a
    checklist of 15 characteristics)

E. Students' views of the six preconditions most necessary for
    achieving success in business life in Hungary (open-ended ques-
    tion).

We first set out the responses of students on the Junior Achievement
Program in each section, then report on correlations and factor
analyses across sections of the questionnaire.

A. Attitudes towards choosing a career in business

The majority (71 per cent) of the respondents, irrespective of gender,
could imagine themselves as business-people. While this number is
very high, it is not surprising in view of the fact that these students
joined the programme voluntarily and expressed interest in the business world right from the beginning. Moreover, studying economics,
business and finance are the most popular subject choices in higher
education in Hungary, and are believed to lead to highly paid jobs.

B. Types of business-people and topics that interest students

Both those who could and those who could not imagine themselves
as business-people said that they would welcome the opportunity to
meet and talk with someone actively involved in business (87 per
cent). They expressed an interest in talking with top managers of
multinational companies (62 per cent), bank directors (43 per cent),
and top managers of Hungarian companies (22 per cent). The preference for managers of multinational rather than Hungarian companies reflects the higher respect for foreign companies. The most
popular among the six topics of conversation listed were starting of
a new enterprise (43 per cent), functions of the market economy (41
per cent), the current situation of the Hungarian economy (38 per
cent), and personal career possibilities as a business-person (38 per
cent).

C. Attitudes towards the market economy, entrepreneurship and business-people

The five-point scale showed that respondents had a rather positive view of the introduction of the market economy, emphasising its positive effects on the development of Hungary (mean score = 3.88). They strongly disagreed with the statement, 'The market economy has only negative consequences' (1.68), but they doubted whether everybody would observe the ethical code of business in a market economy (2.00). Business life is seen as very stressful (4.01) and full of unexpected events (4.21). It is only money that counts (3.74) and there is no space for humanity (3.40) or trust (3.28). Entrepreneurs are considered to be the driving force of the economy (3.53) and their success is attributed to cunning (4.01), nepotism (3.96) and, less importantly, hard work (3.68). Students tend to agree that business-people in Hungary have established close contacts with the political elite (3.22). The entrepreneurs' work is considered to be colourful and interesting (3.61). Successful business-people have high prestige (3.38) and are envied in society (3.37). Financial rewards are believed to be high (3.54). These adolescents tended to disagree with those statements that were similar to socialist doctrine; thus they did not generally agree that business-people get rich at the expense of others (2.75) or that they exploit those who work for them (2.53).

In relation to the attitude scale we noticed an interesting variable. Students could choose whether they wrote their names on the questionnaire or preferred to remain anonymous; only 38 per cent of the respondents gave their names. We found that those who did not give their names had a significantly more negative view of business than those who did. They tended to agree more with the following statements (significant at the p<.01 level):

Business-people get rich at the expense of others
Business-people exploit those who are working for them
The market economy is good only for a small group of people
Being an entrepreneur is very lucrative

and with these (significant at the p<.05 level):

145

Entrepreneurs are immoral

Success in business depends on having connections

They tended to disagree more strongly with the following:

Entrepreneurs work hard to achieve success ($p<.01$) and Business-people are talented people ($p<.05$).

D. The typical Hungarian business-person

Students used a five point scale to rate the characteristics of the typical business-person against 15 positive attributes. Those rated most highly were goal-oriented (mean score = 4.62), self-confident (4.48), determined (4.25), industrious (3.72), and intelligent (3.62). The six least highly rated were reliability (2.85), good sense of humour (2.8), patience (2.61), honesty (2.44), patriotism (1.96) and modesty (1.92). Girls gave more positive ratings than boys, seeing the typical Hungarian business-person as more popular, purposeful and confident, less modest (all $p<.01$), more educated and deter-mined and having more sense of humour ($p<.05$).

E. The six preconditions most necessary for achieving success in business life in Hungary

Students were asked to list six factors that they considered to be the most important to achieving success in business life in Hungary. The most frequently mentioned were competence (63 per cent), connec-tions (52 per cent), capital (49 per cent), confidence (31 per cent), ambition (23 per cent), and persistence (21 per cent). Other factors mentioned by less than 20 per cent of the students were business skills, luck, social skills, good looks and talent. Creativity, self-control, risk taking, aggression, good infrastructure were mentioned by less than 10 per cent of the students. Altogether more than one-fifth mentioned morality; however half that group identified morality as an important factor in business success (11 per cent), and an equal number of students identified immorality (11 per cent). As we have already discussed, morality is not part of the discourse about successful entrepreneurs in the western literature; however it seems to be an important factor to be taken into consideration among adolescents in Hungary.

There was again a difference between the ideas of those students who gave their names and those who did not. Students who gave their names mentioned confidence ($p<.01$), morality and structural preconditions such as infrastructure ($p<.05$) significantly more often. The students who preferred to remain anonymous more often mentioned an extrinsic variable, luck ($p<.05$).

We now turn to our analysis of responses across sections.

Interest in business

We labelled a student as 'interested in business' if s/he answered yes to both 'Can you imagine yourself as a business-person?' and 'Would you like to talk to business-people?' (responses from Sections A and B). Two positive responses were considered reliable indicator of interest. Using this classification, 66 per cent of the total of over 400 students were labelled as 'interested in business'. The remaining 34 per cent included students who had answered negatively to both questions, and those who had answered positively to only one. It was considered that any positive response they gave could be seen as a sign of open-mindedness rather than a strong indicator of interest in business.

Students identified as interested in business had a much more positive view about the market economy, entrepreneurship and business-people than the others. They tended to agree more strongly with the following statements in Section C (significant at the $p<.01$ level):

The job of an entrepreneur is varied and diverse
In a market economy only the hard-working ones will be successful
Entrepreneurs work hard to achieve success
Business-people have high prestige
The market economy has a positive effect on the development of
    Hungary
Business-people are open and flexible

They also tended to agree more with the statements below (significant at the $p<.05$ level):

> Entrepreneurs make the economy work
> Being an entrepreneur is very lucrative
> In a market economy everyone observes the moral rules of business

Those students who were not identified as 'interested in business' tended to agree more strongly with the statements that characterised business negatively:

> Business-people get rich at the expense of others ($p<.01$)
> Business-people exploit those who are working for them ($p<.01$).
> Entrepreneurs are immoral ($p<.05$)
> In business money is the only thing that counts ($p<.05$).

We also found similar differences in the responses of these groups of students to the characteristics checklist (Section D). Students identified as 'interested in business' perceived the typical business-person as being more intelligent, educated, honest, hard-working, more friendly, reliable and modest, and less determined than did the other students ($p<.05$).

Among those identified as 'interested in business' more mentioned persistence, self-control and knowledge among the preconditions for success (Section E) ($p<.01$). However, they also mentioned luck and connections more frequently ($p<.05$). They were more likely to agree that they would like to be successful ($p<.01$) and wealthy ($p<.05$) in ten years' time.

Representation of business life

We found that, at the end of their year studying in the Junior Achievement Program, students had one of three distinctively different, coherent views about business and people dealing with business. We carried out a factor analysis on the 30-item attitude scale (Section C: attitudes towards the market economy, entrepreneurship and business) and found as a first factor a coherent negative, as a second factor a coherent positive and as a third factor a relatively coherent cynical concept of business.

The negative concept sees business-people as getting rich at the expense of others, exploiting those that work for them, and being immoral. According to this view, in business there is no humanity; only achievement counts, no one can be trusted, only money is important, and the market economy is only beneficial for a narrow group of society. It is interesting to note that this combination of ideas resembles the socialist ideology that emphasised equality, and condemned wealth because it derived from exploitation of the majority. Our results show that those students who handed their questionnaires in anonymously agreed with these statements significantly more than those who wrote their names. We can interpret this result as a kind of consistent socialist view of business; it is not seen as acceptable for such a view to be revealed openly by secondary school students who participated in a programme that clearly represents the changed ideological circumstances that emphasise capitalism.

The second factor revealed a coherent positive view of business life and included such statements as: business-people are open and flexible; they are talented; their work is colourful; they are the driving force of economic development; they work hard to achieve success; and everybody follows ethical business practices.

These two factors represent two distinctively different concepts of the market economy, entrepreneurship and business. The first depicts those involved in business as cruel capitalists and the second sees them as positive role models, the heroes of our time.

The third factor revealed a realistic but rather cynical view of business life, emphasising that it is stressful and people working in business often have to face unexpected situations. Connections are the most important element in being successful and the majority of entrepreneurs are believed to have established close connections with political leaders. Successful business-people are very cunning, but they have high prestige and make a lot of money.

A further factor analysis was carried out on the checklist of the characteristics of business-people (Section D). This also resulted in three factors as shown below. The characteristics in brackets have a weaker loading; a minus sign indicates a negative loading.

general positive characteristics	assertiveness	sociability
reliable	confident	popular
intelligent	purposeful	friendly
educated	determined	good-humoured
honest	(-) modest	satisfied
hard-working	(intelligent)	(patient)
patriotic	(educated)	
patient	(hard-working)	

The correlations between the factors from the attitude scale and the attributed characteristics are shown in Table 7.1 (** indicates a $p<.01$ significance level). Attitudes towards the market economy, entrepreneurship and business-people correlated positively with a positive view of the characteristics of the typical business-person. Assertiveness correlated only with the 'cynical' attitude. This may indicate that it is considered acceptable or 'normal' for a business-person, and thus relate to a positive or negative evaluation.

Table 7.1: The realtionship between attitudes towards the market economy and the characterisation of the typical Hungarian business person

	characteristics of the typical Hungarian business-person		
attitudes towards the market economy, entrepreneurship and business-people	General positive characteristcs	Assertiveness	Sociability
Negative attitudes	-.387**	.116	-.063
Positive attitudes	.466**	.041	.332**
Cynical attitudes	.123	.257**	.107

We can conclude that views of the business world and the evaluation of entrepreneurs were in consonance with each other.

We also expected some relationship between students' attitudes towards the market economy, entrepreneurship and business-people (Section C) and their views on what it takes to achieve success in business life in Hungary (Section E). For each precondition for success, we compared the mean scores of the factors described above for those who mentioned that precondition with the scores of those who did not. According to our results, those who had a negative concept of business consider immorality to be a necessary requirement for success in business in Hungary (p <. 01). Knowledge, persistence and luck as requirements of success were in negative relationship with this concept (p<.01). In contrast, those students who had a positive concept of business considered persistence, an ethical approach (p<.01) and knowledge (p<.05) to be necessary to success.

When we compared the characteristics of the typical Hungarian business-person (Section D) with the requirements for achieving success in business in Hungary (Section E), we found that the factor representing general positive characteristics was in a positive relationship with knowledge, confidence, persistence, morality (p<.01) and luck (<.05) while in a negative one with immorality (p<.01). The factor representing assertiveness was in a positive relationship with confidence (p<01), and the factor representing sociability was in a negative relationship with immorality (p<.05).

Summary

During the late 1980s and early 1990s dramatic social, political, and economic changes occurred in Central and Eastern Europe. It was expected that the structural changes in these societies would result in rapid changes in values, attitudes, and ways of thinking, especially among the younger generation. However, it has become increasingly clear that the process of change is complex, and takes place much more slowly than was anticipated. Therefore it is especially important to study how young people, who have been characterised as the 'omega–alpha generation' (Van Hoorn et al., 2000) think about the changes, and how they will continue to shape the outcomes for their countries. While in modern western liberal or market economies there are numerous studies concerned with children's and adolescents' ideas about different aspects of the economic world, there are relatively few that address these questions in those countries that are undergoing a historical change in their ideological and economic structure. Education plays a distinctively important role in establishing knowledge and skills that are required of citizens of any country

151

if they are to participate successfully in the economic reality of their society, but it is even more decisive in the post-socialist countries of Eastern and Central Europe. Research has shown that attitudinal change, or change in the mentality of people, is much slower than structural change. Systematic education of young people can facilitate this process somewhat. However, from our study carried out with students participating in the Junior Achievement Program we learn that education offers limited possibilities. In spite of the fact that the programme places special emphasis on teaching ethical business practices, a significant number of students on the programme view business life in general, and particularly in Hungary, as unethical. The implication of this finding is that the perceived everyday reality of a society can hardly be ignored in the classroom and negative views must be addressed openly. It seems that only those students whose concepts are in harmony with the expressed aims and ideas of the course are prepared to reveal their identity, while those who had a different perception preferred to remain anonymous.

The 'omega–alpha generation', born to become the first generation of the dream future, has become the holder of a heavy heritage. Will they be able to carry out what their parents have so far failed to do, to close the gap between east and west and to lead their society into a stronger and more united Europe? It is the responsibility of this generation to determine the social, political and financial future of this region. Economic education, underpinned by research, is absolutely vital.

Notes

This chapter was completed while the first author was supported by grants received from the Johann Jacobs Foundation and the Hungarian National Research Fund (No. T 029876). The authors would like to thank Ivan Jávorszky, director of the Junior Achievement Program in Hungary for providing the raw data of the research presented here.

The questionnaire was prepared and administered by the Junior Achievement Hungary Office.

8

Pocket money, spending and sharing: young children's economic understanding in their everyday lives

Elisabet Näsman and Christina von Gerber
Linköping University, Sweden

Introduction

Young children are often described as incompetent in economic matters. In their everyday lives, however, they indirectly experience and take part in economic transactions of several kinds. Since children's economic learning is, to a great extent, based on experience, it is important for educators to know what experiences they have, in what contexts, and what understandings they develop from these. As Crawford writes: 'Research is needed – not only into the variety and extent of the economic and industrial understanding which young children possess – but also into the contexts in which they acquire that understanding' (1992, p.206).

In the research project *Children's Economic Understanding*, we interviewed some 70 children aged three to six years at their daycare centre in small groups.[1] We were interested in the children's culture rather than in the responses of each individual. How do a group of pre-school children describe their everyday economic transactions? What kind of ideas, values, experiences and strategies can be found in such a group, and what potential do these have for mutual exchange, and for input into the learning processes of the daycare centre?

The focus of the interview was on the economic transactions that take place in the children's everyday lives, both in their families and at the daycare centre. The children's answers are related to examples of the ways in which staff in daycare centres consider children's competence in economic matters, and these are linked to ideas concerning economic socialisation of young children at daycare centres. The following questions are discussed in this chapter:

- Do young children have money of their own?

- What are their views on this and on children's role in making decisions about their own money?

- Can young children work to earn money?

- How do they use their money in terms of saving and consumption?

- What norms do children identify in relation to transactions involving private property?

- How do daycare staff consider young children's economic competence and what economic norms do they refer to?

The interviews were thematic and offered considerable scope for the children to develop their own thinking under the various themes. The analysis was done in the grounded theory tradition (Glaser and Strauss, 1967). This means that we focus on content rather than on numbers giving any particular response. In any case group interviews make it impossible to quantify individual responses.

Children's own money

In most of the groups children reported that they had experience of money that they defined as being their own. Having their own money could be very important to the children, as they reported in several of the groups. The phrase '*my money*' was stressed by the pitch of the voice as well as by the context in which it was used; for example, they emphasised their right to make decisions concerning the use of their own money. When they described going shopping by themselves, they stressed the fact that the money used was theirs. The issue of having their own money did not arise only when it was initiated by our questions; it was an issue children returned to now and then all through the interviews.

The quantity of money a child possessed also seemed to be important since it was often talked about in detail, even though we did not ask about this. The reactions in the groups when this topic was raised seemed to indicate that it was a matter of social status among the children to have access to money of their own. If one child started talking about it, others joined in and those who did not have money would mention the amount of other property they had.

Some comments linked the children's money to that of their parents, or emphasised that the parents did not have to pay because the children had their own money. This can also be seen as an indication of the importance of the issue. Having money of their own seemed to be a way of getting closer to acquiring a status equal to that of adults. It was with clear expressions of pride that one child explained that his parents had borrowed money from him, since he was the only one in the family who had money to hand. Money seems in this way to be part of children's conception of the status difference between childhood and adulthood.

We asked the children how they could acquire money. The most frequently mentioned source was parents:

> *From their mother.*

> *Or their father. Because I used to ask my father: Will I get money? Then he sometimes used to give me some.*

Pocket money was a familiar phenomenon; in a comparison between our three age groups the proportion of children who received regular money from their parents increased with age. Pocket money was generally paid on a weekly basis. The expressions *week-money* and *month-money* were well-established concepts. In one municipality children also talked about *morning-money* i.e. a coin they were occasionally given in the morning. The sums varied:

I get week-money every Saturday.

I get a fiver every Saturday and Friday.

I get a gold-coin. I get a gold-coin every Saturday.[2]

Well I get a twenty-scrap.

Most children move from week-money to month-money as they grow up; i.e. a larger sum of pocket money is given less frequently (Näsman and von Gerber, 2001a, 2001b). This transition was already taking place for some at these early ages.

I get one hundred kronor in month-money. I used to have week-money and then I got ten.

None of the children described pocket money as a self-evident right of a child at a certain age. It was rather a matter of negotiation between children and parents. They had to ask their parents in order to establish the routine. The young children described how they could influence this decision-making process.

The agreements they came to with their parents concerning pocket money varied not only in relation to amounts and periods; age was also a factor differentiating between these pre-school children. Some were paid according to an age ladder; each year brought an automatic increase in the sum. This rule could include all the children in a family.

Payment in kind was also mentioned in response to the question about having their own money; for example, some children said they got sweets. Since for several children, week-money was linked to buying sweets on Saturday, this makes sense as an alternative to cash. This practice could also take the form of children being allowed to shop for sweets up to a certain sum that the adult then paid. Some were allowed to buy sweets and pay with their mother's money when she was present; they then returned the change to her. The children did not consider the money used during such transactions as belonging to them.

The children did not all receive regular pocket money; some were only given money from time to time, an arrangement that offered considerable scope to the parents. Other arrangements seemed un-reliable in that the children were not paid regularly, even when pocket money had been agreed upon. We found several examples of such uncertainty of income; in our research we have also found this among older children and teenagers (Näsman and von Gerber, 1999, 2001b).

Regular pocket money as an established form of financial contri-bution by parents was not the only way to acquire money. Some children received money from the older generations in their family as birthday or Christmas gifts. Some were given money at the end of a visit to grandparents and great-grandparents. How much children received from the older generations varied considerably; we heard examples ranging from SEK 100 to a one krona coin.

To sum up we can say that children described their lives as having an economic culture with a large variation in norms for acquiring their own money: month-money, week-money, a coin handed out in the shop to buy sweets, payment in kind, money gifts, and so on. The variation in amount of pocket money was also considerable. The highest sum we learned of was 500 per cent more than the lowest, a wide income gap. Moreover, some children told us that they did not get any money regularly. Other children had only a few experiences of ever having received money: *I got some once*. This four-year-old girl was given three coins on this particular occasion, but was not allowed to keep them for long. Asked about what she did with the money she replied: *Mum, she just put them in her pocket*. Some chil-dren simply said: *I never get money*.

Children's decision-making rights

Having money meant that children had scope for economic action:

To buy a little themselves, sweets or something.
I save half my money so I can buy things myself.

When asked what they used their money for, most of the children talked about buying things. The consumption they described was generally typical items bought by children such as sweets, toys and Pokémon cards, but food was also mentioned in some groups. Their shopping could also be planned on a long-term basis involving saving money to buy something more expensive at a later date. There were a few examples of altruistic consumption, though this was restricted to benefiting members of the family:

> *... to buy and give things to their fathers and mothers and sisters and brothers.*

As we have already discussed, most groups stressed that it was up to them to decide how to use their money, though we also encountered examples of children who obviously had no say. Children often emphasised that they bought things themselves, and some developed long stories about times when they went shopping without any adult company. That seemed to be an important milestone, and examples showed that some parents could prohibit it. This was clearly an area of adult regulation and of restriction of the children's freedom of action. Some children explained that they were not permitted to decide what to do with their money. The power rested with their mother.

> *I have my money until my mother allows me to buy something.*

Other children mentioned their own fears as a hindrance. Those who had been shopping on their own told about their experiences with excitement and pride.

> *Once, when we had a lot of money, and then we bought two Kindereggs, one for my little sister and one for me. Then we walked to a shop, hand in hand. Then we went on our own, without mum and dad. Then we got two coins each from mum. Then we were allowed to buy Kindereggs. On our own! Then I saved the chocolate, all for myself.*

The way the children talked about this kind of situation implies that it was important that they were independent economic actors. This was one of the things that made money important for them:

> *I buy what I want to have, I buy things with my own money. And what Mum and Dad want, they buy.*

One story about a child who bought Pokémon for SEK 100 without parental permission confirmed the importance of this kind of event, and also showed the potential for being disobedient or taking individual initiative. Some children responded to the question about what young children need money for by saying that it allowed them to buy things their parents did not want to buy for them, suggesting that this was a matter of independence and power.

To buy some toys if the mother doesn't want to buy them.
Have you ever done that?
Yes.

Several children clearly expressed the view that they ought to have control over their own money and goods.

Because it is their money.

My mother mustn't help me and decide about my money.

Yes, my daddy doesn't decide anything about my money. Nobody decides about my money except me.

Some children phrased their answers in abstract terms as in the quotations above, while others pointed at the most common decision concerning the money: what to buy with it:

Yes I decide that I want to buy.

If it was Saturday, we would buy sweets, I would decide which I would have, which sweets I would have. Otherwise I would never eat the ones I got otherwise.

The possibility of making decisions about how to spend their own money was generalised by some children as a scope for potential action in relation to all the things that they described as their personal belongings:

I decide about myself and my toys and my bed and like that.

We asked the children why they thought children should make decisions about their own money. Some simply said that it was fun, another reason was: *because they don't have anything else to do.* To some children the answer was so self-evident that our question seemed comically absurd.

Why then? [laughter]
It is the children's money [laughter] *and then they must be allowed to decide.*

Justice was the reason given in one group.

It is not fun if only other people decide.

It is unfair.

One boy said that in his opinion children ought to be allowed to decide about their own money and savings, and then he drew a parallel with parents' rights to make similar decisions. Another group made a clear distinction between deciding about their own money and about that of their parents. These examples again show the importance children attach to comparing, and achieving a fair relationship between, their conditions and those of their parents.

The young children made a clear connection between ownership and control; their repeated widening of the discussion to include toys and other property demonstrates this. They also linked control over decision-making to other matters that concerned them, such as the choice of Saturday sweets.

According to some of the young children, restrictions on the powers of children to make decisions could be justified by their lack of competence, or could simply result from the power of parents. Two children mentioned risks children could run as independent economic actors:

You could buy things even though you didn't want to buy.

You don't know if they are expensive or not.

These children didn't think that children should be given money of their own because they lack competence. Several of them obviously accepted or took for granted the subordinate position of children.

Saving and spending

All the groups were familiar with the idea of saving, even though not all children actually saved themselves. The possibility of saving was one reason put forward to support giving pocket money to children.

160

Yes, because then you can save money and then you get more.

Children could explain saving in the basic sense that you put the money away and don't touch it. The money was saved in a receptacle described as a wallet or a piggy bank. When money is put there, you are saving, increasing your fortune until the piggy bank gets full and is emptied.

Several groups described saving as increasing the total sum of money i.e. saving was not a single event, but rather a process over time, involving adding more and more money to the savings. Other children developed a further analytical step, that saving was refraining from or postponing consumption.

For some children the money seemed to be an end in itself: you save so that you accumulate a huge pile of money. But for others saving a large sum of money was a means to an end: you save so that you can buy something really expensive, or a lot of different things:

If you want to buy something that is very expensive then you can save the money, until the money is enough for the thing.

In several groups children described specific consumption goals for which they were saving such as a Lego house, a radio-controlled car, or a Pokémon game. Several mentioned saving for holiday trips abroad. We also found examples of planning for the distant future. Several children saw saving for adult life as something that young children could do, and some said that they were doing that themselves. They did not always specify what they would use the money for. Saving money until you are grown-up seemed to be meaningful in itself. Some children, however, described what they would need the money for as adults: a nice big house to move into, food and a real lorry. One child explained that you needed to save for your adult life because all the people you know now might be dead, and so you would have to depend on yourself.

Overall, the children expressed positive attitudes towards saving, even though some stressed that their opportunities to do so were limited because they did not have enough money. Saving was an established economic strategy, and the children enjoyed talking about it.[3] The children seemed especially interested in talking about the various money receptacles that they had, with all their niceties.

Children also talked about saving in the bank, and put forward two reasons for doing this: that your money would not be stolen or yet lost. They described strategies for hiding money from other people at home. The possibility of money getting lost or being stolen seemed to be the two major concerns about saving among the young children.[4] For example, they explained that a piggy bank had advantages over a wallet, because the wallet could get lost. This emphasis on the risk that their money could just get lost, indicates, again, that some young children saw their age group as incompetent in that they are not able to take care of money in an orderly manner.

Earning money

Pocket money and gifts can be given without demanding anything from children in return, but could pocket money also be a form of payment for work done? Can young children in Sweden earn money? Studies of children's paid work in Scandinavia do not in general include children before school age.[5] This reflects a presupposition that paid work is rare among pre-schoolers. We asked the groups if children could earn money. Some children simply said *No*, while others laughed as an indication of the absurdity of the idea, an explanation being, *Only adults could do that*. Earning money belonged to adulthood. Several groups, however, argued that children do earn money. In general terms *helping adults* was mentioned as one way of doing so, and, when specified, this help was mostly with domestic work. The pocket money contract could include a request for domestic work. Cleaning the house, washing the dishes and gardening were examples mentioned. Many of the tasks that children were paid for would not be seen by adults as work. For example, some children were paid for searching for something that their parents had lost, such as a key.[6] On the other hand when children received money for cleaning the house, they did not always construct this as payment for work; for example, some parents hid money that the children searched for while they did the cleaning.

We should note here that the children described very varied conditions. But although it became obvious that there were differences in whether pay was given for a particular task or not, this did not give rise to any discussion among the children. The differences were simply noted and commented on as matters of fact. Children did not seem to expect any consistency in parental norms in this respect.

The concept of helping parents, with or without payment, also extended to the parents' workplace. In the children's culture there was no clear distinction between work and help, or between paid and unpaid tasks.

Pay for good behaviour

Children said that they were also paid for what one could call self-care tasks, such as making their beds and brushing their teeth. This can be seen as giving monetary value to the fostering of good habits. Payment in cash or kind was also offered as an incentive for refraining from undesirable behaviour such as eating sweets, swearing or nagging. This is earning for non-activity.

> *When I promised not to nag, then I was allowed to go to a movie and see Pokémon.*

More generally, children reported that they were paid when they were good or kind. The repertoire of good behaviour for which payment was given included resisting temptations and refraining from bad behaviour. In some cases children were paid for achievement-oriented behaviour such as swimming training. The children did not all approve of this kind of conditional pay system:

> *Sometimes I get money though I have not done anything, from daddy. I want to be able to get that though I have not done anything, though sometimes I used to get money when I have been nice too.*

However, the young children did not express any moral doubts about being paid for domestic work, self-care tasks or good behaviour, while such concerns have been found to be common among older children (Näsman and von Gerber, 1999, 2001b).

Other sources of income

Money contributions and payment for work were generally restricted to the children's network of relatives, but some children also mentioned that they could get money from other people. For example, children could get paid by strangers for assisting them, or for dancing. Searching for money on the ground could be profitable; this sounds like an idea belonging to a fairy-tale world, a sort of treasure hunt, but in relation to the limited cash flow of young children, finding even a single coin could considerably increase economic resources. In the economic world of these children, it could therefore be quite a reasonable strategy to search for money. Collecting and delivering cans for recycling was another familiar way of earning money, and could prove lucrative.

In two groups begging was mentioned as a way that children could earn money. Begging in the streets has become more frequent in Swedish cities during the last few decades. A more acceptable kind of begging has for a long time been a tradition among children knocking on doors at Easter. The children dress up as witches or old men and walk around the residential areas in groups leaving Easter cards with chickens and eggs, and receiving sweets and coins, sometimes collected in copper coffee pots – an attribute linked to the image of witches in Sweden. The children also mentioned this as a way of earning money.

Children could also increase their scope for economic action by selling things. An explanation of the business transaction could be that: *One gives money and then the other gives something.* Some children knew about organised forms of trade with used or second-hand goods. In several groups children gave examples of how they could earn money by trading. Mostly they sold things that they owned, such as toys and games. They described selling things to each other. Relatives were also customers. According to the children, some parents try to stop this business activity of young children. The children would then either move their trading activities elsewhere, or try to persuade the parent to allow them to continue, by arguing, for instance, that they would never again play with the toy they wanted to sell. It was obvious in the discussions of these trading activities among children that some of them had developed a degree of competence in business.

Bartering and lending

Swapping and borrowing from one another were familiar ways of expanding the scope for economic action without using cash. In several groups children mentioned that the exchange was voluntary.

> What are the rules?
> *That you have to ask first if you may swap it.*
>
> *If Marie for instance has it, then you might say, 'Shall we swap?'*
> *Then she might say, 'Yes'. And then you swap things.*
>
> What do you do when you borrow from someone?
> *You ask, 'May we borrow your things?' Then they say, 'No', or 'Yes'.*
> *Then we listen to what they say.*

Some young children made a clear distinction between swapping and borrowing things from one another. Borrowing means that you get back what you have lent to someone.

> *You take it home, and then you give it back when you don't want to*
> *have it.*

Swapping means that you get another thing in exchange, but then definitely lose what you have given away.

> *Swapping, do you know what swapping is, that you give one thing*
> *and then you get something back.*
>
> *I have swapped a Pokémon and then I got a thing back, then I got*
> *a Pokémon back.*

The principle of voluntary action did not exclude problems in the bartering trade. To give possessions away by swapping rather than lending could cause problems. The difficulty of getting your old Pokémon cards back if you regretted the trade was mentioned in several groups. It seemed hard to accept the irreversibility of swapping, though the principle as such was clear to the children.

> Do you exchange things?

No, it is no fun. You only regret it and then you want them back later.

Maybe you start longing for it.

And then, it is not kind to the other who bought it for you, and then you give it away.

Bartering was a pattern of economic activity that seemed to follow firm rules among the young children. Moral aspects were seen as relevant, and this made some children refrain from taking part. There was a risk that transactions might be regretted, and it was considered morally wrong, and unfair to the donor, to give away what you had received. Both of these kinds of problem resulted from the irreversible nature of swapping. Some daycare centres had rules about swapping, which gave a child the right to get the traded goods back. In such circumstances, the exchange became a loan.

Sometimes we give away some cards but sometimes we want them back then. Then they have to bring them back the next time and if they are not there then you put them on their shelves.
So you swap cards?
Yes, we borrow from one another like that.

On one occasion it was reported to us that a child had broken the rule of reciprocity in bartering. That child was excluded from further participation in such activity. It seems reasonable that this, and the problems mentioned earlier, caused conflicts between children and as a result motivated the regulation or prohibition of bartering that we found in some daycare centres:

Then they may get angry.
Are the teachers angry?
Yes.
When are they angry? ...
If they give out Pokémon cards if you mustn't do that.
Are you not allowed to have Pokémon at the daycare centre?
Yes you may, but not give out ...
No you mustn't give to somebody else. But you may bring them with you. ...

'Emil', maybe the teachers say, like, 'No, now you must go and tell Emil that you will take it back, because you mustn't distribute them'.

When the staff forbade the bartering and actively intervened in order to stop the trade, some children solved this in the same way as mentioned above – by moving the swapping activity to another location.

Borrowing

Some children were negative about borrowing because it could cause conflicts. To others, borrowing from one another was positive. All groups had some experience of borrowing.

An important norm was to ask permission: borrowing was a voluntary transaction. Another basic rule was that the borrowed goods had to be returned.

That you have to give back. And if you hand something over, and if you want it back, when we are playing, then you must give it back or else you get angry.

Some children were only prepared to lend their things to particular children. Based on their experience, young children could see a risk in this kind of transaction even among friends, a risk that the things someone borrowed could get lost because of children's difficulties in keeping things in order.

My friend who is called Nina, who borrowed from me ... She lost a box for make-up ... She has lost it at home

Yes, to my friend, but she has lost them, so I cannot get them back, clothes.

Reciprocity was stressed in relation to borrowing:

If I have something, then I give that to Martin, then I may borrow his things.
Yes, that is borrowing.

Borrowing clothes from one another seemed to be a way of solving problems at the daycare centre when a child did not have suitable clothes or these had become wet. According to the children, this was initiated and practised by them without adult intervention. Children mostly borrowed toys from one another for a short period when they were playing together, but they also borrowed on a long-term basis, taking the borrowed items home with them. The adults were in general not mentioned as initiators or mediators in this kind of business. If, however, a child broke the rules, for instance by taking things without asking, the staff at the daycare centre could intervene helpfully to sort the matter out.

To sum up, young children have a variety of ways of getting access to money and goods. Their income mostly comes from parents and relatives, but the group of children at the daycare centre provided an important market for bartering and swapping collectable objects, toys and clothes, and for some selling and buying.

This description of young children's understanding, experiences, values and strategies in economic issues is, of course, very condensed. Since it does not focus on the individual child, we cannot demonstrate the wide variation between children. One self-evident difference relates to age, though our data does not clearly demonstrate stages of learning about economic issues, or the processes influencing the level of learning in relation to experience. The oldest children in our sample had lived twice as long as the youngest ones. This means, of course, a difference in experiences, but also a difference in understanding and in the competence to take an active part in a group interview. Among the youngest children we found some who contributed very little to the cultural content we are analysing. They included those with the least experience of money, and some who could not describe their fortune in numbers of kronor, but had to find other ways of estimating the amount. But even these children had taken part in economic transactions, and could benefit from a learning process were they could share ideas with others.

The staff

To what extent does the adult world, represented here by members of staff at daycare centres, recognise and understand the learning potential in children's economic culture? How much scope for action are adults willing to offer young children so that they can experience

168

economic activity and use this as a basis for developing their competence and sharing this with others, for instance in a daycare centre? Are those concerned with teaching actively interacting with the children in these matters, and thereby engaging in their processes of economic learning? We will conclude by discussing the interaction between staff and children in daycare centres.

We were not able to interview staff from all the daycare centres we visited; this discussion is therefore based on the children's accounts and on interviews with a few staff members. In the interviews we raised general issues concerning economic socialisation at pre-school level, and we also asked questions that reflected the information that the children had given to us concerning economic transactions and norms, and their interactions about economic issues with the staff. We comment here on the way that the staff described everyday economic activity within the daycare centre, and on their understanding of the children's competence and experience.

The children often described the staff in their responses, identifying them as a source of rules and routines, and as authorities that children could turn to in order to control those who had broken common rules. The staff played the role of a superior authority that intervened both on its own initiative, and when children asked for help (for example, when they encountered problems in economic transactions). Conflicts could thereby be resolved. Staff sometimes prohibited certain categories of economic activity, and some children resolved this problem by conducting such transactions where they were not being supervised. The power of the staff in this context can be seen as parallel to the role the state has in relation to the market. The extent to which children could offer explanations of the motives and norms behind staff interventions varied. Some children just stated the rules as matters of fact. When they did mention a motive, this was often linked to normative frameworks other than those used in the economic sphere. For example, children were not allowed to bring private property into one daycare centre, and the motive the children suggested for this was that if they did, it would be harder for the staff to keep order. It was not obvious to the children that this prohibition also addressed potential problems associated with bartering.

Economic issues were described by the children as moral issues, for instance in relation to the resolution or abolition of conflict over private property or the property of the daycare centre. Staff did not want to take responsibility for children's private property, as this led to the risk of conflict with parents if items got lost or broken. Reducing tensions was a major task for the staff, and this was sometimes done in a way that made the economic issues invisible, contradictory or blurred for the children. Some research has concluded that a major priority for Swedish daycare staff is the avoidance of conflicts and emotional tensions between children (Ehn, 1983). Similarly, in the interviews with us, staff members mentioned this as a major problem, and they said they implemented strategies that were aimed at conflict limitation. Staff members regulated the issues that arose on the pre-school scene, but they did so without any analysis of these from the perspective of economic socialisation.

In addition to conflict avoidance, the staff mentioned other moral motives for their actions. They did not want children to make comparisons between the possessions of different children in a competition for social status, and they were concerned about the impact of differences in economic resources between poor and wealthy parents. This was related to the issues of property management as well as to planning for excursions, birthday celebrations and end-of-term festivities. Staff saw this as a matter of justice between families with different material resources. Children and parents could become the victim of social pressure to buy expensive new toys or other high status items. A related concern that staff mentioned was that children should not 'buy' friendship, for example by giving away or lending their personal possessions in a bid to be allowed to play with a high-status child. These motives suggest that staff aimed to construct the daycare centre as an area protected from market forces. They also show an ethical framework in which the value of an individual or a social relationship is not seen as being for sale on the market. Equality is a basic value. Staff members expressed a generally critical view of 'consumer culture', in which they considered that children become careless and materialistic, and parents fail to take on the responsibility of fostering positive values. Staff regulation was focused on reduction of conflict and tension in the groups of children, and fostering empathy and a positive attitude towards sharing.

This combination of motives can account for both the heavy restrictions on children's scope for action with their personal possessions at some of the centres, and for the regulation of the children's usage of institutional property. The adults lacked awareness and understanding that many aspects of the children's everyday life can be seen as economic, and they did not recognise that these issues could form the basis for a more planned approach to support the children's economic learning. They were not aware that economic issues could form a topic in the adult-driven learning processes. What we see as economic issues were categorised and dealt with as moral education, and the staff did not reflect upon the connections between moral and economic socialisation. This can explain the lack of consistency, reflection and conceptual clarity that appeared in the responses from the staff about these matters.

Another explanation may be that the staff lack economic competence. When some staff members described how they had eventually talked about these matters with the children, their descriptions of economic transactions were often unclear, or in some cases drew on incorrect terminology and showed misunderstandings of the economic processes involved. They were not aware of the need for a better understanding, since they were not focusing on the economic aspects. This is obviously a problem in the role of the staff in the economic socialisation of children at daycare centres.

The fact that the staff did not see economic issues as relevant in the socialisation of the children may also be the explanation for the adults' lack of knowledge about the children's understanding. Generally the staff members were not aware of the richness of these young children's experiences or of the complexity of their ideas, values and strategies in relation to economic issues. They underestimated the potential that children have for economic competence and their interest in these issues. For example, one staff member said that a child could not have any idea of prices, or of how to go shopping until a much later age than that of the children we talked to. Moreover, staff seemed to interpret some of the children's activities and talk about these matters in a way that made the children appear to be driven by fantasies, or alternatively they suggested that the children were simply parrots, repeating things that they had heard without really understanding what they were saying. But we found that during the group interviews some children expressed their ideas in a way that convinced us that they knew what they were talking about. For example, the price of Pokémon cards was very well known; some children clearly knew how to save for future consumption; and most knew how buying and selling things works because they were already involved in trading.

Context of learning

Obviously the daycare centre is a context with considerable potential for economic learning. In conversation, play and other interactions through which children share their understandings, correct each other, and explain to each other, they are actively constructing and reproducing a children's culture in which economic issues are naturally a component. The staff did not recognise the range of economic experience in the children's culture and as a consequence this was not used as a basis for promoting economic learning through interactions among the children and between children and staff. Discussion of economic issues from everyday life with young children at the daycare centre offers staff an opportunity to enhance children's understanding and ability to cope, both in their present-day lives and in the future.

In the exchange of ideas during the interactions between children, their different experiences and understandings meet. Their understanding and competence may develop when they share and reflect upon that of others. In trying to understand the symbolic world of others, they widen their own. Individual interpretations are confronted by alternative or complementary ways of thinking. The children were ready to tell one another about their economic experiences so that they could all share their diverse experiences of access to money, shopping, playing a role in economic decision-making, and so on. This demonstrates that there are good opportunities for exchange of ideas and experiences among children.

Teachers who want to play a part in these learning processes need to deepen their own understanding, as well as the children's economic experiences and thinking. Our research will continue, focusing, on the one hand on the family as an economic context for children, and on the other hand, on developing methods for teachers to work with young children in economic matters, using the communication technique described as 'draw and tell'. This is part of training courses for staff members at daycare centres.

Notes

1. The study uses several methods for data collection. In this chapter we analyse data from interviews where boys and girls in groups of two or three children were interviewed. The sample was selected from three geographical areas: a suburb of a large city, an industrial town and a small town community including countryside; and from two kinds of housing: detached houses and flats. We interviewed 72 children in 25 groups, eight boys' groups, four girls' groups and thirteen mixed groups. The majority of six-year-olds attend compulsory school but those who attended daycare centres have been included here.

2. A so-called 'gold coin' in Sweden is worth SEK 10. At the time of writing the exchange rate was €1 = SEK 9.3.

3. Among the older children (aged between eleven and sixteen) saving was difficult and several labelled themselves as spendthrifts (Näsman and von Gerber, 2001b).

4. Among the older children the major risk mentioned was that they might spend the money carelessly themselves (Näsman and von Gerber, 2001b).

5. In studies of child work it is common to consider only those aged ten and over (e.g. *Barn og ung i Danmark*, Köpenhamn Socialdepartementet, 1992, Facts about Children in Norway, Oslo Barneombudet, 1992). However, Swedish statistics often start at age thirteen, and labour market statistics at sixteen (0-17, Stockholm Rädda Barnen, 1991).

6. This kind of pay was also described by young children in a study by Näsman and von Gerber (1996).

9

Children's reflections on income and savings

Helene Elvstrand

Linköping University, Sweden

Today's children are a significant consumer group; considerable sums are invested every year in marketing merchandise such as toys, clothing, music and sporting goods directly to children. However, there is still limited understanding of how they think about issues related to money. Children's own reflections and perceptions in this area are an important source of knowledge for educators and parents, and are thus worthy of investigation. This chapter focuses on children's narratives about their economic experiences and in particular, their personal income and savings.[1]

The child is part of a family, and inevitably children's finances are dependent on the family economy and parental attitudes toward money. Modern family research indicates that a new child-rearing ideal has emerged, 'characterised by a familial 'culture of negotiation" (du Bois-Reymond, Buchner and Kruger, 1993, p.87), in which the balance of power between parents and children is changing and children are more often regarded as independent subjects with inherent rights. According to Dahlberg (1993), the child in the 'project-oriented child rearing ideal' (p.92) is an integral participant in the family's decision-making process. The parental role becomes one of being present and guiding the child, and the parents hope through this guidance process to help the child form an understanding of the ways in which various circumstances impact on decision-making. As a result it is hoped that the child will become competent to make his or her own decisions.

175

The main questions addressed in this chapter are therefore:

*   How do children describe their income and their opportunities, if any, to increase their income?

*   How do they feel about saving money and, if they save, what do their savings mean to them?

*   What characterises the child's role in the modern 'familial culture of negotiation', and in particular, how do children participate in and understand the economic life of the family?

Research design

This study is based on empirical data consisting of individual interviews with six boys and four girls aged eight to eleven years. All the children are members of the same class; classes with children from more than one grade are common in Sweden. The sample was selected by asking all fifteen children in the class if they would like to participate in the study; ten of them agreed to be interviewed. The children live in a multicultural urban area with mixed housing and socio-economic groups. This heterogeneity is reflected in the living conditions of the children in the sample; there are considerable variations among them with respect to the type of homes in which they live and their parents' occupations. The children who participated in the study were all born in Sweden, though two of them have parents from another Nordic country.

Each child was interviewed in the classroom during school hours. The interviews were based on thematic questions surrounding the children's personal income and savings. The open-ended questions afforded considerable opportunity for the children to be active in the interview process and to describe their own economic experiences freely. The initial interviews were followed up with second interviews with three children, two girls and a boy, to explore further the questions above. The follow-up interviews, which were held in the children's own rooms at home, yielded responses that were very consistent with what the children said in the first interview, particularly when they gave accounts of events or situations, or reasoned at length. This indicates that the children's narratives were genuine and reflective. All interviews were recorded and transcribed. The interviews were analysed using a Grounded Theory approach (Strauss and Corbin, 1998).

Sources of income

To have personal finances, children must have some source of income, which may be money of their own, or income earned through some form of primitive economy. What sources of income do the children in this study describe? As is common in Sweden, all of them stated that they get money of their own in the form of a weekly or monthly allowance from their parents, weekly being the most common. Seven receive a weekly allowance and two receive a monthly allowance. There are significant differences in the amounts that they say they receive, varying from SEK 10 to SEK 70 a week.[2] The girls report generally lower levels (receiving SEK 10–30 per week, in comparison with the boys SEK 20–70). There is an age spread of approximately two years among children in the sample; I found no differences in levels of allowance in relation to age.

During the interviews none of the children complained about the size of their allowance, or said that they did not have enough money for what they wanted to buy. This was true regardless of the amount they received. Nor did any of the children say that their allowances are low because their parents could not afford to give them more. This could be because they are unwilling to describe their families in terms of limited economic resources. Another explanation may be that there is no automatic correlation between the amount of the weekly allowance and the family's financial situation, which could mean that families do not cut back on the children's allowances even when family finances are strained. However, a few children reported that the family's financial situation occasionally impacts on them in that parents may sometimes borrow the children's money, or have to delay giving the allowance because they have no spare cash on the usual day.

The children who receive less money (SEK 10–20 per week) are aware that their allowances may be considered low. In several cases they gave spontaneous explanations for this: the family may have chosen to prioritise other things, such as an expensive hobby, or may be saving for a common goal, such as a family holiday. Tobias (11) explains:

> *We only get twenty because daddy says that's enough. We're supposed to save for our holiday ... and then you can't give away so much if we are going to save.*

In the extract above, Tobias uses the word 'we', thus including himself in the activity of saving and prioritising. He perceives the family as an economic unit, of which he is part, and thus thinks it is reasonable that he is not given as much money on those occasions when the family is saving for something that will benefit them all. This economic argument encompasses not only the child's awareness of why s/he gets a low allowance, but also the knowledge that s/he will share in the family's resources, in the form of a holiday for example. To what extent do the children's explanations of why they do not get a large allowance reflect family discussion of financial priorities? If the children themselves participate in financial decision-making, possibly it is easier to teach them that they cannot have everything they want, and to justify lower allowances.

The data indicate that the economic situation in which children are most involved and influential is discussion with parents about allowances. In several families, an increase in allowance was preceded by family negotiations. I interviewed Maria (10) on two occasions about four months apart. On the second occasion her weekly allowance of SEK 20 had been raised to SEK 120 per month, and she told me that she had been promised a raise to SEK 150. She explains here what happened when her allowance was raised:

> *The first time I had to write down what I was going to do and how much I would need, so first I wrote how much, that was 150 and that I would buy clothes, sweets on Saturdays, and useful things like make-up, things you have to have.*

Maria is aware that setting out how she will use the money to buy useful things is a cogent argument for being given money. It is interesting to note that she describes make-up as a useful thing, something '*you have to have*'!

Personal responsibility

A nine-year-old boy, Petter, has considerably more responsibility for his own consumption than many of the other children. He is given an allowance of SEK 70 per week, which is quite a lot more than the other children, where the usual amounts are SEK 20-30 per week. I asked him how long he had been receiving SEK 70 per week:

Petter: *About a year maybe. Before that I got 50, for about two years, and then I got ten before that.*

HE   *But when you got 70 – what happened so that you got that?*

Petter: *I got older, so I needed more money.*

HE   *Is that so?*

Petter: *Yes, because then you start doing a lot more things, so, so you can, if you want, you can have more clothes or, if the ones that mum and dad buy, if they are really expensive, say 300 kronor or something like that, then you can pay half.*

Petter is aware that his weekly allowance is considered high, and he emphasises the consequences of having a high allowance: '*Yes, but anyway, I buy things for myself, mum and dad don't buy very much for me, I get a high allowance instead.*' When I ask him what he thinks about his allowance, he replies, '*I think it is better to have more money every week because then I can buy whatever I want with it.*' Having his own money gives Petter a tremendous sense of freedom. He shows considerable economic awareness; discussions of what things cost arose in both interviews. He says that he does not often ask his parents for things, since he has his own money.

> *But if I do, then maybe I can pay half. Of course, mum and dad don't buy me that much, I have to save for stuff instead. Like when we go on vacation, I have to pay for everything I want myself, except for food and stuff like that. But if I want a tee shirt or something, I have to buy it myself with no help from my mum or dad.*

He says that he has had more financial responsibility since his allowance was raised. When he had less money, it only had to cover buying sweets. If he wanted something else, he could ask his parents for more. After his allowance was raised that course of action was no longer open to him in the same way. Petter's story is unusual among these informants. The children more often describe a situation like Christian's (9):

> I usually write a wish list and then I give it to my mum and then my dad and mum talk about it after we go to bed so we won't hear them.

Although Petter and Christian are the same age, there is a considerable difference in the scope they have to realise their desires and buy what they want. Christian has to rely on his parents' generosity, hoping that they will decide to accede to his wishes. Petter, on the other hand, has considerable freedom, which he emphasises as positive.

The size of the allowance among children in this sample is not related to age, but is highly dependent on parental attitudes towards children having their own money. In the interviews I asked the children what expenditure their parents think the allowance should cover; what their parents consider to be reasonable and expected expenditure for children; and the extent to which they expect the child to take personal responsibility for his or her finances.

Earning an allowance

Accounts of express demands for children to 'earn' their allowances through good behaviour and performance make it apparent that the allowance is to a great extent a mechanism of socialisation:

> Well, if I haven't cleaned up and don't behave, or if I'm naughty, then I usually don't get an allowance, or I can't have my allowance. (Maria, 10)

> You have to do what mummy and daddy say and not do stuff you're not supposed to. (Evelina, 9)

Some descriptions of what children are expected to do to merit an allowance are vague, especially among the girls. They do not give any concrete examples; instead, several of the children use the terms 'behave' and 'not act up.' There are parallels in international research showing that parents may see the allowance as a means of sanctioning their children. Feather (cited in Warton and Goodnow, 1995) interviewed parents about their views on children's allowances and found that 40 per cent stated that they reduced their children's allowances for bad behaviour, while 30 per cent said they increased the amount for good behaviour. My data include detailed accounts of how children's allowances may be reduced if they do not behave. Some children perceive this as an empty threat, since they always get their allowances in the end, but others say that the withholding of allowances for 'bad behaviour' is practised in their families, and has happened to them. However, none of the children reported that they get more money for good behaviour.

There is also a close correlation between the child's keeping his or her room neat and being given an allowance. For some children this is a condition for receiving money: '*My room has to be all cleaned up when it's time to get my allowance*' (Evelina, 9). In an Australian study, Warton and Goodnow (1995) analysed parental views on allowances in relation to children's jobs in the home and found that parents fell into two groups: those who give their children an allowance independently of their doing any chores at home, and those who set a clear correlation between doing chores and the allowance. These differences in parental attitudes can also be seen through the children's accounts I have collected. Some children say that there is no connection between performance and allowance in their families. However, several children perceive that they are expected to contribute to household work in order to get an allowance. This ideal of doing one's fair share and of working for money is consistent with the Protestant work ethic that is widespread in Swedish society. This view has also had a profound effect on child-rearing; children should not be given an allowance unless they do something to earn it (Norling and Gunnarsson, 1994).

In many families, then, the children's allowance is not simply a matter of the child being given a certain amount of money with which to have fun. It appears that many parents use the allowance as a mechanism for socialising their children into thinking about money and finances.

Selling their possessions

The children have a well-developed understanding of the concept of recycling in relation to possessions; they know that a cast-off possession may be worth something to someone else. They described in detail the recycling practised in their families, for example when outgrown clothing is handed down to a sibling. They also see their things as a potential source of income, since they all believe that one can get money by selling one's possessions. Several have practical experience of having done so:

Maria (10): *Over there somewhere, we stood at a table and sold stuff, me, Grandma and Anna* [older sister] *and we got a lot of stuff together, kids' books and toys, like action figures.*

HE: *What did you do with the money?*

Maria: *Anna and I divided it up, well, no, we didn't really, 'cos we put it all together in a tin. Daddy had taped it shut so we couldn't see what was in it and he taped it so*

we *couldn't open it and when we got money we had to put it in the tin.*

The children who have not sold their possessions say that they plan to do so in the future, like Daniel (10):

Yeah, I am going to sell, I think I'll probably sell a lot of stuff, like cars and stuff like that, and maybe action figures and Legos and I'm thinking of selling them 'cos I don't play with them very much any more.

Some of the children described how they have stood behind a table and sold things, together with parents, siblings, or, in Maria's case, grandmother and older sister. On these public occasions, both children and parents seem to have been active participants. Even if the adult initiated a sale at a flea market, the children were active in that they were allowed to come along and, within certain limits, choose the things to be sold. When the families do such things together, there is often a common purpose, such as saving money for a family trip. The money then belongs to the whole family, and may be treated as special, as in Maria's account of the tin that was taped shut. One or two children recount how their parents did the actual selling through contacts with potential customers, such as work colleagues. The money in such cases may still be given to the child, with the adult playing the part of the broker. The general opinion among the children is that if they sell any of their possessions, the money should rightfully be theirs:

> *Well, but then Karin* [older sister] *and I shared everything we sold and she got a little more than me because she had been there the whole day.* (Petter, 9)

It is obvious to Petter that he should get the money for the things he sold when he worked at the flea market with his family. He explains that he had a business deal with his older sister that they would share the proceeds. He also describes a common norm existing in working life, that the person who does the most work should receive the most money. Petter and Karin applied this to their own sales activity, and Petter is content that Karin got a little bit more. In the neighbourhood where the children live, spontaneous flea markets have been arranged during the summer amongst the children, where they set up a table in the front yard to sell their things. These 'yard sales', which several children describe, are not only about selling possessions to earn money, but are also an entertaining and exciting summer activity. Evelina (9) tells how she would like to be part of such a sale:

> *With my friends, like when they asked me if I wanted to sell stuff with them, but I'm not allowed to, but I still wanted to.*

Evelina stresses the contrast with her friends, whose parents allow the practice. There are many possible reasons why parents may disapprove of their children selling their possessions. We do not know the reason in this case, but it is possible that parents may withhold permission because they do not consider the items in question to be the child's own property. It may be that when toys are bought for the eldest child, they are expected to be handed down to younger siblings. In that case, the toy is not the sole property of the child to whom it was first given, but rather the communal property of all the children. Thus the notion of possessions as realisable capital collides with the 'recycling concept' within the family. Alternatively, it may be that the parents disapprove of children standing outside and selling, believing that this is not an activity that should be part of childhood. Several children described how they have earned money through more informal sales, such as selling to family members:

> *We both took some of our toys that we didn't want any more, the ones that were really old, and we made a deal. My little brother collects erasers, so he bought them all.* (Tina 9)

What reasons do the children give for selling their possessions? Several of them measure the value of their possessions by their value for play, and the most common reason for selling something is that they no longer play with it. In that case, it may be better to exchange it for money. Petter talks about what he charged others to buy his things. He sold his action figures at a flea market for two or three kronor each, even though they cost 20–30 kronor new. When I asked him whether he thinks he got a good price for them, he replied, '*Yes, it was worth it because I don't play with them any more.*' Thus, the play value was an important aspect in setting the price. Compared to the purchase price, Petter was poorly recompensed, but for him, a little money was better than none at all, because he no longer got any pleasure from these toys.

Independent selling

A few of the children describe situations where they made things to sell:

Tina (9):	*Last summer, I think it was, we drew some really pretty pictures.*
HE:	Who did you sell them to?
Tina:	*To an old lady, she used to buy them all the time. She was in the store almost every day, she was 84 years old, she said that she hung up all the pictures on the wall.*
HE:	How much did you sell them for?
Tina:	*One krona each or one krona for two pictures, but she used to give us a whole five kronor.*

Tina, who made drawings specifically in order to sell them, shows once again that there is more involved in the activity of selling than simply earning money. For Tina, the customer was an important person whom she got to know partly because the children repeatedly sold drawings to her. It is also discernible here that some children ascribe sufficient value to things that they have made themselves to believe that they can sell them. Some children have also engaged in selling for a special purpose, such as to get money to go on a school trip.

Um...once I tried to sell those Christmas crafts or Christmas cards but it didn't work very well, 'cos nobody was home then ... and then I sold sweets for Karin's [older sister] class that she had got, Karin sold about five with me and then I went around twice and sold about twelve, for her, and this one person bought four of them.
(Petter, 9)

Petter tells about this selling activity with pride. He has detailed memories of how the event proceeded and how, even though he is several years younger than his sister, he was able to help her earn money to go on her school trip.

Earning money

In addition to allowances and selling possessions, the children describe working to earn money as a third source of income. The most common task the children describe is helping out at home in exchange for payment. Maria (10) has various suggestions about what she can do:

Maria:	*Oh yes, Anna [older sister] and me, we clean the whole house for 30 kronor each. The toilet, the hall, vacuuming and washing the floor ...*
HE:	Can you do anything else to earn money besides cleaning?
Maria:	*Oh, you can get extra jobs, say, like I usually say to my mum, if I shovel the snow so you can get out to the garage, then can I have ten kronor?*

If the children have a garden, they may earn money by mowing the lawn or weeding. Another common job is to baby-sit for their younger siblings. Tina (9) describes how she has earned money:

Sometimes when our little cousin Albin comes to visit us, he's two years old, one time my mum, 'cos she had a really bad headache,

185

she said if you watch him, I'll give you ten kronor ... And if you do a job for them you can get money.

In a study in the United States, Phipps (1996) asked children of various ages how they obtain money to buy the things they want. She found that 97.5 per cent of the nine- and ten-year-olds she interviewed said that they could earn money in some way. Common chores the children listed included baby-sitting and walking the neighbour's dog. In her study there was an age difference; older children were more likely to have expectations of being able to earn money from work. In my data, all the children said that they can work and earn money, regardless of age.

I found that the children believe that they can earn money by doing things that they do not consider to be their ordinary chores. Several of them pointed to the clear boundaries that they perceive between children's jobs and adult jobs. They expect to be paid when they do a task that they perceive as an adult job. As mentioned earlier, most of the children are responsible for cleaning their own rooms:

Daniel: (11):	*But my mum doesn't give me money 'cos I clean my room, that wouldn't be fair.*
HE:	Why not?
Daniel:	*'Cos it's your own room and you're supposed to take care of it yourself.*

In Daniel's view, it is obvious that he would not be not paid to clean his room, because that is his responsibility. None of the children mention cleaning their own rooms as one of the jobs they can do to earn extra pocket money. However, as I described earlier, for many children the allowance is linked to the requirement that they clean and take care of their rooms properly.

Some children, such as Petter, who is given a large allowance, see no need to earn their own money. The opportunity to earn money depends on the parents' financial situation. When I ask Maria if she usually cleans the house to earn money, she answers:

No – 'cos my mum and them don't usually have very much money. My mum goes to school and my daddy works. Sometimes daddy

has to work on the weekends to get enough money to buy food.
(Maria, 10)

The situation is governed here by the parents' ability to pay, which in cases like Maria's can be a significant factor. For a child to be paid for certain kinds of household chores, there must be enough in the family budget. Even if the family can afford to pay the child, there are always tensions, for example, between the child's need to be able to earn and the parents' need for help – and between conflicting educational goals: that the child should learn to be helpful without payment, or that children should learn that one must work in order to obtain money.

Saving

All of the children in the study stated that they save some money, mainly from their allowances. There is no correlation between the amount of the allowance and the children's tendency to save. However, there is a variation in how often children put money aside: some save regularly, others only on certain occasions. The children consider thrift to be a positive character trait and a worthy endeavour.

The researcher Silja Jundin (1988), who surveyed savings patterns in young people, believed that being thrifty is a widespread norm in Swedish society; saving is seen as a virtue. In her research she found that the majority of teenagers stated that they saved money, but that one-third of them had negative attitudes towards saving. This may indicate that while saving is a social norm in the adult world, it is imposed on young people, and although they comply, they do not always do so willingly. Almost half the respondents in Jundin's study had no express goal for the money they saved. This may be designated aimless saving. There are parallels in this research, as some children stated that they save but could not say what they are saving for, or why they save.

Some of the children have an agreement with their parents about saving a certain sum from their allowance. In other cases, the child may decide independently to save in order to accumulate enough money to buy something specific. In these cases, saving is goal-oriented and may also be for a limited period of time.

> *Yes, it was only that thing that I was saving my money for, now it's a lot of other stuff, sweets and stuff.* (Petter, 9)

Several of the children describe the difficulty of living up to the ideal of thrift:

> *Buying sweets, or different things, it feels like my money just disappears like I had a big hole in my pocket or something.* (Robin, 11)

> *Yes, sometimes, but sometimes I can't stop myself from buying something, even though sometimes I really try to.* (Sally, 8)

Even though many of the children say that it is hard to save money, they still perceive it to be necessary. They also see that there can be certain advantages to saving, as Niklas (10) explains:

HE	Is it fun to save money?
Niklas	*Not really, but if you save money then you can buy something a little more important.*

The children are able to manage the disagreeable aspects of saving because it gives them the opportunity to buy something more expensive that they want. Saving is easier when there is a clearly defined goal.

Of the children in the study, Petter is the most enthusiastic about saving and the one who has thought about it the most carefully:

> *I have a lot right now, although it has got less and less. For a while I had almost 2000 kronor there, now I have something like, with the money that I have in the bank that I can take out whenever I want, and so now I have something like 1300 kronor.*

As I described earlier, Petter is highly economically aware, which is certainly connected to his considerable responsibility for his own finances, but he also appears to be interested in his finances. He is the only one of the children to have his own bank account; he reports that he is allowed to make deposits and withdrawals as he chooses. This is in addition to the savings account his parents keep for him.

Several of the children have saved together with their families for some shared project that all members of the family will benefit from or enjoy. On such occasions, there seems to be scope for the children to be involved in decision-making. In some families, this saving takes on a ritualised form, such as the entire family saving together in a piggy bank or a holiday fund. When I asked Maria (10) whether she has yet started saving for an forthcoming trip, she said:

> *Not yet, but we are going to, maybe a week or two weeks before or something, and then we will have to put in five or ten kronor every day, or sometimes a 20 or 100 krona bill and a little bit of everything.*

The children as part of the family economy

The focus of this study is how children perceive their own finances. They sometimes described their finances as a separate component, but also as dependent on the family economy in general. The children have in so doing also directly or indirectly described the family's financial situation. In this context, it is important to note that the descriptions are of the child's perceptions of the family economy. The aim of this study is not to verify whether any individual child's narratives concerning his or her family's finances were true, but rather to describe how the situation is perceived from the child's point of view. If, for example, parents often justify their unwillingness to buy something for a child by saying 'we cannot afford it,' rather than 'I don't want to buy it right now', the child may perceive this to mean that the parent has little money, even if that is not the case.

The children in this sample live in varied economic circumstances: some in detached houses and others in blocks of flats; a few of the parents are unemployed, while others hold highly paid positions. Among this sample there is no correlation between economic circumstances and size of children's allowances, their tendency to save, or their opportunities to have a say in financial matters.

It appears that most of the children play an active part in some family financial decisions. This is particularly clear on occasions when the entire family is to do something together, such as take a family holiday. In those cases, financial priorities may need to be set, and the children are often aware of these.

We can't afford to stay in one of those big hotels, but only the ones that have just one or two stars, so a lot of times we rent a room. (Petter, 9)

The children's activity is also shown in the division of responsibility for various savings goals. There may be discussions in the family about which are the child's and which are the adults' financial obligations:

Mummy and daddy save up for the airline tickets, and they pay for the food, and I pay for things I want myself, or if I buy a present for somebody when we are abroad. (Petter, 9)

Several of the children are also extremely aware of financial priorities in general, such as the most important things that the family needs to buy:

HE: What is most important for the family to buy?
Sally (8): *Food and things like that, so you can live, and then you have to try to save for the rent and then –*
HE: Yes
Sally: *stuff like light bulbs, you know, if a light bulb burns out you have to buy one.*

The involvement of children in the study in these economic activities varies, but is not related to age. Some children feel that they do not have any insight into the situation at all, or believe that they cannot participate in decisions because they are children and know less than adults. However, most believe they have a genuine ability to influence decisions and ascribe importance to their own opinions. This would be consistent with the described characteristics of the project-oriented child-rearing ideal.

There are thus two sides to the children's attitudes towards the family finances. They often feel a sense of freedom, but realise at the same time that their freedom is limited because they are children. Even if they are allowed to sell their possessions, the adults still make the final decision about what they are allowed to sell. The same applies to the children's opportunities to earn money at home, which are based upon their parents having the means and, particularly, the willingness to pay. The children in the study seem to feel a sense of solidarity with their family's financial status and circumstances. This may, of course, result from a wish to present themselves as contented in the context of the interview. However, it may also have to do with children's ability to adapt to their living conditions.

The family emerges in many respects as an economic unit in which the members contribute in various ways. This is consistent with Edin's (1996) description of the postmodern family, in which she says children are allowed to be extremely active in the family's financial situation. If money is tight at the end of the month, everyone has to pitch in and help save. Some children explained that if their parents are short of money, they may postpone giving the children their allowances. The children are also without exception aware of financial priorities. Buying one thing means that one must forego buying something else. This sophisticated reasoning is well developed among the children.

The distinctly moral dimension attached to children and finances, of which the children are aware, is a recurring theme in the children's narratives in response to questions concerning finances in all areas of the study. They demonstrate a strong moral dimension when they describe their personal income. They draw a clear, moral distinction between the tasks that they believe they should be paid for doing, and those jobs that are their responsibility and for which they do not have the right to expect payment. Finally, there is also an apparent moral tone when the children describe saving and the function it serves, as they portray being thrifty as a positive character trait.

With respect to the research field of children and finances, there is relatively copious research on how children think about finances based on stages of development (e.g. Jahoda, 1979; Berti and Bombi, 1981a; Schug and Birkey, 1985). There is also some educational literature on the subject of how children should learn various economic concepts (e.g. Laney, 1988; Schug, 1996). In contrast to developmental research, I found no age correlation in this study indicating that older children have a greater understanding of economic concepts. What emerged instead is that the children who are allowed to participate in the family finances and/or who handle their own finances are more knowledgeable concerning economic issues. The limited size of my sample makes it hard to draw any wide conclusions from this concerning the validity of a stage model of learning. In order to see the impact of children's experiences on their understanding a more through study of the family situation is needed. That was not possible in this limited study.

There is very little current research in which the focus is on children's accounts of their own finances. An obvious conclusion of my study is that children have various beliefs and experiences concerning finances. I believe that this financial knowledge that children possess could be more extensively utilised in schools and that children's daily experiences related to economic issues should form the basis of improved economic education.

Notes

1. The study is part of the research project 'Too little for money' at the Department of Thematic Studies, Linköping University, Sweden, conducted under the direction of Elisabet Näsman. The project is being funded by the Swedish Council for Research in the Humanities and Social Sciences and Linköping University. It will be concluded in 2001. See also Helén Justegård's chapter, which is part of the same project.

2. At the time of writing, the exchange rate was €1= SEK 9.3 .

10

Earning money of your own: paid work among teenagers in Sweden

Helén Justegård
Linköping University, Sweden

Many young people start working while they are still at school. Even though work is part of the lives of so many, our understanding of teenage labour is very limited. Jens Qvortrup (1994b) describes teenage labour as something approaching a public secret, in that everyone knows that it exists, but knows nothing about the conditions in which it takes place or its extent. A Swedish study of young people's lives outside school (Nilsson, 1998) showed that some 68 per cent of the thirteen- to fifteen-year-old respondents had worked outside the home or school; this indicates that it is very common for teenagers in Sweden to have jobs. The ongoing debate in Sweden concerning child/teenage labour is almost exclusively related to the problem of exploitation at an international level. As far as I am aware, there is no debate in the country in which work performed by Swedish children/teenagers is discussed in terms of exploitation, and no discussion about possible negative effects on school attainment.

In many studies of teenage labour, the data is quantitative. Teenagers' relationships to work and money are discussed without their own voices ever being heard in any distinct way. The objective of the research described in this chapter is to allow young people with steady jobs outside the home to speak out and, in their own words, explain how they perceive the reality of their everyday lives, with a particular focus on work and money.[1] The central questions of the study are: Why do teenagers work? How much money do they have at their disposal? What do they spend their money on? How do they feel about saving money? How do their parents feel about them having jobs? How is the close link between work, morals and values found in Swedish society expressed among teenagers? The main part of the chapter addresses these questions; the first section provides information about the Swedish context and the research design.

The Swedish context

Swedish children start school at age seven, and attend compulsory school for nine years. Thereafter, the vast majority elect to attend post-compulsory upper secondary school for three years (Börjesson and Palme, 2000). The secondary school curriculum may be vocational or a preparation for higher education; however, all secondary school graduates have fulfilled the general requirements for admission to Swedish colleges and universities. Primary and secondary education is free.

According to Swedish labour laws, children may be employed for light work from the age of thirteen. However, their tasks may not be of such a nature that they have a negative effect on the child's health, development, or school attendance.

A universal, tax-exempt child benefit is paid monthly in Sweden to the legal guardian of all children up to the quarter in which the child turns sixteen. Thereafter, extended child benefit is paid for those over sixteen who are still attending compulsory school. Young people who are under twenty and are attending post-compulsory secondary school receive a study grant. The study grant is disbursed nine months a year, with no payments in June, July, or August. At the time the study was conducted, the child benefit and the study grant were each SEK 750[2] a month. A child cannot receive both child benefit and study grant at the same time. Swedish school children and teenagers commonly receive pocket money in the form of a weekly or monthly allowance, usually starting in the first grade. The amount is often related to the child's age. Starting at about age fourteen or fifteen, the child's monthly allowance is often equal to the monthly child benefit (i.e. the parents allow the child to have control over spending the child benefit).

Method and sample

The study informants are teenagers who work delivering newspapers for a local newspaper in a small Swedish municipality. The newspaper is published once a week. The publishing company also issues a fortnightly advertising circular. The weekly paper and the circular are both delivered in the afternoon. Throughout most of the paper's nearly 80 years in business, it has been delivered to subscribers by school children. The same is true for the advertising circular. From the newspaper's perspective, it is difficult to get adults to do newspaper delivery because the job only offers about one and a half hours of work per week. The pay rate is SEK 120 per delivery round, which means that those who deliver only the newspaper earn SEK 480 a month. The 21 teenagers who work for the newspaper were invited to participate in the study; seven agreed to be informants.

Each informant was interviewed, and the interviews were recorded and transcribed. Each interview was carefully listened to in its entirety and partially transcribed before the next interview was held. A question guide with a number of overarching questions was used as a point of departure for the interviews. This method provided opportunities to reflect on the content of each interview and add to the question guide as new angles emerged that we found worthy of discussion with other informants. The data material was thereafter sorted and categorized. We used the Grounded Theory approach for our analysis, since the method is predicated on an open and flexible approach, which fits the purpose of this study (see Strauss and Corbin, 1997, 1998).

The informants

The sample consisted of seven teenagers, four girls and three boys aged thirteen to sixteen years. They all worked delivering newspapers, and lived in a small Swedish municipality with a population of about 15,000. The interviews revealed that they had several other circumstances in common. All except one lived in a nuclear family in a detached house. Five attended the same upper-level compulsory school, one attended another upper-level compulsory school and one was in the first year in secondary school. Five of the seven had at least one other job. In terms of age, gender balance and type of home, this sample of seven appeared to be representative of the whole group of 21 teenagers who delivered the newspaper. The teenagers in the sample are referred to as Emma, Filippa, Matilda, Sanna, Erik, Jonas and Karl.

Why work?

The material shows that there is one clear and common basic reason why teenagers work: to earn money. Jonas says that the reason he started working was the desire to *'make money, I didn't have very much'*. Karl's answer is similar, but somewhat more detailed:

> *To earn my own money ... if I didn't have that job, I wouldn't be able to buy as much stuff as I usually do. It's not like I would be asking for some huge amount from home anyway, 500 kronor would be more than enough.*

Karl thinks he would have enough money even if he did not work. Earning money to cover his own expenditure does not seem as important to him as it is to some of the others. Karl uses his wages to *'buy the extras'*. Unlike several of the others, he does not have to buy his own clothes; his mother buys them for him. If he happens to buy a garment once in a while, it is something extra, something that he does not believe he really needs.

The desire to buy something special can also be the impetus that makes young people take the step into working life. That was the case with Matilda. She says: *'I wanted to have a bicycle too. It started with wanting to get the money together for a bike.'* In Matilda's case, her desire for a bicycle led to her taking on so much work that her parents no longer give her money regularly. She does not control the child benefit, nor does she express any wish to do so. She earns SEK 1,500 a month by working. This amount, which must be considered high in the context, is the reason that Matilda does not express any need for additional money from her parents. In addition to working as a newspaper delivery person, she works in a kiosk, which must be seen as her main job, since it requires more of her time and provides the most income. In her view, the money gives her the freedom to make her own decisions; it makes her independent. She says that her parents sometimes think she buys too many clothes, but she dismisses their comment, saying, '*I earned it, so it's up to me to decide how much to spend on what.*'

Matilda is not alone in talking about freedom in relation to her wages. Karl, who believes he would have enough money even if he did not work, explains why he chooses to do so: '*I guess it's mostly the freedom – it's just fun.*' By earning money outside the family circle, the teenagers forge an independence that they call freedom. There is a sense that it is 'me who decides'. The family sometimes discusses purchases and the teenagers get advice from their parents, but they make the final decisions themselves. Regardless of whether their parents also give them money as a monthly allowance or child benefit, wages from a job of one's own create independence. This is a major reason contributing to teenagers' decisions to work.

Five of the teenagers describe work as fun, but at the same time, several of their statements indicate that the fun relates to earning, rather than to the work itself. When Sanna went with her brother to try out delivering newspapers, she thought it was very hard work and was not sure she could handle it on her own. Matilda says that it is not a lot of fun to work in the kiosk at weekends, because the hours are so awkward, and are the downside of the job. When asked if her friends are envious of her job, Matilda says: '*Not when I have those awful hours, but – getting so much money – yeah, sure. Of course I get pretty jealous of them too, because they get money just for the asking, if you know what I mean.*' It is not always fun to work. Jobs that require a great deal of time mean that other things have to be given up, but in Matilda's case that is not enough to make her quit. The money she earns outweighs any of the negative aspects of the job, and makes the effort worthwhile.

Work can also offer other benefits. Two of the girls describe how they get exercise by delivering newspapers. Emma says that she does the job to earn money, but adds, '*and then of course I get a lot of exercise, since it seems like I have to run almost all the time*'. It is unlikely that the exercise that a job may provide would be an overwhelming reason to start working. In this context, it would be more accurate to see exercise as a positive side effect of the job, and a justification for the physical strain that the job entails.

Work during one's teenage years may also be a strategy for succeeding in one's career as an adult. In addition to her job at the newspaper, Emma works as a waitress in a restaurant. Her plans for the future are to work in the hotel and restaurant industry. She believes that experience in the business may advantage her in her future profession. At the same time, the money is a strong motivator for her as well. Emma says that she can earn up to 700 kronor for one evening's work. Erik, who wants to go to college to become a mechanical engineer, also sees his current job in relation to his future career. During school holidays, he works part time for an engineering firm. This has given him experience and insight into industrial work that he believes will be useful to him in the future.

Several informants bring a moral dimension into their explanations of why they work. They compare themselves and their personal situations with those of other teenagers. Few of Emma's friends work. When asked why they don't work, she states bluntly that they are '*lazy*' but does not explain further. Sanna explains sarcastically how teenagers who do not work expect to get money from their parents as a matter of course:

> *Oh yeah, they just ask at home and they get money just like that – ooh, Mama, I'm gonna go shopping, can I have a few bucks – and just like that – oh, sure, honey – and they get the money and that's that.*

Sanna says that she has never asked her parents for extra money; she saves her money so that she does not need to ask. Even before she started working, she saved her monthly allowance. She believes personal responsibility is important. When asked why some teenagers work and others do not, she answers:

For those who – those who – I want to be the kind of mother that my mother is ... but I also thought it was a drag in the beginning, helping out at home, that it was boring. But now I know that it has helped me a lot that ... Now I'll know what to do when I get a place of my own and like that. For those who don't – well, there is this one guy in the class and he doesn't lift a finger at home, doesn't do anything! All he has to do is ask and they give him tons of money and then he still doesn't do anything. He isn't going to have a clue when he has to live on his own.

In this instance, Sanna begins talking immediately about work in the home. Of all the informants, she has been employed for the shortest time, which may be why she immediately associates the question about work with chores at home. Sanna has scheduled chores to do at home, which may make what she does at home have more similarity to paid work than the chores the other teenagers do. This is also the only excerpt where it can be implicitly seen that the money teenagers get from the family may be linked to performance of chores. When the teenagers were asked about such a connection, they all denied that there is one, including Sanna, who claims: '*No-o, no, no, it's just because Mum and Dad want help and like that*'. Possibly parents *do* expect some performance from their teenagers in the form of household chores or other work in the home in exchange for their monthly allowance or child benefit, but that expectation is not clearly expressed.

The other informants also perform household chores to a lesser or greater extent. They all think that this is something to be expected and for which they should not automatically be paid. The scope of this work varies among the teenagers. Filippa says that she takes care of her room and that her parents are satisfied with that. Jonas says that he cleans up after himself when he eats, puts the dishes in the dishwasher, and carries out other minor chores. If he mows the lawn or paints the fence, he expects to get a little extra money from his parents because these tasks are not regular and are not among those that he is normally expected to do.

Erik thinks that what he calls '*will*' or '*determination*' affects the attitudes teenagers have towards working. According to him, not everyone has that quality; he believes that he does, but says he does not really know where it comes from. In his view it may come from his parents, whom he resembles. He believes that parental views on upbringing affect children's attitudes towards work and responsibility.

Matilda thinks along similar lines. She sees personal traits as determining whether teenagers work or not:

> *Well, it probably has a lot to do with – well, how you are at – um, responsibility, you know ... some of them may not think about the fact that they have to earn their own money, they, like just take and take – and you know, their parents give them money.*

Matilda believes that the home environment can affect *'how you are'* in this context, but in her view teenage employment is not linked to family financial status. She is careful to point out that she works even though her family *'doesn't have any money problems'*. She also talks about how some teenagers from affluent homes *'don't even need to think about what money is used for'*, but still choose to work.

One of the other informants, Filippa, is an example. She shows through her actions and her attitude towards work that she also possesses something that could be called 'will', or personal traits that inspire her to work. Filippa is thirteen and has two jobs. In addition to the newspaper round, she also delivers bread. She collects orders in her neighbourhood during the week, then gets up at five o'clock on Saturday mornings to deliver the bread. She sought out the job herself and claims that she does it for the money. But she also points out that she could manage perfectly well without her earnings, and that it is easy to get extra money from her parents. For her, work seems to be a way of spending her leisure hours, and she indirectly compares her work with other pastimes such as athletic activities. She says that many of her friends work, and explains why others do not: *'They have other things to do. Like this friend of mine, she would definitely like to hand out fliers or something, but she has a horse and that takes up a lot of time – so that's probably why.'* The other informants gave a variety of reasons why some teenagers work and others do not. Jonas and Karl both believe that many want to work, but that it can be hard to find a job.

Erik is the only one who makes it clear that his work outside the home is partly an act of solidarity towards the family. He says on several occasions, '*my parents aren't made of money, you know*'. By earning his own money, he relieves his parents of some costs; they do not have to give him as much money as they would if he did not work. In the same way, Emma started working because her monthly allowance was low: '*I didn't get my child benefit before; my mum took care of that*'. By starting to work, she reduced her need for money from her parents. But when she started post-compulsory school, her parents turned over her study grant to her and circumstances changed. Combined with her wages, she believes that she now has a lot of money compared with her friends.

How they got jobs

Some of the teenagers in the study were inspired to work by their friends who had jobs. They found jobs by actively looking, with help from their parents, or via contacts at companies. Many of them got the newspaper delivery job by telephoning the newspaper and putting their names on a waiting list. Those new to the job often start as substitutes before they are given a district of their own. This system may be seen as a trial by the newspaper, allowing the employer to determine whether the teenagers are suited to the task. Erik explains:

> *The guy who was delivering XX wanted to have two weeks off during the summer. So I did the deliveries for those two weeks and it went really well and then when he started again, it turned out that he wasn't delivering all the papers, he was skipping some, and so I got the job instead. That's how I got it.*

Several of the teenagers emphasize the importance of contacts and personal initiative in getting a job. Emma has acquired several short-term jobs through taking classes in the hotel and restaurant programme at school. Erik knows someone on the employer side at both his workplaces. Reiterating the theme of determination as a positive trait in relation to work, he said that if he had not had those contacts, he would have '*applied at other places – it might not have been as easy – but I tried to stay determined, but not everybody is like that*'.

201

All the teenagers believe that their parents approve of them working. From our findings, we can say that they believe that parents fill an important function with respect to teenage employment, both during job hunting and once they have jobs. The extent of parental involvement varies. Some of the parents were actively involved in finding jobs for their children; they identified advertisements, accompanied their children when they applied for jobs, or simply showed approval when told that they had got a job or were thinking about getting one. Filippa says: '*My dad found the ad. ... I had told him that it would be cool if he could find some kind of job for me passing out fliers or whatever and then he checked around a little and like that.*' Sanna simply mentioned at home that she was thinking about applying for a job delivering newspapers. She assumed that her parents would approve, since they approved of her older brother's job.

Erik decided independently that he wanted a job. Both his parents worked when they were at school, which may have influenced Erik's attitudes concerning part-time work. To get a factory job, Erik called a business owner whom he knows through family friends. He describes how his parents supported him:

> *Um, they encouraged me when I started talking about it and saying that maybe I should call Magnus and ask him. I was really nervous about calling and asking for a job. It's really nerve-racking when you start out like that and they really supported me, said, 'Of course you should call', but I thought, what if he gets mad if I just call out of nowhere like that. They said, 'Oh, no he won't', and so they really encouraged me.*

Erik's hesitation was not about the job, but rather how the business owner would treat him. He handled the contact with the business owner himself, but knew that his parents were supporting him in the background.

Sometimes the parents take a more active role, especially in relation to newspaper delivery. They may pick up the papers ready for delivery, and occasionally substitute for their children when they cannot do a round. Siblings do the same, often without the paper's knowledge. This may be seen as the teenagers being responsible for their jobs even when they cannot carry out the work themselves. Another reason may be that this keeps the wages in the family.

None of the informants feel that they are living in difficult financial circumstances. They can all get money from their parents. Several of them are given their entire child benefit or study grant to spend, but they still choose to work. In this light, parental support does not seem to be related to financial factors. In the families where the parents were most actively involved in helping the teenagers find a job, there are also siblings who work. There seems to be a belief in these families that through having a job, teenagers learn to take responsibility both for doing the work and for the money that they earn. Active parental involvement in this context may be seen as a strategy for socialising teenagers into an adult relationship with work and money.

Money and consumption

The teenagers in this study have between 700 and 1,500 kronor at their disposal every month. This is not related to age, but varies depending on the hours they work; those who work most have the most to spend. The amount includes wages from employment and money received from their parents in the form of a monthly allowance and/ or child benefit or study grant. All of the teenagers in the study are given money by their parents except Matilda, who earns 1,500 kronor a month by working.

All of the teenagers believe that, compared to other teenagers, they have a lot of money. On a scale from poor to rich, they put themselves in the middle, or else consider themselves rich. Erik says:

In a way I guess you could say I don't have that much money. But I still feel rich ... I feel rich even if I'm not rich compared to older people. But if I compare myself with my friends, I'm pretty rich. I earn 1,000 kronor a month and I think that's pretty good.

When he uses the word '*earn*' Erik is also counting the child benefit, which his parents recently turned over to him.

There are considerable differences among the teenagers when it comes to how their money should be spent and what the money is supposed to cover. All of them are expected to pay for what they call *'entertainment'* themselves. This includes going to the movies or dance clubs, eating in the school cafeteria and, for the girls, buying make-up. A few report clear limits between what they are expected to pay for themselves and what their parents will help with, while others have more flexible limits. Those, like Eric and Sanna, who have been given charge of their child benefit, have an oral agreement with their parents about what they are supposed to pay for (including their clothes), and they do not consider asking their parents for more money as a matter of course. Sanna says that her parents would probably give her extra money if she asked for it, but she never has because *'I save my money, so I've never had to ask them'*. Eric and his parents agreed, when he was given control of the child benefit, that he would meet all his daily needs (apart from food and household expenditure) from his own income.

Matilda, who earns SEK 1,500 from working, is in a different situation. Her parents do not give her money on a regular basis, but instead help pay for more expensive purchases. We can only speculate about why her parents choose to help pay for those kind of purchases, even though Matilda could probably pay for them on her own. Parenthood entails an obligation to provide support, which includes material responsibility for the child. Matilda's parents may for that reason feel that they should help pay for more expensive purchases, even though there is no real need to do so.

Filippa has about 1,500 kronor a month to spend. Her main reason for working is to get money to support her snowboarding hobby. She says, *'I've been up in the mountains a bunch of times this year, which costs a lot, and snowboards cost a bomb, so my parents help pay for it, but I also pay for it myself.'* Filippa is not required to pay for things she calls 'real needs', by which she means clothing and other items for which her parents pay. Apart from what she spends on snowboarding, she says she uses her money for *'Well, fun stuff like going to the dance club or buying presents for my friends' birthdays, that's the kind of stuff I pay for myself – but not things I really need, you know.'* She puts herself in the middle of the rich–poor scale, because she only counts the 240 kronor a month that her parents give her. There is a difference here between Filippa and Erik; when he compares himself to others, he counts the entire amount he has at his disposal.

Since Erik's parents allow him to spend his child benefit, they contribute a larger amount to his disposable income than do Filippa's parents to hers. And Erik is expected to pay for a much larger proportion of his needs than is Filippa, even though she has about 500 kronor more a month at her disposal. One explanation for this may be that Filippa earns more by working than Erik does, which means that she is in charge of a larger amount over which her parents have no influence. The data shows, then, that parents have a say in how allowances and child benefit, which come from the parents, are spent, but the teenagers themselves decide how to spend the money they earn, with no parental influence. Naturally, the family's financial situation may affect the extent to which parents expect teenagers to take personal responsibility and the extent to which they are able to finance the teenagers' expenses.

Lending, borrowing and consumption

All the study subjects attend schools that have cafeterias or else are close to kiosks or stores. Whether the teenagers take money to school with them or not varies from day to day. Some have money with them much of the time, and others less frequently. Several say that they can sometimes borrow money from their friends and that they lend money in return. According to Jonas, it can sometimes be difficult to get back the money he lends. Sometimes he has to nag his friends about repaying the loan, and it usually takes quite a while.

Emma does not have the same problem getting her money returned. This may be because she is always careful to pay back money she borrows from others quickly. She says, '*I always pay it back as soon as I can because it's – better to have things square.*'

When they borrow money from friends, the loans involve small amounts to buy a snack or sweets. The teenagers also describe more long-term borrowing. Matilda started working because she wanted a new bicycle. When she got a job, her parents lent her the money to buy the bicycle, which she then began paying back. When Jonas was asked what he uses his money for, he answered, '*I bought a new moped for 17,000 kronor, so now I'm making payments on it.*' He borrowed the money from his grandfather and pays him back when he can. Jonas describes how the loan was arranged: '*Well, I asked him, and wrote a contract that if he lent me the money I wouldn't start smoking and using snuff and drinking, but would instead use the money to pay him back.*' Jonas was the one who came up with the terms of the contract with his grandfather. When asked directly, he admits that he had tactical motives behind his contract proposal. He was sure that it would be easier to get his grandfather to lend him the money if he promised not to start smoking, for instance.

Other earning opportunities

Most of the teenagers think it is a good idea for parents to offer money in exchange for not smoking or as a reward for good grades. Money can be an incentive to perform better or to refrain from a harmful practice. Karl thinks that '*you should tempt them by saying that the better your grades the more money you can get from us and things like that*'. Filippa is the only one who expresses doubt about the idea of money promised for good grades:

> *Well, I don't think it's right to get money for your grades. If you are sitting at home and studying and doing your best and ... what if school is hard for some people? It shouldn't have an effect on what you get, on money from your parents, anyway.*

She considers doing your best to be more important than a good end result.

Two of the boys talk about how they make a profit by buying and selling mopeds; one way of getting a newer and more expensive moped is to start by buying one in poor condition, fix it up and sell it for a profit, then buy one in better condition and do the same thing again. Working on mopeds seems to be a common interest among the boys.

Karl has another job in addition to the newspaper delivery job. He says: '*Yeah, there's this guy and I kind of work with him, fixing bikes and stuff.*' Here, Karl combines one of his main hobby interests with work. At first he does not define it as a job, because he does not earn money doing it. But after he thinks about it, he changes his mind and says that it is a job. Rather than being paid wages, he is allowed to take spare parts worth about 20 kronor for every hour of work. Like the other teenagers, Karl believes that money is the main incentive for working. This example shows that it can be difficult to define something as work if money does not change hands.

Saving

All the teenagers want to save and they all try to do so with varying degrees of success. They save for a variety of reasons: to have enough money for more expensive things they have seen and want to buy; to accumulate an emergency fund so they can buy or do something that comes up suddenly; and for longer term needs, such as a driving licence, car or an apartment of their own. The boys are more likely to talk about long-term savings; a driving licence and a car are their main goals. Some of them are aware that in addition to their own savings, their parents are saving money on their behalf. One is not sure that this is so, but believes it is, and one knows that the parents do not save any money.

Emma has a goal of saving money, but does not succeed as well as she would like. She laughs when she says that she does not do very well when it comes to saving: '*I always manage to find something I want to buy, you know how it is.*' Emma does not think it is particularly common for teenagers to save money if they do not have a specific goal. She believes that when they save, it is short term and for a particular goal. You save when you want something a little more expensive than you can afford at the moment. Not all the teenagers in the study share her view. Some of them are much more goal-oriented in their saving and see the saving itself as an incentive to save. Sanna's attitude is diametrically opposed to Emma's. She sees saving as fun, saying: '*I save and save and save and then when I am about to buy something I think – no – I want to save a little more and that's that.*' When asked why she saves, she says:

'Cos it's fun to count the money [laughter] – *no, well, yeah, a little. But it feels a little like, well, I want to buy a stereo, a little bit newer stereo and then I save a little towards that and then maybe I'll want to go to the movies, so I save a little towards that, and then maybe a little extra for that blouse I want and I don't quite have enough, so I have to save a little more, and then maybe, maybe sometime I'll want to go somewhere.*

The others do not express the same enthusiasm for saving as Sanna. Filippa says that she does not save much during the winter, when most of her money gets spent on snowboarding, but that she probably saves a few hundred kronor per month in the bank. She does not seem to care about her savings in the same way as Sanna. It may be that it is more important for Sanna to have control over her assets and a financial buffer against unforeseen expenses, since her parents give her the child benefit and she knows that together with her wages, this is essentially all the money she can count on. She knows that her parents expect her to take responsibility for her own consumption. At the same time, she seems to think it is fun and exciting to take that responsibility herself.

Filippa has a different attitude towards saving: '*I save the bread money at home, but it ends up in the bank sooner or later, 'cos my dad puts it in my bank account for me.*' She does not feel the same need to control her money as Sanna does. Instead, she counts on her parents contributing money when she needs it. Filippa explains: '*Well, it's not like I get everything I point my finger at, but if there is something I really, really want, they give it to me.*' These differences in attitudes to saving were not related to age, but rather appeared to result from parents' views on child rearing and the strategies they have chosen to socialise their children towards taking a more adult view and approach towards money.

Discussion

The study shows clearly that these teenagers work mainly to earn money, thus gaining freedom and independence. Other reasons must be seen as less important. It is unlikely that teenagers would consider these important enough to motivate them to work if they were not paid. By earning money outside the family, they create an arena of action to which their parents are barred admission. The teenagers do not have to negotiate to get money, or report to their parents how it will be spent. Certainly they may discuss spending plans, but the teenagers make the final decisions themselves. Thus, there are different meanings attached to money received from parents, and money that is earned.

The teenagers express the view that having a job demonstrates initiative and drive, qualities charged with positive meaning. They also report moral stances in relation to money and work, for example, distancing themselves from other teenagers who do not work, whom they sometimes characterise as lazy.

They use their money for running expenses, for buying durable goods, and for short- and long-term savings. The way the teenagers handle their finances does not differ significantly from how adults act in relation to their financial circumstances, although teenagers deal with smaller sums of money, and have their parents' money for fixed expenses such as housing and food, and as security in case they spend beyond their means or make errors. It may seem easy to criticise these teenagers for putting so much emphasis on money and consumption. But it is important to remember that they live in a society that is strongly characterised by consumption and materialism. They are also part of a school system in which they have few opportunities to influence their daily lives until they are almost twenty years old. Consumption is thus one of the few areas in which teenagers have the opportunity to act freely and independently.

From a parental perspective, teenage labour may be seen as a way to socialise young people into a relationship with money that is representative of the society in which they live. According to the teenagers in the study, their parents without exception approve of them working. In most cases, the parents actively supported and helped the teenagers find jobs. This indicates that work is valued highly by parents and that they approve of their children spending some of their non-school hours working.

Allowing the teenagers to comment on the questions provides an understanding of contemporary young people's relationships to work, consumption and saving. This creates opportunities to gain insight into their daily lives, of which working is a part, and the way in which they handle their personal finances. Listening to children's and teenagers' own thoughts is an important basis for learning. An issue that the schools must consider is the extent to which they could make use of the opportunities for learning about economics, ethics and morals that are offered by teenagers' experiences of employment and financial management.

Notes

1. The study is part of the research project 'Too little for money', at the Department of Thematic Studies, Linköping University, Sweden, under the direction of Elisabet Näsman. The project is being funded by the Swedish Council for Research in the Humanities and Social Sciences and Linköping University. It will be completed in 2001.

2. At the time of writing, the exchange rate was €1= SEK 9.3 .

Notes on contributors

Anna Maria Ajello is full professor of Educational Psychology in the University of Rome 'La Sapienza'. She researches in educational psychology in three main areas: implementation of social science curricula; analysis of cognitive problems in the acquisition of knowledge in schools; and implementation of curricula for adults in organisational contexts.recent publications include *Le abilità di studio* (ed.), Nucleo monotematico di Studi di Psicologia dell'Educazione, N.1 (1998); La motivazione ad apprendere: aspetti teorici, implicazioni educative, in C. Pontecorvo (ed.) *Psicologia dell'educazione*, Bologna: Il Mulino (1999); and *Orientare dentro e fuori la scuola* (with S. Meghnagi and C. Mastracci), La Nuova Italia (2000).

Mihaly Berkics is an assistant researcher at the Institute for Psychology of the Hungarian Academy of Sciences. He also is a PhD student in psychology at Eötvös Loránd University, Budapest. Areas of research include social psychology of competition, cognitive psychology and pragmatics.

Anna Silvia Bombi is Professor of Developmental Psychology at the University of Rome 'La Sapienza', where she also teaches techniques for interviewing children. She was one of the first scholars to investigate the development of children's ideas about economics, and with A. E. Berti she published a seminal book in the field (*The Child's Construction of Economics*, Cambridge University Press, 1988). With other colleagues at Rome University she has conducted field studies about the teaching of economics in elementary schools. She has studied children's representations of friendship using their drawings as a source of data (see A. S. Bombi and G. Pinto *Los colores de la amistad. Estudios sobre las representaciones pictoricas de la amistad entre los ninos*, Madrid: Visor, 1998).

Helene Elvstrand is a research assistant at Linköping University. Her main research interests are children, childhood and children's rights. She has conducted a study of democracy at a daycare centre and now works on a project about participation and democracy among teenagers in compulsory school.

Márta Fülöp is a senior research fellow in the Institute for Psychology of the Hungarian Academy of Sciences, Budapest, Hungary and a Széchenyi Professor of Social Psychology in the Department of Psychology of the University of Szeged, Hungary. Her main research interest is the psychology of competition with a special attention to adolescents and young adults and cross-cultural aspects. She has carried out research on competition in Japan, the USA, Canada, Costa Rica and Great Britain. She is a member of the CiCe Steering Group and chairs the Network's Data Group.

Adrian Furnham is Professor of Psychology at University College London where he has taught for twenty years. Previously a lecturer at Pembroke College Oxford, he is also visiting Professor at Henley Management College. He has three doctorates (DPhil, DSc, DLitt) and three masters degrees (MA, MSc, MScEcon). He is author/editor of 35 books and over 400 peer reviewed papers. He has many interests in applied psychology particularly culture shock, economic socialisation and job satisfaction. He has written books on money, managerial incompetence and personality theory. Among other papers he is currently working on is one on young people's understanding of taxation.

Merryn Hutchings is Reader in Education at the University of North London. Her PhD thesis, Children's Constructions of Work, was winner of the British Educational Research Association's Dissertation Prize for 1997. Her research interests continue to focus around careers and inequalities, and include social class and widening participation in higher education, and teacher supply and retention.

Helén Justegård is a research assistant at Linköping University. Her main research interests are children, childhood and children in politics. She now works on a project about participation and democracy at secondary school, focusing on teenagers with special needs.

Elisabet Näsman is Professor of Social and Cultural Analysis at Linköping University. Her main research interests are children, childhood, families and the generational order. In relation to children's perspectives, she has studied work-life conditions, unemployment, everyday life economic understanding and standards of living. She also leads a project on participation and democracy in school.

Christine Roland-Lévy has a PhD in psychology (obtained in 1980 at the Sorbonne). She became Senior Lecturer in Social Psychology in 1990 at the University of Paris 5, where she still works. She is an active member of national, European and international associations, and she was president of the International Association for Research in Economic Psychology. A former head of a department of psychology with 2,700 students, she is head of a research group in economic psychology (GRASP). Her current research interest focuses on the study of economic socialisation as well as on social representations of economic concepts, and especially how they change. She recently co-edited two books in this field, *Psychologie Economique: Théories et Applications*, Paris: France (1998), and *Everyday Representations of the Economy*, Vienna: Austria (2001).

Anne-Marie Van den dries (Lic. Business and Consular Sciences and Aggr. HSE) teaches Economics and Social Law in the Business School KATHO-HANTAL, Katholieke Hogeschool Zuid-West-Vlaanderen. Since 1987 she has been involved in the European Exchange Programmes. She is currently head of the international office of KATHO and member of the steering group for international cooperation from the Council of Flemish Hogescholen, VLHORA. Special interests include curriculum development for incoming students on entrepreneurship, constitutional and social law, sociology and politics. She publishes regularly on various aspects of internationalisation in Belgian and international education journals.

Christina von Gerber is a researcher and psychologist at Linköping university. Her main research interests are in children and families. She has studied unemployment and everyday life economy from a children's perspective using a qualitative approach. She also works as a consultant, specialising in stress, coping with crises and supervision.

Bibliography

Abramovitch, R., Freedman J. L. and Pliner, P. (1991) Children and money: Getting an allowance, credit versus cash, and knowledge of pricing, *Journal of Economic Psychology*, 12, pp. 27–45.

Ahier, J. (1988) *Industry, Children and the Nation*, Lewes: Falmer.

Ahier, J. (1992) Economics for children in the United States and Britain, in M. Hutchings and W. Wade (eds) *Developing Economic and Industrial Understanding in the Primary School*, London: PNL Press.

Ajello, A. M. (1991) L'insegnamento dell'economia: problemi e prospettive, in A. S. Bombi (ed.) *Economia e processi di conoscenza*, Torino: Loescher.

Ajello, A. M., Bombi, A.A., Pontecorvo, C. and Zucchermaghro, C. (1986a) Insegnare l'economia nella scuola elementare: cosa e come?, *Orientamenti Pedagogici*, 30, 1, pp. 78–87.

Ajello, A. M., Bombi, A. S., Pontecorvo, C. and Zucchermaglio, C. (1986b) Understanding agriculture as an economic activity: The role of figurative information, *European Journal of Psychology of Education*, 1, pp. 67–80.

Ajello, A. M., Bombi, A. S., Pontecorvo, C. and Zucchermaglio, C. (1987) Teaching economics in the primary school: The concepts of work and profit, *International Journal of Behavioural Development*, 10, pp. 51–69.

Ajello, A. M., Bombi, A .S., Pontecorvo, C. and Zucchermaglio, C. (1988) Prezzi alti, prezzi bassi, dove, quando e perché? *Età evolutiva*, 29, pp. 62–74.

Andorka, R., Healey, B. and Krause, P. (1994) A Gazdasági és a politikai követelmények szerepe a rendszerváltozásban: Magyarország és Kelet-Németország 1990–1994, *Szociológiai Szemle*, 4, pp. 61–82.

Anthony, P. (1977) *The Ideology of Work*, London: Tavistock.

Apple, M. with King N. (1990) Economics and control in everyday school life, in M. Apple, *Ideology and Curriculum* (2nd edition: first published 1979), New York: Routledge and Kegan Paul.

Archbishop of Canterbury's Commission on Urban Priority Areas (1985) *Faith in the City: A call for action by church and nation*, London: Church House Publishing.

Argyle, M. (1972) *The Social Psychology of Work*, Harmondsworth: Penguin.

Atherton, M., Davis, M. and Parr, S. (1992) Industry education and economic and industrial understanding: A hard hat approach? in M. Hutchings and W. Wade (eds) *Developing Economic and Industrial Understanding in the Primary School*, London: PNL Press.

Atkinson, J. W. (1957) Motivational determinants of risk–taking behavior, *Psychological Review*, 64, pp. 359–372.

Bakacsi, Gy. (1998) Szervezeti kultúra és léeadership nemzetközi összehasonlításban, *50 éves a Budapesti Közgazdaságtudományi Egyetem Jubileumi tudományos ülésészak*, Október 1–3, III, pp. 2163–2172.

Bakacsi, Gy. and Takács, S. (1998) Honnan–hová? A nemzeti és szervezeti kultúra változásai a kilencvenes évek közepének Magyarországán, *Vezetéstudomány*, 12, pp. 15–22.

215

Bamford, S. (2000) Entrepreneurship education: Should it be taught? can it be taught? in A. Ross (ed.) *Developing Identities in Europe: Citizenship education and higher education*, London: CiCe.

Barneombudet (1992) *Facts about Children in Norway*, Oslo: Barneombudet.

Bas, J. (1996) *Parent Power: Raising children in a commercial world*, London: Advertising Association.

Bas, J. (1998) *Parent Power 2: A practical guide to children, shopping, and advertisements*, London: Advertising Association.

Benenson, J. F. and Dweck, C. S. (1986) The development of trait explanations and self-evaluation in the academic and social domain, *Child Development*, 57, pp. 1179–1187.

Benfield, E. (1988) Exploring 'working community', in D. Smith (ed.) *Industry in the Primary School Curriculum: Principles and practice*, Lewes: Falmer.

Berk, S. F. (1985) *The Gender Factory*, New York: Plenum Press.

Bernstein, B. (1970) Social class, language and socialisation, in P. P. Giglioli (ed.) *Language and Social Context* (1972), Harmondsworth: Penguin.

Berti, A. E. (1993) Fifth-graders' ideas on bank functions and interest before and after a lesson on banking, *European Journal of Psychology of Education*, VIII, 2, pp. 183–193.

Berti, A. E. (1999) Knowledge restructuring in an economic subdomain: banking, in W. Schnotz, S. Vosniadou and M. Carretero (eds) *New Perspectives on Conceptual Change*, Oxford: Elsevier Science Publishers.

Berti, A. E. and Benesso, C. (1998) The concept of the nation–state in Italian elementary school children: Spontaneous concepts and effects of teaching, *Genetic, Social and General Psychology Monographs*, 124, pp. 185–209.

Berti, A. E. and Bombi, A. S. (1979) Where does money come from? *Archivio di Psicologia*, 40, pp. 53–77.

Berti, A. E. and Bombi, A. S. (1981a) The development of the concept of money and its value: A longitudinal study, *Child Development*, 52, pp. 1179–1182.

Berti, A. E. and Bombi, A. S. (1981b) *Il Mondo Economico nel Bambino*, Firenze: La Nuova Italia.

Berti, A. E. and Bombi, A. S. (1988) *The Child's Construction of Economics*, Cambridge: Cambridge University Press.

Berti, A. E., Bombi, A. S. and de Beni, R. (1986) Acquiring economic notions: profit, *International Journal of Behavioural Development*, 9, pp. 15–29.

Berti, A. E., Bombi, A. S. and Lis, A. (1982) The child's conceptions about means of production and their owners, *European Journal of Social Psychology*, 12, pp. 221–239.

Berti, A. E. and Ciccarelli, R. (1996) Gli effetti a breve e a lungo termine di un curricolo di economia per la quarta elementare, *Scuola e Città*, 47, 3, pp. 121–129.

Berti, A. E. and Monaci, M. G. (1998) Third graders' acquisition of knowledge of banking: Restructuring or accretion? *British Journal of Educational Psychology*, 68, pp. 357–371.

Berti, A. E. and Ugolini, E. (1998) Developing knowledge of the judicial system: A domain-specific approach, *Journal of Genetic Psychology*, 159, pp. 221–236.

Blanchet, T. (1996) *Lost Innocence, Stolen Childhoods*, Dhaka: University Press.

Blyth, W. A. L. (1984) *Development, Experience and Curriculum in Primary Education*, London: Croom Helm.

Blyth, A. (1990a) *Making the Grade for Primary Humanities*, Buckingham: Open University Press.

Blyth, A. (1990b) Some implications of assessment in primary industry education, in A. Ross (ed.) *Economic and Industrial Awareness in the Primary School*, London: PNL Press.

Bodnar, J. (1997) *Dr. Tightwad's Money–Smart Kids*, Washington: Kiplinger.

Bombi, A. S. (1996a) The child conception's of ownership: The case of public monuments, XXVI Congress of the J. Piaget Society 'The growing mind – La pensée en evolution', Genève (Suisse), 14–18 September.

Bombi, A. S. (1996b) Social factors of economic socialization, in P. Lunt and A. Furnham (eds) *Economic Socialization: The economic beliefs and behaviours of young people*, Cheltenham: Edward Elgar.

Bombi, A. S., Cacciamani, S. and Pieramico, A. (1990) Economic conceptions and moral judgments in children 6 to 11 years old, Symposium 'Economic socialization: Cross–cultural and developmental perspectives', XXII International Congress of Applied Psychology, Kyoto, July 1990.

Bombi, A. S. and Cannoni, E. (1995) Ricchi e poveri: Conflitto, aiuto, o mondi separati? Rappresentazioni pittoriche del rapporto tra classi sociali in bambini dai 6 agli 11 anni, *Rassegna di Psicologia*, 2, 11, pp. 79–95.

Bombi, A. S. and Pinto, G. (1993) *I colori dell'amicizia: Studi sulle rappresentazioni pittoriche dell'amicizia tra bambini*, Bologna: Il Mulino. (Spanish translation: 1998, *Los colores de la amistad. Estudios sobre las representaciones pictoricas de la amistad entre los ninos*. Madrid: Visor).

Börjesson, M. and Palme, J. (2000) Skillnader, profilering och elevers utbildningsstrategier i gymnasieskolan under 1990–talet, in *Välfärd och skola* (Swedish Government Report), SOU 2000:39, Commission on A Balance Sheet for the Welfare of the 1990s, Stockholm.

Bowes J. M. and Goodnow, J. J. (1996) Work for home, school or labour force: The nature and sources of changes in understanding, *Psychological Bulletin*, 119, 2, pp. 300–321.

Bowles, S. and Gintis, H. (1976) *Schooling in Capitalist America*, London: Routledge and Kegan Paul.

Burris, V. (1976) The Child's Conception of Economic Relations: A genetic approach to the sociology of knowledge, unpublished doctoral thesis, Princeton University, Princeton NJ.

Burris, V. (1981) The child's conception of economic relations: A study of cognitive socialisation, paper presented at the annual meeting of the American Sociological Association, Toronto, and described in S. E. G. Lea., R. M. Tarpy and P. Webley (1987) *The Individual in the Economy*, Cambridge: Cambridge University Press.

Burris, V. (1983) Stages in the development of economic concepts, *Human Relations*, 36, pp. 791–812.

Butorac, A. (1988) Children's Work Code, unpublished PhD thesis, University of Western Australia, Perth, Western Australia.

Butorac, A. (1989) Children's work code: A Western Australian study, *Early Child Development and Care*, 52, pp. 171–84.

CACE (Central Advisory Council for Education) (1967) *Children and their Primary Schools* (the Plowden Report), London: HMSO.

Callaghan, J. (1976) Speech made at Ruskin College, Oxford, *The Times Educational Supplement*, 3203, 22 October 1976, pp. 1 and 7.

Cannoni, E. (1993) La rappresentazione di somiglianze e differenze nei disegni infantili di figure umane, *Rassegna di Psicologia*, X(2), pp. 79–97.

Carey, S. (1985) *Conceptual Change in Childhood*, Cambridge, MA: MIT Press.

Carey, S. (1991) Knowledge acquisition or conceptual change? in S. Carey and R. Gelman (eds) *The Epigenesis of Mind: Essays on biology and cognition*, Hillsdale NJ: Erlbaum.

Carraher, T., Carraher, D. and Schliemann, D. (1985) Mathematics in the streets and in schools, *British Journal of Developmental Psychology*, 3, pp. 21–9.

Chell, E., Haworth, J. M. and Brearley, S. A. (1991) *The Entrepreneurial Personality: Concepts, cases and categories*, London: Routledge.

Cohen, L. (1981) Political literacy and the primary school: A Dutch experiment, *Teaching Politics*, 10, 3, pp. 259–267.

Cole, M. (ed.) (1988) *Bowles and Gintis Revisited: Correspondence and contradiction in educational theory*, Lewes: Falmer.

Coleman, J. (1968) The concept of equality of educational opportunity, *Harvard Educational Review*, 38, 1, pp. 7–22.

Connell, R. W. (1977) *Ruling Class, Ruling Culture*, Melbourne: Cambridge University Press.

Consultative Committee of the Board of Education (1931) *Report on the Primary School* (the Hadow Report), London: HMSO.

Costello, P. (1992) Down to business: Economic understanding and critical thinking in the primary school, in M. Hutchings and W. Wade (eds) *Developing Economic and Industrial Understanding in the Primary School*, London: PNL Press.

Cram, F. and Ng, S. H. (1989) Children's endorsements of ownership attributes, *Journal of Economic Psychology*, 10, pp. 63–75.

Cram, F. and Ng, S. H. (1994) Children's understanding of public ownership, *European Journal of Social Psychology*, 24, pp. 469–480.

Crawford, K. (1992) Beyond the numbers: Exploring primary children's economic and industrial socialisation, in M. Hutchings and W. Wade (eds) *Developing Economic and Industrial Understanding in the Primary School*, London, PNL Press.

Crites, S. (1986) Storytime: Recollecting the past and projecting the future, in T. R. Sarbin (ed.) *Narrative Psychology: The storied nature of human conduct*, New York: Praeger.

Cromie, S. (2000) Assessing entrepreneurial inclinations: Some approaches and empirical evidence, *European Journal of Work and Organizational Psychology*, 9, 1, pp. 7–30.

Crook, C. (1998) Technology, media and social development, in A. Campbell and S. Muncer (eds) *The Social Child*, Hove: Psychological Press.

Cullingford, C. (1991) *The Inner World of the School*, London: Cassell.

Cummings, S. and Taebel, D. (1978) The economic socialization of children: A neo–Marxist analysis, *Social Problems*, 26, pp. 198–210.

Dahlberg, G. (1993) Modern barnuppfostran och modernt familjeliv: en komplex och sofistikerad förhandlingsprocess, in A. Agnell, B. Arvé-Parès and U. Björnberg (eds) *Modernt familjeliv och familjeseparationer en antologi från ett forskningsseminarium,* Stockholm: Allmänna förlaget.Komm. för FN:s familjeår, Socialdepartmentet.

Dalgard, B. (1993) *Comparing student perceptions of economic competition across cultures: Hong Kong, Japan and the United States*, paper presented at the Midwest Economic Association Meetings, Indianapolis, April 1–3.

Danziger, K. (1958) Children's earliest conceptions of economic relationships, *Journal of Social Psychology* (Australia), 47, pp. 231–240.

Davis, K. and Taylor, T. (1979) *Kids and Cash: Solving a parent's dilemma*, La Jolla: Oak Tree Publications.

DeFleur, M. L. and DeFleur, L. B. (1967) The relative contribution of television as a learning source for children's occupational knowledge, *American Sociological Review,* 32, pp. 777–789.

Delval, J. and Denegri, M. (1999) *La formación de las ideas sobre el origen y fabricación* manuscript quoted with permission of the authors.

DES (1984) Initial Teacher Training: Approval of courses (Circular 3/84), London: Department of Education and Science.

Despierre, J. and Sorel, N. (1979) Approche de la représentation du chômage chez les jeunes, *L'Orientation Scolaire et Professionnelle*, 8, pp. 347–364.

Dickinson, J. and Emler, N. (1996). Developing ideas about distribution of wealth, in P. Lunt and A. Furnham (eds) *Economic Socialization: The economic beliefs and behaviours of young people*, Cheltenham: Edward Elgar.

Dismorr, B. (1902) Our children to be paid for domestic services? *Studies in Education*, 2, pp. 62–70.

Dittmar, H. (1996) Adolescents' economic beliefs and social class, in P. Lunt and A. Furnham (eds) Economic Socialization: *The economic beliefs and behaviours of young people* Cheltenham: Edward Elgar.

Donaldson, M. (1978) *Children's Minds*, London: Fontana.

du Bois–Reymond, M., Buchner, P., Kruger, H–H. (1993) Modern family as everyday negotiations: Continuities and discontinuities in parent–child relationships, *Childhood*, 1, pp. 87–89.

Dustmann, C., Micklewright, J., Rajah, N. and Smith, J. (1996) Earning and learning: Educational policy and the growth of part–time work by full–time pupils, *Fiscal Studies, 17*, 1, pp. 79–103.

Ealy, C. and Lesh, K. (1999) *Our Money Ourselves,* New York: Anacom.

Echikson, W. (1992) Bloc buster, in L. Legsters (ed.) *Eastern Europe: Transformation and revolution,* Lexington: D. C. Health and Co.

Edin, L. (1996) Köpa, leka, lära, in H. Brembeck (ed.) *Postmodern barndom,* Göteborg: Etnologiska föreningen i Västsverige.

Ehn, B. (1983) *Ska vi leka tiger?* Stockholm: Liber.

Eisenberg–Berg, N., Haake, R. and Bartlett, K. (1981) The effects of possession and ownership on the sharing and proprietary behaviors of preschool children, *Merrill–Palmer Quarterly* 27, 1, pp. 61–68.

Elder, G. (1974) *Children of the Great Depression*, Chicago: Chicago University Press.

Emler N.(1986) Perception of occupation–related income differences in middle childhood: A cross–national comparison of class differences, Symposium 'Economic Socialization in Developmental Context', 2nd European Congress of ISSBD, Roma.

Emler, N. (1992) Childhood origins of beliefs about institutional authority, *New Directions for Child Development, 56*, pp. 65–77.

Emler, N. (1998) Socio–moral understanding, in A. Campbell and S. Muncer (eds) *The Social Child*, Hove: Psychological Press.

Emler, N. and Dickinson, J. (1985) Children's representation of economic inequalities: The effect of social class, *British Journal of Developmental Psychology*, 3, 2, pp. 191–198.

Engestrom, Y. (1991) Non scholae sed vitae discimus: towards overcoming the encapsulation of school learning, *Learning and Instruction, 1*, 3, pp. 243–259.

Enright, R. D., Bjerstedt, A., Enright, W. F., Levy, V. M., Jr., Lapsley, D. K., Buss, R. R., Harwell, M. and Zindler, M. (1984) Distributive justice development: Cross–cultural, contextual, and longitudinal evaluations, *Child Development*, 55, pp. 1737–1751.

Estes, P. and Barocas, I. (1994) *Kids, Money and Values*: Creative ways to teach your kids *about money,* Cincinnati: Betterway Books.

Feather, N.T. (1991) Variables relating to the allocation of pocket money to children: Parental reasons and values, *British Journal of Psychology*, 30, pp. 221–234.

Feldman, S. and Ruble, D. (1981) The development of person perception: Cognitive and social factors, in S. S. Brehm, S. M. Kassin and F. X. Gibbons (eds) *Developmental Social Psychology: Theory and research*, New York: Oxford University Press.

Fitzpatrick, S. (1988) The 'we make' projects, in D. Smith (ed.) *Industry in the Primary School Curriculum: Principles and practice*, Lewes: Falmer.

Ford, K. (1992) Cross–curricular themes in the whole curriculum: The contribution of economic and industrial understanding, in M. Hutchings and W. Wade (eds) *Developing Economic and Industrial Understanding in the Primary School*, London: PNL Press.

Forman, N. (1987) *Mind over Money: Curing your financial headaches with money sanity*, Toronto: Doubleday.

Fox, C. (1993) *At the Very Edge of the Forest: The influence of literature on storytelling by children*, London: Cassell.

Fox, K (1978) What children bring to school: The beginnings of economic education, *Social Education*, 10, pp. 478–481.

Francis, B. (forthcoming 2002) Is the future really female? The impact and implications of gender for 14–16 year olds' career choices, *Journal of Education and Work*, 15,1.

Fülöp, M. (1999) Students' perception of the role of competition in their respective countries: Hungary, Japan and the USA, in A. Ross (ed.) *Young Citizens in Europe*, London: CiCe.

Furby, L. (1978) Possessions: Toward a theory of their meaning and function throughout the life cycle, *Life Span Development and Behaviour*, 1, pp. 298–336.

Furnham, A. (1982) The perception of poverty among adolescents, *Journal of Adolescence*, 5, pp. 135–147.

Furnham, A. (1984) Getting a job: School–leavers' perceptions of employment prospects, *British Journal of Educational Psychology*, 54, pp. 293–305.

Furnham, A. (1990) *The Protestant Work Ethic: The psychology of work–related beliefs and behaviours*, London: Routledge.

Furnham, A. (1993) *Reading for the Counter. The New Child Consumers: Regulation or Education*, London: Social Affairs Unit.

Furnham, A. (1996) Attitudinal correlates and demographic predictors of monetary beliefs and behaviours, *Journal of Organisational Psychology*, 17, pp. 375–396.

Furnham, A. (1997) The half–full or half–empty glass: The views of the economic optimist vs. pessimist, *Human Relations*, 50, 2, pp. 197–209.

Furnham, A. (1999a) Economic socialisation: A study of adult's perceptions and uses of allowances (pocket money) to educate children, *British Journal of Developmental Psychology*, 17, pp. 585–604.

Furnham, A. (1999b) The saving and spending habits of young people, *Journal of Economic Psychology*, 20, pp. 677–697.

Furnham, A. (2001) Parental attitudes to pocket money/allowances for children, *Journal of Economic Psychology*, 22, pp. 397–422.

Furnham, A. and Argyle, M. (1998) *The Psychology of Money*, London: Routledge.

Furnham, A. and Cleare, A. (1988) School children's conceptions of economics: prices, wages, investments and strikes, *Journal of Economic Psychology* 9, pp. 467–479.

Furnham, A. and Jones, S. (1987) Children's view regarding possessions and their theft, *Journal of Moral Education*, 16, 1, pp. 18–30.

Furnham, A. and Kirkcaldy, B. (2000) Economic Socialisation: German parents' perception and implementation of allowances to educate children, *European Psychologist,* 5, pp. 202–215.

Furnham, A., Kirkcaldy, B. and Lynn, R. (1994) National attitude to competitiveness, money, and work among young people: First, second, and third world differences, *Human Relations,* 47, 1, pp. 119–132.

Furnham, A. and Thomas, P. (1984a) Pocket Money: A study of economic education, *British Journal of Developmental Psychology,* 2, pp. 205–212.

Furnham, A. and Thomas, P. (1984b) Adult perceptions of the economic socialisation of children, *Journal of Adolescence,* 7, pp. 217–231.

Furth, H. G. (1978) Young children's understanding of society, in H. McGurk (ed.) *Issues in Childhood Social Development,* London: Methuen.

Furth, H. G. (1980) *The World of Grown–Ups,* New York: Elsevier.

Gibb, A. A. (1987) Enterprise culture: Its meaning and implications for education and training, *Journal of European Industrial Training,* 11, pp. 1–38

Ginzberg, E. (1972) Towards a theory of occupational choice: A restatement, *Vocational Guidance Quarterly,* 20, pp. 169–176.

Giron, C. (2001) In search of social representations of unemployment, in C. Roland–Lévy, E. Kirchler, E. Penz and C. Gray (eds) *Everyday Representations of the Economy,* Vienna: WUV.

Glaser, B. G. and Strauss, A. L. (1967) *The Discovery of Grounded Theory: Strategies for qualitative research* Chicago: University of Chicago Press.

Godfrey, N. (1994) *Money Doesn't Grow on Trees,* New York: Fireside.

Godfrey, N. (1996) *A Penny Saved: Teaching your children the values and life skills they will need to live in the real world,* New York: Simon and Schuster.

Goldstein, B. and Oldham, J. (1979) *Children and Work: A study of socialization,* New Brunswick NJ: Transaction Books.

Goldstrom J. D. (1972) *Education: Elementary education 1780–1900,* Newton Abbott: David and Charles.

Goodnow, J. J. (1988). Children's household work: Its nature and functions, *Psychological Bulletin,* 103, pp. 5–26.

Goodnow, J. J. (1996) From household practices to parents ideas about work and interpersonal relationships, in S. Harkness and G. Super (eds) *Parents Cultural Belief Systems,* London: Guilford Press.

Goodnow, J. J. and Burns, A. (1985) *Home and School: Child's eye view,* Sydney, Australia: Allen and Unwin.

Goodnow, J. J. and Delaney, S. (1989) Children's household work: Differentiating types of work and styles of assignment, *Journal of Applied Developmental Psychology,* 10, pp. 209–226.

Goodnow, J. J. and Warton, P. (1991) The social bases of social cognition: Interactions about work and their implications, *Merrill–Palmer Quarterly,* 37, pp. 27–58.

Goodnow, J.J. and Warton, P. (1992) Contests and cognitions: Taking a pluralist view, in P. Light and G. Butterworth (eds) *Context and Cognition: Ways of learning and knowing,* Hemel Hempstead: Harvester Wheatsheaf.

Goswami, U. (1991) Analogical reasoning: what develops? A review of research and theory, *Child Development,* 62, pp. 1110–1123.

Gottfredson, L. (1981) Circumspection and compromise: A developmental theory of occupational aspirations, *Journal of Counselling Psychology,* 28, pp. 545–579.

Gruenberg, S. and Gruenberg, B. (1993) *Parents, Children and Money*, New York: Viking Press.

Grusec, J. E., Goodnow, J. J. and Cohen, L. (1996) Household work and the development of concern for others, *Developmental Psychology*, 32, 6, pp. 999–1007.

Gumpel, W. (1993) The mentality problem in the transition process from centrally planned economy to market economy, in R. Schonfeld (ed.) *Transforming Economic Systems in East Central Europe*, Munich: Sudosteuropa–Gesellschaft.

Gunter, B. and Furnham, A. (1998) *Children as Consumers*, London: Routledge.

Habermas, J. (1989) *The structural transformation of the public sphere: An inquiry into a category of bourgeois society* (trans. T. Burger with F. Lawrence), Cambridge MA.: Cambridge University Press.

Halsey, A. H. (ed.) (1972) *Educational Priority*, London: HMSO.

Hámori, B. (1998) *Érzelemgazdaságtan*, Budapest: Kossuth Kiadó.

Hanson, K. (1988) Prospects for the good life: Education and perceptive imagination, in K. Egan and D. Nadamer (eds) *Imagination and Education*, Milton Keynes: Open University Press.

Harbaugh, W.T. and Krause, K. (1997) *Contributions to Public Goods by Children: An experimental study*, available via the Internet from harbaugh@oregon.uoregon.edu or kkrause@unm.edu

Harris, D. B. (1963) *Children's Drawings as Measures of Intellectual Maturity*, New York: Harcourt Brace.

Hartup, W. W. (1998) The company they keep: Friendships and their developmental significance, in A. Campbell and S. Muncer (eds) *The Social Child*, Hove: Psychological Press.

Hatano, G. and Inagaki, K. (1992) Desituating cognition through the construction of conceptual knowledge, in P. Light and G. Butterworth (eds) *Context and Cognition: Ways of learning and knowing*, Hemel Hempstead: Harvester Wheatsheaf.

Hobbs, S. and McKechnie, J. (1997) *Child Employment in Britain: A social and psychological analysis*, Edinburgh: The Stationery Office.

Hobbs, S. and McKechnie, J. (1998) Children and work in the UK: the evidence, in B. Pettit (ed.) *Children and Work in the UK: Refocusing the debate*, London: Save the Children Fund and CPAG.

Hofmeister Tóth, Á. and Bauer, A. (1996) A magyar marketingvezetk helye a nemzetközi kulturális térképen, *Vezetéstudomány*, 6, pp. 37–44.

Hofstede, G. (1995) *Culture's Consequences: International differences in work–related values*, Beverly Hills, CA: Sage.

Hutchings, M. (1995) Children's ideas about payment for work, *Economic Awareness*, 7, 2, pp. 28–34.

Hutchings, M. (1996) What will you do when you grow up? The social construction of children's occupational preferences, *Children's Social and Economics Education*, 1, 1, pp. 15–30.

Hutchings, M. (1997) *Children's Constructions of Work*, unpublished PhD thesis, University of North London.

Hutchings, M. (1999) Children's constructions of work in manufacturing industry: The contribution of experiences at school, in A. Ross (ed.) *Young Citizens in Europe*, London: CiCe.

Jackson, R. (1972) The development of political concepts in young children, *Educational Research*, 14, pp. 51–55.

Jahoda, G. (1979) The construction of economic reality by some Glaswegian children, *European Journal of Social Psychology*, 9, pp. 115–127.

Jahoda, G. (1981) The development of thinking about economic institutions: The bank, *Cahiers de Psychologie Cognitive*, 1, pp. 55–73.

Jávorszky, I. (1999) *Business Plan 2000*, Budapest: Junior Achievement Foundation Magyarország.

Jeffs, T. (1988) Preparing young people for participatory democracy, in B. Carrington and B. Troyna (eds) *Children and Controversial Issues*, Lewes: Falmer.

Jundin, S. (1988) Ungdomars konsumtion och sparande, in K.E. Wärneryd, S. Jundin and R. Wahlund (eds) *Sparbeteende och Sparattityder, expertrapport Spardelegationen*, Stockholm: Stockholms Allmänna Förlag

Kahneman, D. and Tversky, A. (1974) Judgement and uncertainty: Heuristics and biases, *Science*, 185, pp. 1124–1131.

Kelly, A. (1989) 'When I grow up I want to be...': A longitudinal study of development of career preferences, *British Journal of Guidance and Counselling*, 17, pp. 179–200.

Kirzner, I. M. (1979) *Perception, Opportunity and Profit: Studies in the Theory of Entrepreneurship*, Chicago: University of Chicago Press.

Klingander, B. (1998) The status of consumer economics in compulsory school in Sweden, Proceedings of Second Conference of the International Association for Children's Social and Economics Education, Malmo, Sweden, June 1997.

Koh, H. C. (1996) Testing hypotheses of entrepreneurial characteristics, *Journal of Managerial Psychology*, 11, pp. 12–25.

Kourilsky, M. (1974) *Beyond Simulation: The mind–society approach to instruction in economics and other social sciences*, Los Angeles: Educational Resource Association.

Labov, W. (1969) The logic of non–standard English, in P. P. Giglioli (ed.) *Language and Social Context (1972)*, Harmondsworth: Penguin.

Laney, J. D. (1988) Can economic concepts be learned and remembered? A comparision of elementary students, *Journal of Educational Research*, 82, pp. 99–105.

Lassarre, D. (1996). Consumer education in French families and schools, in P. Lunt and A. Furnham (eds) *Economic Socialization. The economic beliefs and behaviours of young people*, Cheltenham: Edward Elgar.

Lassare, D., Ludwig, D., Roland-Lévy, C. and Watiez, M. (1987) *Education du Jeune Consommateur: Les sources d'information économiques des enfants de 11-12 ans*, Paris: Paris University Press.

Lassarre, D. and Roland–Lévy, C. (1989) Understanding children's economic socialization, in K. G. Grunert and F. Olander (eds) *Understanding Economic Behaviour*, Dordrecht, Netherlands: Kluwer Academic Publishers.

Laughlin, M. A. and Odorzynski, S. J. (1992) Introducing young people to economics: Video programmes for young learners, in M. Hutchings and W. Wade (eds) *Developing Economic and Industrial Understanding in the Primary School*, London: PNL Press.

Lautrey, J. (1980) *Classe sociale, milieu familial et intelligence*, Paris: PUF.

Lavalette, M (1999) The new sociology of childhood and child labour: Childhood, children's rights, and 'children's voice', in M Lavalette (ed.) *A Thing of the Past: Child labour in Britain in the nineteenth and twentieth centuries*, Liverpool: Liverpool University Press.

Lave, J. (1988) *Cognition in Practice: Mind, mathematics and culture*, Cambridge: Cambridge University Press.

Lave, J. and Wenger, E. (1991) *Situated Learning: Legitimate peripheral participation*, Cambridge: Cambridge University Press.

Lawson, E. D. (1963) Development of patriotism in children: A second look, *Journal of General Psychology*, 55, pp. 279–286.

Lea, S. E. G., Tarpy, R. M. and Webley, P. (1987) *The Individual in the Economy*, Cambridge: Cambridge University Press.

Lea, S.E.A. and Webley, P. (1991) Vers une psychologie plus réelle de la socialisation économique, in D. Lassarre (ed.) *Connaître les Modes de Vie et de Consommation des Jeunes*, Paris: Colloque Européen.

Leahy, R. (1981) The development of the conception of economic inequality, *Child Development*, 52, pp. 523–32.

Leahy, R. L. (1983) *The Child's Construction of Social Inequality*, New York: Academic Press.

Leiser, D. (1983) Children's conceptions of economics: The constitution of the cognitive domain, *Journal of Economic Psychology*, 4, pp. 297–317.

Leiser, D. and Ganin, M. (1996) Economic participation and economic socialisation, in P. Lunt and A. Furnham (eds) *Economic Socialization: The economic beliefs and behaviours of young people*, Cheltenham: Edward Elgar.

Leiser, D., Roland–Lévy, C. and Sevòn, G. (eds) (1990) Special issue on Economic Socialisation, *Journal of Economic Psychology*, 11, 4.

Leiser, D., Sevòn, G. and Levy D. (1990) Children's economic socialization: Summarizing the cross–cultural comparison of ten countries, *Journal of Economic Psychology*, 11, pp. 591–614.

Lewko, J. H. (ed.) (1987) How children and adolescents view the world of work, *New Directions for Child Development*, 35.

Linton, T. (1990) A Child's–Eye View of Economics in A. Ross (ed.) *Economic and Industrial Awareness in the Primary School*, London: PNL Press.

Livesley, W. J. and Bromley, D. B. (1973) *Person Perception in Childhood and Adolescence*, London: Wiley.

Lumpkin, G. T. and Dess, G. G. (1996) Clarifying the entrepreneurial orientation construct and linking it to performance, *Academy of Management Review*, 21, pp. 135–172.

Lunt, P. (1996) Introduction: Social aspects of young people's understanding of the economy in P. Lunt and A. Furnham (eds) *Economic Socialization: The economic beliefs and behaviours of young people*, Cheltenham: Edward Elgar.

Lunt, P. and Furnham, A. (eds) (1996) *Economic Socialization: The economic beliefs and behaviours of young people*, Cheltenham: Edward Elgar.

Lynn, R. (1991) *The Secret of the Miracle Economy*, London: Sage.

Maital, S. (1982) *Minds, Markets and Money: Psychological foundations of economic behavior*, Basic Books: New York.

Mannetti, L. and Tanucci, G. (1988). The meaning of work for young people, *Rassegna di Psicologia*, 5, 3, pp. 5–21.

Marshall, H. (1964) The relation of giving children an allowance to children's money knowledge and responsibility, and to other practices of parents, *Journal of Genetic Psychology*, 104, pp. 35–51.

Marshall, H. and Magruder, L. (1960) Relations between parent's money, education practices and children's knowledge and use of money, *Child Development*, 31, pp. 253–284.

Matthews, A. (1991) *If I Think about Money so Much, Why Can't I Figure it Out?* New York: Summitt.

McClelland, D. C. and Winter, D. G. (1969) *Motivating Economic Achievement*, New York: Free Press.

McCullagh, S. K. (1959) *The Three Pirates*, Book 1, Griffin Readers, Leeds: E. J. Arnold.

McKechnie, J., Lindsay, S., Hobbs, S. and Lavalette, M. (1996) Adolescents' perceptions of the role of part–time work, *Adolescence*, 31, 121, pp. 193–204.

Meadows, S. (1993) *The Child as Thinker: The development and acquisition of cognition in childhood*, London: Routledge.

Medrich, E. A., Roizen, J., Rubin, V. and Buckley, S. (1982) *The Serious Business of Growing Up: A study of children's lives outside school*, Berkeley and Los Angeles: University of California Press.

Micromegas (1993) *Money*, Paris: Micromegas.

Middleton, S., Shropshire, J. and Croden, N. (1998) Earning your Keep? Children's work and contributions to family budgets, in B. Pettitt (ed.) *Children and Work in the UK: Reassessing the Issues*, London: Save the Children Fund / Child Poverty Action Group.

Miller, J. and Yung, S. (1990) The role of allowances in adolescent socialisation, *Youth and Society*, 22, pp. 137–159.

Mookherjee, H. N. and Hogan, H. W. (1981) Class consciousness among young rural children, *Journal of Social Psychology*, 114, pp. 91–98.

Morrow, V. (1994) Responsible Children? Aspects of children's work and employment outside school in contemporary UK, in B. Mayall (ed.) *Children's Childhoods: Observed and experienced*, London: Falmer Press.

Mortimer, J. and Shanahan, M. (1994) Adolescent experience and family relationships, *Work and Occupation*, 21, pp. 369–384.

Moscovici, S. (1984) On social representations, in R. Farr and S. Moscovici (eds) *Social Representations*, Cambridge: Cambridge University Press.

Näsman, E. and von Gerber, C. (1996) *Mamma pappa utan jobb*, Stockholm: Rädda Barnen förlag.

Näsman, E. and von Gerber, C. (1999) *Räkna med oss!* Linköping: Unitryck.

Näsman, E. and von Gerber, C. (2001a) *Mina pengar!* Linköping: Unitryck.

Näsman, E. and von Gerber, C. (2001b) *Typ pank*, Linköping: Unitryck.

National Curriculum Council (1990) *Curriculum Guidance 4: Education for Economic and Industrial Understanding*, York: National Curriculum Council.

Neisser, U. (1992) The psychology of memory and the sociolinguistics of remembering, *The Psychologist*, 5, 10, pp. 451–2.

Newson, J. and Newson, E. (1976) *Seven-year-olds in their home environment*, London: Allen and Unwin.

Ng, S. H. (1983). Children's ideas about the bank and shop profit: Developmental stages and the influence of cognitive contrasts and conflict, *Journal of Economic Psychology*, 4, pp. 209–221.

Ng, S. H. (1985) Children's ideas about the bank: A New Zealand replication, *European Journal of Social Psychology*, 15, pp. 121–123.

Nilsson, P. (1998) *Fritid i skilda världar: en undersökning om ungdomars fritid i ett nationellt och kontextuellt perspektiv*, Ungdomsstyrelsens uredningar 11, Stockholm: Ungdomsstyrelsen.

Norling, I. and Gunnarsson, M. (1994) *Fritid som socialt fenomen*, Stockholm: Liber Utbildning

O'Donnell, C. and White, L. (1998) *Invisible Hands? Child employment in North Tyneside*, London: Low Pay Unit.

Pahl, R. (1984) *Divisions of Labour*, Oxford: Blackwell.

Pahl, R. (ed.) (1988) *On Work: Historical, comparative and theoretical approaches*, Oxford: Blackwell.

Parker, I. (1992) *Discourse Dynamics: Critical analysis for social and individual psychology*, London: Routledge.

Phipps J. B. (1996) Work, income and human capital: Beliefs and knowledge of urban elementary schoolchildren, *Children's Social and Economics Education*, 1, 3, pp. 175–193.

Piaget, J. (1932) *The Moral Judgement of the Child*, London: Routledge and Kegan Paul.

Pinto, G., Bombi, A. S. and Cordioli, A. (1997) Similarity of friends in three countries, *International Journal of Behavioral Development*, 20, 3, pp. 453–469.

Pliner, P., Freedman, J., Abramovitch, R. and Drake, P. (1996) Children as consumers: In the laboratory and beyond, in P. Lunt and A. Furnham (eds) *Economic Socialization: The economic beliefs and behaviours of young people*, Cheltenham: Edward Elgar.

Polacek, K. and Carli, D. (1977) *Test della figura umana di Goodenough–Harris*, Firenze: OS

Pollard, A. (1985) *The Social World of the Primary School*, London: Holt, Rinehart and Winston.

Pollio, H. and Gray, T. (1973) Change–making strategies in children and adults, *Journal of Psychology*, 84, pp. 173–179.

Potter, J. (1996) *Representing Reality: Discourse, rhetoric and social construction*, London: Sage.

Potter, J. and Wetherell, M. (1987) *Discourse and Social Psychology: Beyond attitudes and behaviour*, London: Sage.

Prevey, R. (1945) A quantitative study of family practices in training children in the use of money, *Journal of Educational Psychology*, 36, pp. 411–428.

Qvortrup, J. (1994a) Childhood Matters: An introduction, in J. Qvortrup, M. Bardy, G. Sgritta and H. Wintersberger (eds) *Childhood Matters*, Aldershot: Avebury.

Qvortrup, J. (1994b) *Barn halva priset: Nordisk Barndom i ett samhällsperspektiv*, Esbjerg: Sydjysk Universitetsförlag.

Qvortrup, J. (1995) From useful to useful: the historical continuity of children's constructive participation, in A. Ambert (ed.) *Sociological Studies of Children, Volume 7*, Greenwich, Conn.: JAI Press.

Rädda Barnen (1991) *0–17*, Stockholm: Rädda Barnen förlag.

Reinke, R. (1992) An American perspective on economics education in English primary schools, in M. Hutchings and W. Wade (eds) *Developing Economic and Industrial Understanding in the Primary School*, London: PNL Press.

Rendon, M. and Krantz, R. (1992) *Straight Talk about Money*, New York: Facts on File.

Rheingold, H. (1982) Little children's participation in the work of adults: a nascent pro–social behavior, *Child Development*, 53, pp. 114–125.

Roberts, K. (1975) The developmental theory of occupational choice: A critique and an alternative, in G. Esland, G. Salaman and M.A. Speakman (eds) *People and Work*, Edinburgh: Holmes McDougall.

Roberts, R. J. and Dolan, J. (1989) Children's perceptions of 'work': an exploratory study, *Educational Review*, 41, pp. 19–28.

Roland-Lévy, C. (1990a) A cross–national comparison of Algerian and French children's economic socialisation, *Journal of Economic Psychology*, 11, pp. 567–581.

Roland-Lévy, C. (1990b) Economic socialisation: Basis for international comparisons, *Journal of Economic Psychology*, 11, pp. 469–482.

Roland-Lévy, C. (1991) Les jeunes et le crédit à la consommation, in D. Lassarre (ed.), *Connaître les Modes de Vie et de Consommation des Jeunes*, Paris: Colloque Européen.

Roland-Lévy, C. (1994) Savings and debts: The impact of the family structure on the processes of money management, in F. van Raaij (ed.) *Integrating Views on Economic Behavior*, Rotterdam: University Press.

Roland-Lévy, C. (1998a) Economic socialization, in P.E. Earl and S. Kemp (eds) *The Elgar Companion to Consumer Research and Economic Psychology*, Cheltenham and Northampton: MA: Edward Elgar.

Roland-Lévy, C. (1998b) Psychologie économique de la consommation et de l'endettement, in C. Roland–Lévy and P. Adair (eds) *Psychologie Economique: Théories et Applications*, Paris: Economica.

Roland-Lévy, C. (2000) Developing identities via different social representations: Teenagers, unemployment and ideology, in A. Ross (ed.) *Developing Identities in Europe*, London: CiCe.

Ross, A. (1983) The bottle-stopper factory: Talking all together, *The English Magazine*, 11, pp. 14–18.

Ross, A. (1988) Studying the world of work: An inevitable controversy? in B. Carrington and B. Troyna (eds) *Children and Controversial Issues*, Lewes: Falmer.

Ross, A. (1990a) Economic and industrial awareness and the primary school child, in A. Ross (ed.) Economic and Industrial Awareness in the Primary School, London: PNL Press

Ross, A. (1990b) Children's perceptions of industrial hierarchies, in A. Ross, (ed.) *Economic and Industrial Awareness in the Primary School*, London: PNL Press.

Ross, A. (1992a) Promoting the enterprise culture or developing a critique of the political economy? Directions for economic and industrial understanding, in M. Hutchings and W. Wade (eds) *Developing Economic and Industrial Understanding in the Primary School*, London: PNL Press.

Ross, A. (1992b) Children's perceptions of capital, in M. Hutchings and W. Wade (eds) *Developing Economic and Industrial Understanding in the Primary School*, London: PNL Press.

Ross, A. (1995) The whole curriculum, the National Curriculum and social subjects, in J. Ahier and A. Ross (eds) *The Social Subjects within the Curriculum*, London: Falmer.

Ross, A. and Hutchings, M. (1987) *The Primary Schools and Industry Kit*, London: PNL Press.

Rudmin, F. W. (1994) Cross–cultural psycholinguistic field research: Verbs, of ownership and possession, *Journal of Cross–Cultural Psychology*, 25, 1, pp. 114–132.

Sarbin, T. R. (1986) *The narrative as a root metaphor for psychology*, in T. R. Sarbin (ed.) Narrative Psychology: The storied nature of human conduct, New York: Praeger.

Schug, M. C. (1996) Teaching economic reasoning to children, *Children's Social and Economics Education*, 1, 1, pp. 79–88.

Schug, M. C. and Armento, B. J. (1985) Teaching economics to children, in M. C. Schug (ed.) *Economics in the School Curriculum*, K–12 Washington DC: NEA Professional Library.

Schug, M. C. and Birkey, C. J. (1985) The development of children's economic reasoning. *Theory and Research in Social Education*, 13, pp. 31–42.

Schug, M. C. and Lephardt, N. (1992) How do children reason about international trade?, in M. Hutchings and W. Wade (eds) *Developing Economic and Industrial Understanding in the Primary School*, London: PNL Press.

Scribner, S. (1984) Studying working intelligence, in B. Rogoff and J. Lave (eds) *Everyday Cognition: Its development in social context*, Cambridge, MA: Harvard University Press.

Selman R. L. (1980) *The Growth of Interpersonal Understanding*, New York: Academic Press.

Sevòn, G. and Weckstrom, S. (1989) The development of reasoning about economic events: A study of Finnish children, *Journal of Economic Psychology*, 10, pp. 495–514.

Shepelak, N. J. and Alwin, D. F. (1986) Beliefs about inequality and perceptions of distributive justice, *American Sociological Review*, 51, pp. 30–46.

Shields, M. M. and Duveen, G. M. (1983) *The young child's representation of persons and the social world*, Phase 2: The child's representations of social roles, SSRC End–of–Grant Report C 0023 0027.

Shotter, J. (1993) *Conversational Realities: Constructing life through language*, London: Sage.

Siegler, R. S. (1978) The origins of scientific reasoning, in R. S. Siegler (ed.) *Children's Thinking: What develops?* Hillsdale, NJ: Erlbaum.

Sigelman, C. K. and Waitzman, K. A. (1991) The development of distributive justice orientations: Contextual influences on children's resource allocations, *Child Development*, 62, pp. 1367–1378.

Singer, M. S. and Stacey, B. G. (1986) Causal attributions, perceived consequences of unemployment, and perceptions of employment prospects among adolescents in New Zealand, *Journal of Genetic Psychology*, 147, pp. 559–565.

Slomczynski, K. M., Janicka, K., Mach, B. W. and Zaborowski, W. (1999) *Mental Adjustment to the Post–Communist System in Poland*, Warsaw: IFIS Publishers.

Snare, F. (1972) The concept of property, *American Philosophical Quarterly*, 9, pp. 200–206.

Socialdepartementet (1992) *Barn og ung i Danmark*, Copenhagen: Socialdepartementet.

Solberg, A. (1990) Negotiating childhood: Changing constructions of age for Norwegian children, in A. James and A. Prout (eds) *Constructing and Reconstructing Childhood: Contemporary issues in the sociological study of childhood*, London: Falmer.

Sonuga–Barke, E. and Webley, P. (1993) *Children's Saving: A study in the development of economic behaviour*, Hove, UK and Hillsdale NJ: Lawrence Erlbaum Associates.

Stacey, B. and Singer, M. (1985) The perception of poverty and wealth among teenagers, *Journal of Adolescence*, 8, pp. 231–241.

Strauss, A. (1952) The development and transformation of monetary meanings in the child, *American Sociological Review*, 17, pp. 275–284.

Strauss, A. and Corbin, J. (eds) (1997) *Grounded Theory in Practice*, Thousand Oaks, Ca.: Sage.

Strauss, A. and Corbin, J. (1998) *Basics of Qualitative Research: Techniques and procedures of developing grounded theory*, Thousand Oaks, CA.: Sage.

Strauss, S. (1986) Three sources of differences between educational and developmental psychology, in L. S. Liben (ed) *Development and Learning*, Hillsdale NJ: Erlbaum.

Strike, K. (1982) *Liberty and Learning*, Oxford: Martin Robertson.

Sutton, R. (1962) Behaviour in the attainment of economic concepts, *Journal of Psychology*, 53, pp. 37–46.

Takahashi, K. and Hatano, G. (1989) *Conceptions of the Bank: A developmental study*, JCSS Technical Report No.11, Tokyo, Japan.

Thompson, D. R. and Siegler, R. S. (2000) Buy Low, Sell High: The development of an informal theory of economics, *Child Development*, 71, 3, pp. 660–677.

Van Hoorn, J. L., Komlósi, Á., Suchar, E. and Samelson, D. A. (2000) *Adolescent Development and Rapid Social Change*, Albany: State University of New York Press.

Vári–Szilágyi, I. (1992) Public and private spheres of morality in the democratic and totalitarian countries, *Human Affairs*, 2, 1, pp. 18–31.

Vári–Szilágyi, I. and Solymosi, Zs. (1999) *A siker lélektana*, Budapest: Hatodik Síp.

Vergès, P. (1992) L'évocation de l'argent: Une méthode pour la définition du noyau central d'une représentation, *Bulletin de Psychologie*, 405, pp. 203–216.

Vergès, P. (1998) Représentations socials en psychologie économique, in C. Roland–Lévy and P. Adair (eds) *Psychologie Economique: Théories et applications*, Paris: Economica.

Vergès, P. and Bastounis M. (2001) Towards the investigation of social representations of the economy, in C. Roland–Lévy, E. Kirchler, E. Penz and C. Gray (eds) *Everyday Representations of the Economy*, Vienna: WUV.

von Salish, M. (1996) Relationship between children: Symmetry and asymmetry among peers, friends and siblings, in A. E. Auhagen and M. von Salish (eds) *The Diversity of Human Relationships*, Cambridge: Cambridge University Press.

Vosniadou, S. (1994) Capturing and modeling the process of conceptual change, *Learning and Instruction*, 4, 1, pp. 45–69.

Vosniadou, S. and Brewer, W. F. (1992) Mental models of the earth, *Cognitive Psychology*, 24, 4, pp. 535–585.

Voss, J. (1988) Problem–solving and reasoning in ill–structured domains, in C. Antaki (ed) *Analysing Everyday Explanation*, London: Sage.

Voss, J. F., Blais, J., Means, M. L., Greene, T. R., and Ahwesh, E. (1986). Informal reasoning and subject matter knowledge in the solving of economics problems of naive and novice individuals, *Cognition and Instruction*, 3, pp. 269–302.

Walkerdine, V. and Lucey, H. (1989) *Democracy in the Kitchen*, London: Virago.

Walls Ltd. (2000) *Monitor: The authoritative survey on British children's pocket money*, Walton–upon–Thames, Surrey: Birds Eye Walls Ltd.

Ward, S., Wackman, D. B. and Wartella, E. (1977) *How Children Learn to Buy*, London: Sage.

Warnock, M. (1976) *Imagination*, London: Faber and Faber.

Warton, P. M. and Goodnow, J. J. (1991) The nature of responsibility: Children's understanding of 'your job', *Child Development*, 62, pp. 156–65.

Warton, P. M. and Goodnow, J. J. (1995) Money and children's household jobs: Parents' views of their interconnections, *International Journal of Behavioural Development*, 18, 2, pp. 335–350.

Watiez, M. (1987) Comportements économiques sur les lieux de vente: Observations et questionnaires dans les supermarchés, in D. Lassarre, in D. Lassarre, D. Ludwig, C. Roland-Lévy and M. Watiez, *Education du Jeune Consommateur: Les sources d'information économique des enfants de 11–12 ans*, Paris: University Press.

Webley, P. (1983) Growing up in the modern economy, Paper at *Sixth International Conference on Political Psychology*, Edinburgh.

Webley, P. (1996) Playing the market: The autonomous economic world of children, in P. Lunt and A. Furnham (eds) *Economic Socialization: The economic beliefs and behaviours of young people*, Cheltenham: Edward Elgar.

Webley, P. and Lea, S. E. G. (1993) Towards a more realistic psychology of economic socialisation, *Journal of Economic Psychology*, 14, pp. 461–472.

229

Webley, P., Levine, R. M. and Lewis, A. (1991) A study in economic psychology: Children's saving in a play economy, *Human Relations*, 44, pp. 127–46.

Webley, P. and Webley, E. (1990) The playground economy, in P. Webley and S. E. A. Lea (eds), *Applied Economic Psychology in the 1990s*, Exeter: Washington Singer Press.

Webley, P. and Wrigley, V. (1983) The development of conceptions of unemployment among adolescents, *Journal of Adolescence*, 6, pp. 317–328.

Wells, G. (1986) *The Meaning Makers: Children learning language and using language to learn*, London: Hodder and Stoughton.

Wetherell, M. and Potter, J. (1992) *Mapping the Language of Racism: Discourse and the legitimation of exploitation*, Hemel Hempstead: Harvester Wheatsheaf.

White, A. R. (1990) *The Language of Imagination*, Oxford: Blackwell.

White, J. (1997) *Education and the End of Work: A new philosophy of work and learning*, London: Cassell.

White, L. and Brinkerhoff, D. (1981) Children's work in the family: Its significance and meaning, *Journal of Marriage and Family*, 43, pp. 789–798.

Wiener, M. (1981) *English Culture and the Decline of the Industrial Spirit*, 1850–1980, Cambridge: Cambridge University Press.

Willig, C. J. (1990) *Children's Concepts and the Primary Curriculum*, London: Paul Chapman Publishing.

Willis, P. (1977) Learning to Labour: *How working class kids get working class jobs*, London: Saxon House.

Winocur, S. and Siegal, M. (1982) Adolescents' judgement of economic arguments, *International Journal of Behavioural Development*, 5, pp. 357–65.

Witryol, S. and Wentworth, N. (1983) A paired comparisons scale of children's preference for monetary and material rewards used in investigations of incentive effects, *Journal of Genetic Psychology*, 142, pp. 17–23.

Woodhead, M. (1999) Combating child labour: Listen to what the children say, *Childhood*, 6, 1, pp. 27–50.

Wosinski, M. and Pietras, M. (1990) Economic socialisation of Polish children in different macro–economic conditions, *Journal of Economic Psychology*, 11, pp. 515–529.

Wyatt, E. and Hinden, S. (1991) The Money Book: *A smart kid's guide to savvy saving and spending*, New York: Somerville House.

Youniss, J. (1978) The nature of social development: A conceptual discussion of cognition, in H. McGurk (ed.) *Issues in Childhood Social Development*, London: Methuen.

Zamagni, S. (1992) Obbiettivi e contenuti di una cultura economica di base, in A. S. Bombi (ed.) *Economia e processi di conoscenza*, Torino: Loescher.

Zelizer, V. (1985) *Pricing the Priceless Child*, New York: Basic Books.

Zigler, B. and Child, I. (1968) Socialization, in G. Lindzey and E. Aronson (eds) *Handbook of Social Psychology*, Vol. 3, Reading MA: Addison–Wesley.

Zinser, O., Perry, S. and Edgar, R. (1975) Affluence of the recipient, value of donations, and sharing in pre–school children, *Journal of Psychology*, 89, pp. 301–305.

Index